NOT AS THE WORLD GIVES

The Way of Creative Justice

BY THE SAME AUTHOR

The Power of the Ring:
The Spiritual Vision Behind The Lord of the Rings
(Crossroad, 2005, 2011)

The Seven Sacraments:
Entering the Mysteries of God
(Crossroad, 2006)

Beauty for Truth's Sake:
On the Re-enchantment of Education
(Brazos, 2009)

All Things Made New:
The Mysteries of the World in Christ
(Angelico Press/Sophia Perennis, 2011)

Beauty in the Word:
Rethinking the Foundations of Education
(Angelico Press, 2012)

The Radiance of Being:
Dimensions of Cosmic Christianity
(Angelico Press, 2013)

Stratford Caldecott

NOT AS THE WORLD GIVES

The Way of Creative Justice

Foreword by
ADRIAN WALKER

Peace I leave with you;
my peace I give to you;
not as the world gives
do I give to you
(John 14:27)

First published
by Second Spring, 2014
www.secondspring.co.uk
an imprint of Angelico Press
© Stratford Caldecott 2014
Foreword © Adrian Walker 2014

For information, address:
Angelico Press
4709 Briar Knoll Dr.
Kettering, OH 45429
angelicopress.com

978-1-62138-054-2

Cover image: Duccio Di Buoninsegna
The Washing of the Feet, 1308–1311
Cover design: Michael Schrauzer

To Our Daughters

Teresa, Sophie, and Rosie

Moral action, therefore, means the creation of something, not in stone, color, or sound, but in the stuff of real life. The world is always incomplete. It is always meeting us in the shape of the situation, in order that we may fill up those things that are wanting in it by moral action, by molding the Good out of it. The moral life has largely become waste. The creative powers have largely been diverted into "anaesthetized" art, into political work divorced from all moral principles, into mere economics, or something similar. It is time for us to recognize moral action once again as a creative work, and to allow the living moral powers to enter into it.

—Romano Guardini[1]

I believe that the one who worships God has, through that experience, a mandate of justice towards his brothers. It is an extremely creative justice because it invents things; education, social progress, care and attention, relief, etc. Therefore, the integral religious man is called to be a just man, to bring justice to others. In this aspect the justice of religion, or religious justice, creates culture. The culture made by a woman or man that worships the living God is not the same culture made by the idolater. John Paul II had a very bold phrase: a faith that does not produce culture is not a true faith. He emphasized this: creating culture. Today, for example, we have idolatrous cultures in our society: consumerism, relativism, and hedonism are examples of this.

—Pope Francis[2]

1. Romano Guardini, *Conscience* (London: Sheed & Ward, 1932), p. 34.
2. Jorge Mario Bergoglio and Abraham Skorka, *On Heaven and Earth: Pope Francis on Faith, Family, and the Church in the Twenty-First Century* (New York: Image, 2013), pp. 22–3.

Acknowledgments

The book includes material that I have published over many years in *Communio* and *Second Spring*, on my blog at http://theeconomyproject.blogspot.co.uk, and at www.theimaginativeconservative.org. It is there that I tend to work out my thoughts, so it is not really strange to find this material eventually condensing into book form. This book owes a lot to my work with the *Chesterton Review* and to a period when I taught a course on Christianity and Society at Plater College.[1] I am therefore grateful to Fr. Ian Boyd CSB, founding editor of the *Chesterton Review*, and Michael Blades, one-time Principal of Plater College, along with the late Fr. Roger Charles SJ. I am grateful to my publishers John Riess and James Wetmore of Angelico Press for encouraging me to gather this material and develop it into book form.

I must also mention my colleagues at *Communio* and the John Paul II Institute for Studies on Marriage and Family, and many others from whom I have learnt or with whom I have discussed some of these subjects over the years, including Angelo Scola, Aidan Mackey, Edward Hadas, Michael Black, Mary Taylor, Frances Hutchinson, Winston and Barbara Elliott, Connie Lasher, Russell Sparkes, Charlotte Ostermann, Marco Sermarini, Adrian Walker (with thanks especially for his Foreword and editorial advice), and Léonie Caldecott, with whom I am united in a state of life that underpins all the work we have tried to do together for the Church. Léonie's advice, conversation, and inspiration have been the decisive influences on this book from beginning to end, though its faults are mine.

---

1. The Catholic Workers' College in Oxford founded in 1921 by the Catholic Social Guild in memory of Fr Charles Plater SJ. The College closed in 2005.

CONTENTS

APPENDIX: Essays

Foreword

Adrian Walker

Stratford Caldecott's new book completes the work that he began with quiet mastery in *The Radiance of Being*. Just as the first volume was an exploration of Catholic metaphysics in light of the Trinity, the second is an exploration of Catholic social theory in light of the same triune mystery. Like twin panels of a diptych that share a common motif, the two books join to display the Trinitarian communion illuminating cosmos and society through the purified bodies of the saints. "Above all," Caldecott writes in his introduction to the new book, "I want to show how the *radiance* I spoke of in the earlier book"—the radiance of Trinitarian gift—"can shine through not just the natural but also the social and cultural worlds."

Again and again, *Not As the World Gives* gently draws our attention to the mystery of purity as the matrix of the just society in the image and likeness of the triune God. As Caldecott explains in the first chapter of the book, the pure in heart who behold the Trinitarian light shining through all things, and whose "whole bodies light up" (Matt. 6:22) with the same luminous ardor, necessarily become in their turn "the light of the world" (Matt. 5:14), a "city set on a hill" that "cannot be hid" (ibid.). The "simple eye" (Matt. 6:22) that perceives the triune glory in the cosmos (the theme of the first book) is also the "lamp" (ibid.) that irradiates the same light into society (the theme of the second). And it is *this* radiation of glory (in the midst of suffering), Caldecott argues, that opens a "way" for "creative justice," which the world cannot give, yet which the world both desperately needs and, despite its often dogged resistance, secretly desires.

Not As the World Gives is less an account of Catholic Social Teaching than a reminder of its properly theological context: man's vocation to lift the whole of nature "into the freedom of the glory of God's children" (Rom. 8:21), and so into the Trinitarian *communio personarum* which that glory reflects. Set against this immense eschatological backdrop, earthly justice appears as a fleeting glimpse of the "new heavens and new earth in which righteousness"—the sophianic economy of triune gift—is finally fully "at home" (2 Pet. 3:13). But Caldecott's great merit is to reveal this fleeting glimpse as a solid practical ideal, i.e., as a "way of creative justice" at once more revolutionary than worldly utopianism and more realistic than worldly cynicism. His new book is thus a timely reminder that the freshest source of right order, its most luminous pattern, lies less in programs and techniques than in the Beatitudes, the Church's characteristic way of being in the world precisely by *not being of it.*

According to Caldecott, the "way of creative justice" passes through observance of the evangelical counsels of poverty, chastity, and obedience, which give the love revealed in the Beatitudes its three-fold form. This form, he stresses, governs not only religious consecration, but also, analogously, Christian marriage, whose very *raison d'être* is to embody the *spirit* of the three vows and irradiate it into the world. For the same reason, Caldecott can present Christian marriage as the manifest truth of what he calls the "mystery of gender," which finds its densest expression in the fruitful communion of man and wife, the conjoint *imago Trinitatis.* This communion stands, in turn, at the source of his own thinking, as he himself hints in his opening acknowledgment of "Léonie Caldecott, with whom," he writes, "I am united in a *state of life that underpins all the work we have tried to do together for the Church*" (emphasis added).

By setting chastity within the solemn play of conjugal communion, Caldecott recovers the true splendor of sexual purity as the beautiful integrity of embodied souls. But chastity, he goes on to explain, both shapes and reflects the luminous pattern of all truly human polity. Indeed, one of the great lessons of Caldecott's new book is precisely that personal purity, social justice, and worship coinhere within the undivided wholeness of the "radiant city," i.e., the social microcosm of a world reconciled in the Trinity. This coinherence underscores, in turn, the book's central insight that justice is primarily an effulgence of triune *communio,* rather than simply the vindication of "rights" or even the rightly proportioned *cuique suum* (though it is of course not less than these things). The communion of the Father and the Son in the Holy Spirit that ensouls the Church, Caldecott argues, is also meant to animate our pursuit of earthly justice, whose highest expression is friendship with God, with one another, and with our fellow creatures.

Although Caldecott has a rare perception of the fundamental unity of our current problems—he is a keen, yet sober critic of what George Grant called the "package deal" of modernity—he keeps his gaze calmly focused on the radiant consummation of justice in the rightly ordered *polis* and *kosmos*. This timely vision of cosmo-political justice retrieves an ancient, especially Platonic, contemplation of *dikaiosunê* as a social expression of the radiance of being. And yet, Caldecott suggests, the splendor of justice finds its brightest reflection in the mirror of human "creativity," i.e., of the "sub-creative" imagination located in the distinctively human middle between intellection and sensation. One of the most beautiful implications of Caldecott's argument, then, is that *justice itself is poetic*, even as this poetry finds its supreme inspiration and grandest theme in the Trinitarian gift glimpsed through the purity of Christian marriage and consecrated virginity. Far from bypassing created nature, this triune inspiration enables the world to open itself to the fulfillment it longs for, but cannot give itself apart from God.

Like the Colombian philosopher Nicolás Gómez Dávila, who once defined man as a problem lacking any human solution, Caldecott rejects every merely human attempt to master the *conditio humana*. True creativity lies not in technological despotism, but in "creative justice," the radiance of freedom reborn as pure self-gift from the heart of the Trinity. Because the Holy Spirit is always seeking to enkindle this radiance in us, Caldecott reminds us, the radically new beginning needed for social regeneration requires no more and no less than a pure heart to see and welcome his presence in our mortal flesh. The most practical lesson of this eminently practical book, then, lies not in some program or technique, but in the hope it inspires: the joyful confidence that every circumstance of our embodied existence, however painful or however hidden, can hasten the radiant manifestation of God's "creative justice"—the beautiful order of his own Trinitarian communion—throughout the whole of cosmos and society:

> Justice is the key to order. But it requires imagination to create a just society, and to build a culture of life in which the beauty of God's love shines through, in which every mother is supported, every child protected, every sick person helped, every stranger welcomed. Man is a microcosm, and a fallen, broken one at that. Our ideal city is a dream, a fantasy, until we see it arriving like an impossible resurrection. Plato and the others were right: the soul is the key. The ugly struggle for power, the lies and hypocrisy that are so common in the realm of Caesar, can only be defeated by an "inner struggle" like that of the hesychasts in the desert—though even monks rarely attain the social harmony of the earliest disciples. Nothing is possible without prayer, but with God all things are indeed possible. A Christian society may seem a long way off, but that is a mistake: it exists already, in and among those who show mercy and kindness to those around them.

Introduction

In my previous book (*The Radiance of Being*) I was concerned with the nature of nature, and the relationship between God and the cosmos. That book and this belong together, even though they can be read perfectly well separately. In *Radiance* I found in the doctrine of the Trinity "a key that unlocked everything." In the present volume I try to apply this universal key to the question of a Christian society, as Western civilization in the 21st century begins to face its gravest challenges. Above all, here I want to show how the *radiance* I spoke of in the earlier book can shine through not just the natural but also the social and cultural worlds.

This supernatural light does not just illuminate but transforms the world from the inside out. It opens us to grace and draws us into the life of the Trinity. Purged, illuminated, and united with God, the true Christian or New Man gives rise to a new civilization, healing whatever is blighted and distorted in this fallen world and allowing God to "make all things new." If that sounds like crazy idealism, we must remember we are not talking about any merely human achievement, but about divine promises that can never fail. We act not out of any kind of *hubris* but out of the supernatural virtue of hope. We are planting seeds, not raising towers.

Pope Francis has changed both the style and the focus of Catholic teaching, though not, of course, its substance. His insistence that the Church—all the way from the Cardinals through to the youngsters at World Youth Day—should serve the poor and vulnerable and protect the environment merges with the concern for New Evangelization, revealing the latter to be nothing other than a renewal of the Church's very life in what he calls the "maternal womb" of mercy. It is this synthesis that I hope to draw out in the present book.

Not As the World Gives

So much for an overview of the book. By why—looking at the title and subtitle—do I call it "Not As the World Gives," and why give such prominence to the "Way of Creative Justice"?

The main title is taken from John 14:27: "Peace I leave with you; my peace I give to you. Not as the world gives do I give to you. Let not your hearts be troubled, neither let them be afraid." Jesus is about to be arrested. This speech comes right after the promise of the Holy Spirit who will *teach us all things.*

Jesus promises peace. He promises to give "his" peace. He promises to give it in a special way, "not as the world gives." The world gives, only to take away again. The world gives peace, but that peace does not last. Nor is it a peace that frees the heart from trouble or fear. When Jesus gives, he gives the Holy Spirit, and with it comes freedom from fear—a lasting peace. His gift frees our hearts from trouble, so that we may see God (*Blessed are the pure in heart, for they shall see God*), and in him learn "all things."

The title takes us to the Beatitudes, but our emphasis is on the word "gives" rather than "peace." The idea of *gift*, seemingly so mundane, has an extraordinary depth. Pope Benedict XVI writes in section 34 of *Caritas in Veritate*: "*Charity in truth* places man before the astonishing experience of gift. Gratuitousness is present in our lives in many different forms, which often go unrecognized because of a purely consumerist and utilitarian view of life. The human being is made for gift, which expresses and makes present his transcendent dimension." Giving is what we are *made for*. The metaphysics and theology of gift restores a dimension to nature long ago stripped away by Nominalism and its successors. It re-establishes the priority of relationship over object, of person over thing, and therefore a sense of natural interiority, of true metaphysical depth, and the wonder that is the root of philosophy.[1]

---

1. Heidegger's influential critique of medieval "onto-theology" is really a critique of the separation of nature and grace, nature and the supernatural, that took place in late Scholasticism in reaction to Nominalism and Voluntarism and laid the foundations for the disenchanted, graceless cosmos of modernity. The approach I am trying to describe reintegrates nature and the supernatural by allowing theology

Introduction

The idea of gift is rooted in the Trinity. *God is love* (1 John 4:7), and love is self-giving. It is the Trinity that shows us what it means to give *not as the world gives*. The Son, dying for us on earth, shows us what it means to give *as God gives*. The Father and Son do not cling to their own nature but give everything to each other, and rejoice in the giving. Creation itself is a participation in the Trinitarian act of being—an act of giving, receiving, and being given.

The Trinity illuminates a rather important fact about giving. Think for a moment about what we mean by the term in everyday life. To *give* means intentionally to separate something from myself in order to make it someone else's. I separate it from what belongs to me, I choose it with the recipient in mind, I perhaps wrap it up nicely, and I hand it over. It is no longer mine, as soon as the other has accepted it. But at the same time, there is a sense in which the gift is never "separate" from me at all, even after it has been handed over. It carries me with it, thanks to the spirit of love in which it was offered and accepted. A gift *participates* in the giver, or carries the giver with it—just as in the Trinity (but more perfectly) the gift is the Person.

We acknowledge that fact in everyday life by recognizing our need to give *thanks* for what has been given to us. If we simply grunt or sigh and shove the wretched thing in a corner, we are not treating it as a gift, and the giver may understandably feel like taking it back. Thus it seems that to accept a gift properly establishes a communion between the giver and the receiver. A *true* gift is something that will ever afterwards remind us of the giver's affection. Every gift, in a sense, "has strings attached," and to a large extent human society is *held together by these strings*. It is the giving of the self, not just the giving of "things," that creates society.

As for "Creative Justice," this phrase comes from Pope Francis and Romano Guardini, in the two quotations or epigraphs that open the book. There Pope Francis writes, "I believe that the one who worships God has . . . a mandate of justice towards his brothers. It is an

to illuminate and reveal the true nature of the "God of the philosophers," avoiding the misinterpretations of Plato and Aquinas that have become all too common in the literature of postmodernism.

3

extremely *creative justice* because it invents things; education, social progress, care and attention, relief, etc. Therefore, the integral religious man is called to be a just man, to bring justice to others. In this aspect the justice of religion, or religious justice, creates culture." The quotation seems to capture the heart of what I am trying to say in this book: that to be just to others, or to build a just society, it is not enough to be fair, or to balance one person's rights against another's. We need to be inventive. We need to create something new—a new culture, effectively.

Pope Francis is saying that the justice that Christians are called to is "religious justice." Religious justice does not simply restore things the way they were. It does not just improve them a little. It changes them—often radically. In *The Radiance of Being* I made the point that creativity flows from the heart when human nature blossoms and flowers. It is the use we make of our freedom; it is the fruit of freedom. God does not impose it upon us, but he gives us this power and rejoices in it with us. *Be fruitful and multiply*, we are told. This can be read not only as an instruction to have children, but to be creative with what we have received; to cultivate the soil of our own nature, and to produce more than we were given—like the man with five talents who made five more (Matt. 25:16).

There is a brief discussion of "creative justice" at the end of Chapter 6. "Insofar as justice is required of us personally, and not simply as a society, we need to rise to a new level, to do something fresh, as though breaking the pattern of the past, or at least the pattern set by sin." This establishes an important principle: that the *social doctrine* of the Church cannot or should not be separated from *spirituality and the moral life*—specifically the Beatitudes, which offer a portrait of Christian existence lived to the full. "It is time for us to recognize moral action once again as a creative work, and to allow the living moral powers to enter into it" (from the epigraph by Guardini).

Catholics sometimes talk of "Catholic Social Teaching" (CST). There is a danger of treating this as a kind of ideology—a system of ideas—as though we were gleaning from the Church a body of advice to be applied to secular society. The Church's teaching becomes functionalized, and the secular world is treated as primary. We can prevent this not only by avoiding the acronym, but by refusing to separate the subject itself from ethics, spirituality, and the creation of culture.[2]

Structure of the Book

Not As the World Gives can be roughly divided into three groups of three chapters (followed by the Appendices). The first triad is about Catholic social doctrine, its history, and the nature of human society and the Church. From a Catholic point of view, the primary human society is the Church herself. Constituted by Baptism and the Eucharist, the Church is the sacrament of unity between men, as she is also between man and God. She is mankind on the way to being transformed into the City of God. In the third chapter, I look at the Church's formal teaching up to Pope Benedict's *Caritas in Veritate*, and end by trying to get a sense of where Pope Francis is leading us.

The second triad addresses the present-day challenges to this teaching, and broadens the scope of the book accordingly. Chapter 4 confronts a new historical era dominated by technological power. Our counter to the Order of the Machine is presented in Chapter 5—an understanding of human nature as metaphysical and organic rather than mechanical. (This chapter is essentially an exposition of John Paul II's "theology of the body" and its implications.) Chapter 6 goes more deeply into notions of moral order and freedom, picking up the spiritual theme from the first chapter.

The third triad of chapters is concerned with evangelization, understood not as proselytism but as the creation of a culture. In other words, this is *creative justice* in action. Pope Francis is seeking the renewal of the Church's life in the "maternal womb" of mercy.

2. Two other commonly used phrases must be distinguished: Catholic social doctrine, and Catholic social thought. The first refers to what the Church teaches, and the second to what Catholics think. The first is (for Catholics) authoritative, the second not so much. For a complete presentation of social doctrine, the reader should look to the *Catechism of the Catholic Church* and the *Compendium of Social Doctrine*. My own attempt to summarize the doctrine is available in *Catholic Social Teaching: A Way In*. Rodger Charles SJ's magisterial two-volume historical study, *Christian Social Witness and Teaching* and his short *Introduction to Catholic Social Teaching* are also listed in the Bibliography.

The Radiant City

"You are the light of the world. A city set on a hill cannot be hid. Nor do men light a lamp and put it under a bushel, but on a stand, and it gives light to all in the house. Let your light so shine before men, that they may see your good works and give glory to your Father who is in heaven."
                                                            ⁓Matt. 5:14–16

The Bible begins with a garden and ends with a city. But the city the Bible shows us descending from heaven is flowing with water and full of trees—it seems to be a garden as well as a city—and it is full of light, since "the glory of God is its light, and its lamp is the Lamb" (Rev. 21:23).

There are other cities that we know only too well, cities of squalor and concrete, full of hunger and violence, and it is there that darkness reigns.

The places we inhabit are projections. We make the world like ourselves, for better or worse. A "city" is that part of the world that we have shaped to the purposes of social life; a place in which large numbers of us can live and share resources, working and playing together. In order for a city to be worthy of human beings, it must take account of human nature and destiny. It must be a radiant city, a *just* city, a city where Justice reigns. But what does that mean?

City with a Fever

In the *Republic*, a model society or "city" is presented that is rather remote from anything we would call Christian. Commentators disagree as to whether Plato intended it to be taken literally, or whether (as I believe) it was an ironic portrait of the kind of inferior society that emerges when the soul is pursuing the wrong goals. For me, the clue comes in Book II (368c–369b). Socrates is proposing to construct a theoretical model of an ideal city in order to explore the notion of justice in the human soul, projected outwards (see e.g.,

7

443d–e). But Glaucon objects that the city Socrates describes first (see 372a–c) is lacking in luxury—such things as couches and sugary desserts. To this Socrates replies that he now understands Glaucon to be interested not in a healthy city but in a luxurious city, a "city with a fever" (372e).

In the rest of the dialogue he goes on to develop this second city in great detail, and this is the city we normally associate with the *Republic*. It is this city that needs to be defended from enemies, outside and within, who are jealous of its possessions; which therefore needs Guardians trained and prepared for their task; and which must be continually purified of its tendencies to corruption. In light of the discussion in Book II, it may be that Plato intended these prescriptions to be taken no more seriously than the reincarnation myth he presents at the end of the dialogue (or the joke at the expense of Pythagorean numerology he throws in at 546b–c).

The moral seems to be very clear. The desire to have *more than we truly need* is incompatible with true justice, which is defined as a state in which everyone receives his due. Under those circumstances the attempt to impose it will only lead to lies, propaganda, eugenic breeding, and the destruction of the family. In Books VIII and IX Plato traces the way his "ideal" aristocracy (more like a meritocracy in modern terms) will inevitably degenerate into a timocracy (that is, a state ruled by the strong), an oligarchy (one ruled by the rich), a democracy (ruled by the mob), and finally the worst sort of tyranny (ruled by a dictator). To this in the modern age we may add a final humiliation: technocracy, a state ruled by machines.

This may or may not be a correct reading of Plato. However much we may wish to give him the benefit of the doubt, we must remember that he was writing without the help of Christian revelation and the doctrine of the human person. In projecting the divisions of the human soul on to the canvas of the state, he was applying a strict analogy between the two (IV, 434). The various classes each have their own work to do, and each corresponds to a part of the human soul—elements symbolized by gold, silver, bronze, and iron. They must be kept in order in the same way, in order to serve the good of the whole. The best of the "cities with a fever" is the one in which the golden element is dominant and the classes unmixed. But as soon as the ruling class contains traces of the one below it, conflict will arise and eventually the military caste will become dominant. In this way the whole social order begins to unravel.

The mistake here, from a Christian point of view, is that each individual member of society and each member of every class is a person—therefore a whole and not merely a part—and should be treated as such. The harmony of society cannot be ensured by forcing each member of each of the four classes or races to conform to just one of the four elements that are found in everyone. Perhaps Plato would respond that my comment merely demonstrates that I am writing at a time when the worst has already happened, and the classes have become completely mixed. But it may also be that he intended his description of the Golden Age as a myth, pointing towards the ideal of the healthy city, the "city without a fever," which is the city of the just soul.[1]

Full of Light

Whatever we make of the *Republic* as a whole, in the context of his discussion of the Cave in Book 7, Plato makes some remarks about the essence of education that transcend their literary and historical context.

> Education isn't what some people declare it to be, namely, putting knowledge into souls that lack it, like putting sight into blind eyes.
> —*They do say that.*
> But our present discussion, on the other hand, shows that the power to learn is present in everyone's soul and that the instrument with which each learns is like an eye that cannot be turned around from darkness to light without turning the whole body. This instrument cannot be turned around from that which is coming into being without turning the whole soul until it is able to study that which is and the brightest thing that is, namely, the

---

1. When Christians describe the unfallen state as one of "original justice," we are reminded that, according to divine revelation, there was indeed a Golden Age on this earth, even if it consisted of no more than two people! More importantly, justice is not just harmony, but *truth*; that is, a state of affairs in which reality at its deepest level is accurately represented.

one we call the good. Isn't that right?

—*Yes.*

Then education is the craft concerned with doing this very thing, this turning around, and with how the soul can most easily and effectively be made to do it. It isn't the craft of putting sight into the soul. Education takes for granted that sight is there but that it isn't turned the right way or looking where it ought to look, and it tries to redirect it appropriately.[2]

The Christian doctrine that corresponds most closely to this Platonic insight is the Beatitude *Blessed are the pure in heart, for they shall see God* (Matt. 5:8). The Sermon on the Mount, where the Beatitudes are preached right at the start, also includes the instructions on prayer, in which Jesus tells his disciples that "The eye is the lamp of the body. So, if your eye is sound, your whole body will be full of light; but if your eye is not sound, your whole body will be full of darkness" (Matt. 6:22). The word translated "sound" here also means "single" or "undivided." We have here a teaching that purity or singleness of heart forms the *organ of perception* by which we can see the good, which is God. The Christian teaching on purity, and on the "eye of the heart," corresponds to the Platonic teaching on the education of the whole person as a turning of the body and soul towards the good.

The theme of purity will run through this book and emerge in different ways as essential to the living of a Christian life and the creation of a Christian society. "So, my brothers and sisters, our whole business in this life is the healing of the eye of the heart, that eye with which God is seen. It is for this the holy mysteries are celebrated, for this the word of God is preached, to this that the Church's moral exhortations are directed" (St. Augustine).[3] Purity, as a way of *seeing God in all things*, is the seed or foundation of the

---

2. Plato, *Republic*, Bk 7, 518c–d.

3. St. Augustine of Hippo, Sermon 88, 5 on Mark 10:46–52. Pope Benedict XVI, in his book *Jesus of Nazareth* (the volume on Holy Week), remarks that over half of Augustine's commentary on the Sermon on the Mount is focused on "this basic idea of the purified heart" and the word *misericordia* (mercy), because what is involved here is not a new norm to replace the Commandments, but a new "interiority," the possibility of immersion in Jesus Christ (pp. 64–5).

new civilization. The other Beatitudes fill out the image of the Christian citizen, whose life is graced by the theological virtues of Faith, Hope, and Love. For reference, let's list them all here.

Blessed are the poor in spirit, for theirs is the kingdom of heaven.
Blessed are those who mourn, for they shall be comforted.
Blessed are the meek,[4] for they shall inherit the earth.
Blessed are those who hunger and thirst for righteousness, for they shall be satisfied.
Blessed are the merciful, for they shall obtain mercy.
Blessed are the pure in heart, for they shall see God.
Blessed are the peacemakers, for they shall be called sons of God.
Blessed are those who are persecuted for righteousness' sake, for theirs is the kingdom of heaven. Blessed are you when men revile you and persecute you and utter all kinds of evil against you falsely on my account. Rejoice and be glad, for your reward is great in heaven, for so men persecuted the prophets who were before you.[5]

"Beatitudes"—that is, statements about how we may be "blessed" or "happy"—take us to the heart of Revelation. God wants us to be happy. Through the prophets he reveals that we can only be happy through union with him. He also reveals the way to attain this goal: not by our own efforts (which is impossible), but by cooperation with grace. The Bible describes the different stages of that cooperation in terms of a Covenant, a union between God and man, culminating in the Hypostatic Union. And so we find God constantly reiterating, reminding us, that the way to happiness lies with him alone, through the Law, which must not simply be followed blindly, but *lived*. That is why at the heart of the Bible we find the Wisdom books and the Book of Psalms. And it is why the Book of Psalms opens with a Beatitude:

---

4. The Greek word *praus* translated as "meek" does not mean "weak" or "soft," but refers to *strength brought under control*, like a wild horse that has been tamed.

5. Matt. 5:3–12. I have grouped the Beatitudes as St. Augustine does, with a list of seven followed by two referring to persecution. Another important collection of four Beatitudes and four curses or "Woes" may be found at Luke 6:20–26. It is followed by the instruction to love one's enemies, not to judge others, and to build one's house on solid foundations.

"Blessed [Hebrew: *makarios*] is the man who walks not in the counsel of the wicked, nor stands in the way of sinners, nor sits in the seat of scoffers; but his delight is in the law of the Lord, and on his law he meditates day and night."

The opening of the Psalms reflects the teaching of the Bible as a whole. It describes the three obstacles that make our happiness impossible, represented by walking, standing, and sitting. The order, of course, is significant, because as we progress from merely taking the advice of sinners to settling into an identification with sin we become less and less able to "move," to change. This is the consequence of the Fall, and of yielding to the three archetypal temptations that we will be discussing later.

It is no mere chance, then, that the second psalm contains a prophecy of the coming of Christ to Zion, the Holy Mountain: He said to me, "You are my son, today I have begotten you. Ask of me, and I will make the nations your heritage, and the ends of the earth your possession." In other words, as soon as the Goal has been revealed, the Way to that Goal must also be revealed, at least implicitly. The second Psalm then concludes with another Beatitude—"Blessed are all who take refuge in him"—while the third broadens this blessing to apply to the whole people. Thus the Psalms are linked directly to the Beatitudes that Jesus preaches on the mountain, and form the basis for the "social teaching" of both Old and New Testaments.

Life in the Spirit

The Christian life is most succinctly described in the double commandment to love God with all one's strength and one's neighbor as oneself (Matt. 22:37–40). Among Catholics, this is regarded as a summary of the Ten Commandments—the first three of which concern our worship of God, and the second series of seven commandments concern our love of neighbor. This "second tablet" of the Law is transformed by the statement of Jesus in the Gospel of John: "This is my commandment: love one another, as I have loved you" (John 15:12). It ceases to be abstract and becomes concrete: Jesus himself becomes a living example, an embodiment of the Law.

This is expanded further in the Beatitudes, which contain a more detailed portrait of the human person transformed by the Holy Spirit. According to the Beatitudes, blessedness accrues to those who are "poor in spirit"—that is, sufficiently detached from whatever wealth they possess to be able to give generously to others. It accrues to those who mourn—that is, those who remember the dead, and who remain loyal to tradition. It accrues to the meek and to those who hunger and thirst for righteousness—that is, for justice. The merciful shall obtain mercy, the pure in heart will see God, and peacemakers will be adopted as God's sons.

Blessedness is the bright shadow cast by love. We tend to recognize it when we see it. But, as we have seen, the Beatitudes end with a warning:

> *Blessed are those who are persecuted for righteousness' sake, for theirs is the kingdom of heaven.*
> *Blessed are you when men revile you and persecute you and utter all kinds of evil against you falsely on my account. Rejoice and be glad, for your reward is great in heaven, for so men persecuted the prophets who were before you.*

Christians today live in an age when persecution for righteousness' sake is just around the corner, if not already here.

The Beatitudes were preached in the context of a long sermon recorded by the Evangelist Matthew in his fifth chapter. St. Augustine calls it simply "The Lord's Sermon," as we call the Our Father "The Lord's Prayer."[6] In his commentary Augustine treats the first seven Beatitudes as a group (not too far-fetched, given Matthew's propensity for groups of seven), which he then interprets in terms of the Gifts of the Holy Spirit enumerated in Isaiah 11.[7] In this way he abolishes any distinction between morality and spirituality, demonstrating that the moral life is in continual need of the help and grace of the Holy Spirit.

---

6. The Lord's Sermon corresponds to the third of the Mysteries of Light, "The Preaching of the Kingdom," added to the Rosary by Pope John Paul II.

7. Servais Pinckaers OP remarks that later scholastic theologians, "taking as their moral foundation the theological and cardinal virtues," retained Augustine's idea, relating them "to the gifts and Beatitudes in the manner of St. Augustine. St. Thomas, notably, would introduce this concept of morality into the very structure

Beatitudes in Slow Motion

Let me, then, just quickly go through the first seven Beatitudes in slow motion to show how they—as Augustine puts it—"build the house upon rock."

Blessed are the poor in spirit, for theirs is the kingdom of heaven.—This Beatitude is directed against pride, which is the foundation of all sin. The poor in spirit are not "puffed up," says Augustine; they do not take themselves to be more than they are, nor rely on their material possessions.

Blessed are those who mourn, for they shall be comforted.—Those who mourn do so because they have lost temporal things, on which we cannot rely, but they are comforted by the Holy Spirit who assures them of an eternal reward. The gift of tears flows from knowledge.

Blessed are the meek, for they shall inherit the earth.—The meek are the gentle, those who do not use violence to get what they want. They overcome evil with good. The meek person is an image of the Incarnation, and Christ is the one who "inherits."

Blessed are those who hunger and thirst for righteousness, for they shall be satisfied.—Lovers of the true and indestructible good are those who feed primarily on the will of God, and drink of the "living water," their courage and patience strengthened by divine grace. Hunger and thirst for justice are a measure of the distance between earth and heaven, and a sign of the reality of the latter against which the former must always be measured.

Blessed are the merciful, for they shall obtain mercy.—We must learn to forgive in order to be forgiven. Without forgiveness there is no love. Mercy is the complement of justice, and goes beyond it, reaching into the very heart of God, giving where nothing is due.

Blessed are the pure in heart, for they shall see God.—God can only

---

of his *Summa*. He would base morality on the connections among the virtues, gifts, and Beatitudes, adding to them the fruits of the Holy Spirit mentioned in the Letter to the Galatians"—*The Sources of Christian Ethics* (Washington, DC: CUA Press, 1995), pp. 154-5. The Lord's Prayer was also brought into this scheme, after Augustine divided it into seven petitions. Pinckaers speaks of the patterns of seven in Matthew (pp. 143-4).

be seen with a single or undivided heart, Augustine tells us; a heart that loves only God in all things.

Blessed are the peacemakers, for they shall be called sons of God.—Augustine has much to say on this Beatitude. They are peacemakers who,

> by bringing in order all the motions of their soul, and subjecting them to reason—i.e., to the mind and spirit—and by having their carnal lusts thoroughly subdued, become a kingdom of God: in which all things are so arranged, that that which is chief and pre-eminent in man rules without resistance over the other elements, which are common to us with the beasts; and that very element which is pre-eminent in man, i.e., mind and reason, is brought under subjection to something better still, which is the truth itself, the only-begotten Son of God. For a man is not able to rule over things which are inferior, unless he subjects himself to what is superior. And this is the peace which is given on earth to men of goodwill; this the life of the fully developed and perfect wise man. From a kingdom of this sort brought to a condition of thorough peace and order, the prince of this world is cast out, who rules where there is perversity and disorder.[8]

We see that each of the Beatitudes, though distinct, reflects aspects of every other, and each unfolds from the central notion of love, which is the principle at the heart of all Christian teaching. This principle is far from abstract—it is incarnate in Jesus Christ, of whom the Beatitudes are a description. It is by following him, and allowing him to live his life in us, that the work of the Holy Spirit is accomplished, and human work is transformed into the work of God.

Thus each of the Beatitudes throws a shaft of light from the heart of the Gospel. Take the fifth as an example: *Blessed are the merciful.* The word "mercy" (Hebrew *chesed*) is associated with the first day of creation—the day of Light. The Greek equivalent *eleos* refers to the oil or balm used to soothe or heal a wound, and thus to restore it to its original wholesome state. Purity, light, healing—mercy is

---

8. Augustine of Hippo, *On the Sermon on the Mount* (ebook at limovia.net), Book 1, Ch. 2, Para. 9.

often paired with justice, but mercy reveals how love goes further than justice, and deeper. In the end, justice serves love.

Pope John Paul II wrote an entire encyclical on mercy (*Dives in Misericordia*, 1980), in which he says that love "is transformed into mercy" or expresses itself as mercy "when it is necessary to go beyond the precise norm of justice" (DM, n. 5),[9] as in the parable of the Prodigal Son. And so mercy reveals the Father by revealing his love for his Son. Christ on the Cross suffers the full weight of justice (on our behalf) precisely in order to reveal the Father's mercy.

> Do not the words of the Sermon on the Mount: "Blessed are the merciful, for they shall obtain mercy," constitute, in a certain sense, a synthesis of the whole of the Good News, of the whole of the "wonderful exchange" (*admirable commercium*) contained therein? This exchange is a law of the very plan of salvation, a law which is simple, strong and at the same time "easy." Demonstrating from the very start what the "human heart" is capable of ("to be merciful"), do not these words from the Sermon on the Mount reveal in the same perspective the deep mystery of God: that inscrutable unity of Father, Son, and Holy Spirit, in which love, containing justice, sets in motion mercy, which in its turn reveals the perfection of justice? (DM, n.8)

Blessed Are the Peacemakers

But is Christ really a "peacemaker"? "Do not think that I have come to bring peace to the earth," he tells us. "I have not come to bring peace, but a sword" (Matt. 10:34). Between this saying of Jesus and the seventh Beatitude lies the tension of a paradox. But paradox does not mean contradiction. Jesus is talking of the hostility and persecution his disciples will meet even within their own families. The Gospel will not be everywhere accepted, and those who do not accept will often violently reject—sometimes with open hatred and fear, because of the fact that the Gospel implies a judgment against them. The presence and message of Jesus is the beginning of a war.

---

9. So he says also: "the equality brought by justice is limited to the realm of objective and extrinsic goods, while love and mercy bring it about that people meet one another in that value which is man himself, with the dignity that is proper to him" (DM, n. 14).

"Peace I leave with you; my peace I give to you. Not as the world gives do I give to you. Let not your hearts be troubled, neither let them be afraid" (John 14:27). Here Jesus is talking about the interior peace, the peace of the heart, a peace that transcends all such warfare. This peace is not like any gift of the world. It is the peace of God himself, the peace of the one who has created and saved all things.

"Blessed are the peacemakers, for they shall be called sons of God" (Matt. 5:9). Which kind of peace is being referred to here? It doesn't seem to be simply peace of the heart. But how can it be the peace that Christ has come to disturb, the peace of worldly compromise and the status quo? We need to reflect more deeply, and we are helped in this by Pope John XXIII:

> The world will never be the dwelling-place of peace, till peace has found a home in the heart of each and every man, till every man preserves in himself the order ordained by God to be preserved. That is why St. Augustine asks the question: "Does your mind desire the strength to gain the mastery over your passions? Let it submit to a greater power, and it will conquer all beneath it. And peace will be in you—true, sure, most ordered peace. What is that order? God as ruler of the mind; the mind as ruler of the body. Nothing could be more orderly."[10]

In other words, the "peacemaker" of the Beatitudes is the one who bridges the tension in the paradox of peace. The peace of the heart—beginning with peace in the heart *of the peacemaker*—is the key to peace in the world, the exterior peace, where a person's enemies are liable to be "those of his own household." Though the primary reference here is to the violence that comes as the result of preaching the Gospel, it can be applied more broadly too.

In the first centuries of the Christian era, believers were at loggerheads with the emperors and with the state religion that enshrined them as gods for the sake of civil order. Christianity stripped divinity away from the state as such. But once the emperors themselves began to be converted, and a Christian polity emerged, war became more of an issue: should a Christian fight in defense of the realm,

---

10. *Pacem in Terris* (1963), n. 165.

kill in defense of peace? Later, when the empire had divided into nation states, could a Christian fight against other Christians in defense of one particular homeland?

St. Augustine's solution is well known, especially in the systematic form presented by Thomas Aquinas and the School of Salamanca in the Renaissance. The doctrine of the "just war"—originally developed in ancient India and Rome (Cicero)—specified that fighting was licit when done in a just cause, for a just end, using just means, and under a just authority. The teaching on war is an extension of the principle of self-defense. Christians may resort to violence to protect their families from assault, if faced with no alternative. Something similar applies to the state. The authority must be legitimate, there must be a reasonable chance of success, and the means used must be "proportionate" or measured to fit the objective (the violence must be minimized). War must be fought in self-defense or to punish a guilty tyrant—not for glory or gain or even conversion of the infidel. Innocents, non-combatants, prisoners, etc. must be protected and mass destruction is condemned.

After the Second World War and well into the Atomic Age, it is not hard to see why the popes have argued that the conditions for a just war can no longer realistically be met.[11]

Rules such as these, and all the others that are designed to cover the various contingencies and grey areas that arise in a complicated, fallen world, flow from the underlying principle of the *peaceful heart*, which is the seat of all virtue. It is here that the Beatitude promising divine sonship to the peacemaker (who thereby enters into the identity of the Son) joins up with the fifth of the Ten Commandments, "You shall not kill," which governs all forms of murder, including abortion, suicide, and euthanasia. But as our Lord explains, his teaching applies primarily to the heart:

---

11. See William L. Portier, "Are We Really Serious When We Ask God To Deliver Us From War? The *Catechism* and the Challenge of Pope John Paul II," *Communio: International Catholic Review* 23:1 (Spring 1996), pp. 47–63. Portier also discusses the recent strengthening of the Church's critical view of capital punishment (*Catechism of the Catholic Church*, n. 2267). Portier notes, however, that the *Catechism* tries to avoid use of the term "just war" (p. 49).

You have heard that it was said to those of old, "You shall not murder; and whoever murders will be liable to judgment." But I say to you that everyone who is angry with his brother will be liable to judgment; whoever insults his brother will be liable to the council; and whoever says, "You fool!" will be liable to the hell of fire.

Warfare, too, is interior before it is exterior (and in the next chapter we will look into the interior dimension of chivalry), as is peace, but all of this should be understood in the context of what is known about the relationship of nature to grace. The interior and exterior are distinct but not separate. The human heart is the meeting point of the natural and the supernatural—the loom, if you like, where the two are woven together. What we must do, and what John Paul II was trying to do by making more absolute the strictures against war and capital punishment, is not just taking account of the changed conditions of modern life and the power of technology, but once again reading the Commandments in the light of the Beatitudes, in the light of the model or portrait of Christ—a living model in which the power of the Holy Spirit allows us to participate. As he writes in *Veritatis Splendor* (n. 23), "Love and life according to the Gospel cannot be thought of first and foremost as a kind of precept, because what they demand is beyond man's abilities. They are possible only as the result of a gift of God who heals, restores, and transforms the human heart by his grace: 'For the law was given through Moses; grace and truth came through Jesus Christ' (John 1:17)."

Instead of separating grace from nature, and treating the question of killing as one of legitimacy, John Paul II insists that we must go deeper. "Thus the commandment 'You shall not murder' becomes a call to an attentive love which protects and promotes the life of one's neighbor" (VS, n.15).[12] Similarly with the other commandments, of course—those directed not against the person of our neighbor but his wife or his property.

In the heart these things are real. This is why Jesus tells us that to be angry with our neighbor is enough to deserve judgment: to be angry is to kill, just as to imagine sleeping with another man's wife

12. John Paul II, *Veritatis Splendor* ("The Splendor of the Truth," 1993), n. 15.

can be the equivalent of adultery. All the Commandments are calling us to perfect love; impossible though that may seem before Christ comes onto the scene. International war cannot be ended, though it may be restricted, by attempted obedience to codifications of the natural law—that for us is only the beginning.

At this deep level, there is a stark choice. We can either hate or love, kill or give life. If we do not love we are hating; we are beginning to kill. If we renounce hatred, it must be in the name of a love that gives life, that protects and nurtures, that gives to the other what is his due, that even gives more than his due, because he is worthy of love in God's eyes.

The Cross and the Tomb

The birth of a new world, and the secret of the peacemaker, that which *makes* him a "son of God," is forgiveness. Only forgiveness can create reconciliation and heal relationships that have been broken. The violence that destroys peace throughout the world and in every historical era, a violence that begins when Cain murders Abel—in other words with anger and jealousy (fruits of the first sin)—cannot be overcome Pelagian-style without the help of grace. But forgiveness is impossibly difficult. To understand this we need to contemplate the Cross and the Tomb, which is where all these sins lead, and which also mark the place where they are definitively overcome.

Without Christ, forgiveness in the true sense could not exist. We are incapable of it—or capable only of feeble imitations of it, for example when we decide to "forget" a slight for the moment, or overlook it for the sake of avoiding some trouble. This is like weeding a garden but leaving the roots of the weeds under the soil. Christ, on the other hand, grasps the roots. He takes upon himself the full consequences of the anger and jealousy of the world. He is the two tablets made by God that Moses cast down in anger, shattered as a consequence of the infidelity of the people (Gen. 32:15–19). He is beaten and whipped, crowned with thorns, stripped and pieced through the heart. On the Cross he asks his Father to forgive his enemies. He is laid in the tomb as a dead body.

The difficulty we have in forgiving can be traced back to fear. If we were all invulnerable, there would be no problem. It is easy to be magnanimous from a position of strength. In reality we are all damaged goods, we are all wounded. To forgive in the full sense means to open ourselves up to being hurt again—and what if the person we are trying to forgive shows no signs of repentance? Will not our scars soon be re-opened?

Christ knew fear, and yet was able to forgive. But he was not vulnerable in the way sinners are vulnerable, because sinners are separated from God—even if they are trying to find their way back to him. Fear immediately follows from the first sin, because sin made us vulnerable: as soon as they had sinned, Adam and Eve felt the need to hide in the forest from God. Sin separates us, makes the other an alien to us, a potential threat. Marked by sin, damaged by it in ways we are hardly aware, we are no longer able simply to receive what happens to us—if it is something "bad"—as a gift to be grateful for, because permitted by God. This is the struggle we see in Christ in the garden of Gethsemane, when he prays to be able to accept the cup of suffering that comes to him from the Father. And he succeeds.

So when Jesus promises to give his peace to the disciples, he links it to the release from fear. "Peace I leave with you; my peace I give to you. Not as the world gives do I give to you. Let not your hearts be troubled, neither let them be afraid" (John 14:27). To forgive fully and to be truly reconciled with the other—to establish peace, the tranquility of order inside ourselves and outside in society—is possible for those who participate in the Resurrection, which places us beyond the reach of harm of every kind by reuniting us with God. "For you have died, and your life is hidden with Christ in God" (Col. 3:3).

This identification with Christ is made possible by the Holy Spirit, whose role in all this is often forgotten—the Spirit who is the gift of divine nature, the gift from Christ, the source of all grace, making us one with the Son and the Father. The gift of the Spirit that Christ bestows is the confirmation of his forgiveness of us—for every sin ever committed is directed against him, and this is why we are cut off—and the two streams that flow from his side, that is of blood and water, are the streams of forgetfulness and of memory, enabling us to forget our sins as no longer belonging to us, and to remember all our good actions as those that Christ is doing in us.[13]

Thus St. Paul writes to the Colossians:

> Put on then, as God's chosen ones, holy and beloved, compassion-ate hearts, kindness, humility, meekness, and patience, bearing with one another and, if one has a complaint against another, for-giving each other; as the Lord has forgiven you, so you also must forgive. And above all these put on love, which binds everything together in perfect harmony. And let the peace of Christ rule in your hearts, to which indeed you were called in one body. And be thankful.[14]

Sons in the Son

The intimate relationship between the Beatitudes and the Com-mandments is spelled out by Pope John Paul II in his major encycli-cal on moral theology in 1993, *Veritatis Splendor*. Here are some further extracts:

> *The Beatitudes* are not specifically concerned with certain particu-lar rules of behavior. Rather, they speak of basic attitudes and dis-positions in life and therefore they *do not coincide exactly with the commandments*. On the other hand, *there is no separation or oppo-sition* between the Beatitudes and the commandments: both refer to the good, to eternal life. The Sermon on the Mount begins with the proclamation of the Beatitudes, but also refers to the com-mandments (cf. Matt. 5:20–48). At the same time, the Sermon on the Mount demonstrates the openness of the commandments and their orientation towards the horizon of the perfection proper to the Beatitudes. These latter are above all *promises,* from which there also indirectly flow *normative indications* for the moral life.

13. Dante, *The Divine Comedy*, Purgatorio, Canto 28 (124–33). The streams from Christ's side are mentioned at John 19:34 and are much commented upon. As I read it, connecting the two references, Dante's stream Lethe represents the forget-fulness of death, just as we die with Christ and leave our old life behind us—the stream of water represents Baptism. The other, Eunoe, is equivalent to the stream of blood, signifying the Eucharist and the sacrament of Reconciliation. Immersed in the one, remade by a draft of the second, Dante is now "pure and prepared to climb unto the stars."

14. Colossians 3:12–15.

In their originality and profundity they are a sort of *self- portrait of Christ,* and for this very reason are *invitations to discipleship and to communion of life with Christ.* (n. 16)

Those who live "by the flesh" experience God's law as a burden, and indeed as a denial or at least a restriction of their own freedom. On the other hand, those who are impelled by love and "walk by the Spirit" (Gal. 5:16), and who desire to serve others, find in God's Law the fundamental and necessary way in which to practice love as something freely chosen and freely lived out. Indeed, they feel an interior urge—a genuine "necessity" and no longer a form of coercion—not to stop at the minimum demands of the Law, but to live them in their "fullness." This is a still uncertain and fragile journey as long as we are on earth, but it is one made possible by grace, which enables us to possess the full freedom of the children of God (cf. Rom. 8:21) and thus to live our moral life in a way worthy of our sublime vocation as "sons in the Son." (n. 18)

This is true, but there is also a deeper level to which we must penetrate. The philosopher Michel Henry guides us to this level in his book *Words of Christ.*[15] He points out that many, perhaps the majority, of Christ's words in the Gospels (including the Beatitudes) are directed not towards the building up of the social fabric—even that of the family or tribe—but rather its total dissolution. This implies that the Gospels do not offer a "social doctrine" in the worldly sense we might at first imagine, but something much more far-reaching and all-embracing.

Social life is based on a certain conventional reciprocity.[16] We do good to others (or at least refrain from doing evil to them) so that they will do the same to us. But when Jesus says he has come to kindle a blazing fire, and tells us to hate our family; when he commands us to seek the highest place by becoming the servant of all and washing their feet, and tells us that those who mourn are

---

15. M. Henry, *Words of Christ* (Grand Rapids: Eerdmans, 2012).

16. The market economy depends on exchange, as do most political systems, in which we grant power to a leader in return for protection; even the peace of a household or neighborhood depends on each being prepared to help the other from time to time.

"happy" (and so on for the rest of the paradoxical Beatitudes), something other than reciprocity is involved.

> Do not think that I have come to bring peace on earth; I have not come to bring peace, but a sword. For I have come to set a man against his father, and a daughter against her mother, and a daughter-in-law against her mother-in-law; and a man's foes will be those of his own household. He who loves father or mother more than me is not worthy of me; and he who loves son or daughter more than me is not worthy of me; and he who does not take his cross and follow me is not worthy of me. He who finds his life will lose it, and he who loses his life for my sake will find it.[17]

This passage alone demolishes the most common interpretations of Catholic social teaching. What is going on here, Henry suggests, is that conventional morality is being swept away. Jesus condemns it as so much hypocrisy: a mask for self-interest. In so doing—in looking deep within the human heart that has deceived itself into thinking all is well—he exposes something that needs to be overthrown, a "human nature" or "old Adam" that needs to be discarded or burned away so that the true human being (the Son of God who is *the relation to God as such*")[18] can come into his own. This filial relationship with the Father to which Christ admits us is primarily vertical, interior, because it is the very root of our being. That is why all "horizontal" relationships must be discarded first, and if there is to be a Christian society, it will be built on different foundations—a different kind of reciprocity. "Whoever does the will of God is [now] my brother, and sister, and mother" (Mark 3:35).

Thus Jesus demolishes our superficial human notions of reciprocity in the name of this deeper relationship to God the Father, who tells us to love our enemies, and in his own providence does not merely reward those who do good but has mercy on sinners, and sends his sunshine and his rain both on the evil and on the good (Matt. 5:45). In Luke we find:

17. Matthew 10:34–9 (cf. Luke 9:23–5).
18. Henry, *Words of Christ*, p. 44. Henry speaks of an "abolition" of human nature, in order to accomplish "the *substitution of a divine genealogy for a natural genealogy*" (p. 41).

If you love those who love you, what credit is that to you? For even sinners love those who love them. And if you do good to those who do good to you, what credit is that to you? For even sinners do the same. And if you lend to those from whom you hope to receive, what credit is that to you? Even sinners lend to sinners, to receive as much again. But love your enemies, and do good, and lend, expecting nothing in return; and your reward will be great, and you will be sons of the Most High; for he is kind to the ungrateful and the selfish. Be merciful, even as your Father is merciful.[19]

We must by all means possible resist the tendency to interpret the Beatitudes "ideologically." That would be to use them to construct a world in which we feel (intellectually) comfortable, rather than actually *living* them as Christ intended. For the Beatitudes themselves are followed by a kind of "commentary" by Jesus, in which he draws out and illustrates the implications of each one. First (5:13–14), the Christian is exhorted to be "salt" and "light"—not to hide his difference from others but to live according to the Gospel. The laws and prophecies of the past are not to be neglected but fulfilled (5:17–20). Commandments of the Law against murder and anger must be obeyed not just in the exterior realm but applied to the heart (5:21–26), as must those against adultery (5:27–32). The Christian must be straightforward and honest (5:33–37), generous (5:38–42), loving towards enemies and friends alike (5:43–48).

Furthermore, the Christian must be generous in secret, acting not for earthly reward or approbation but for the approval of his Father in heaven (6:1–4). This leads into the teachings on prayer. And if our souls are integrated, unified, and purified in this way (so that we "serve one master" not two: 6:24) we have nothing to fear or be anxious about (6:25–34). With the kingdom in first place, all else will take care of itself.

The final teachings of the Sermon, in Chapter 7, apply to those who are following the Christian path just outlined, but who will for that very reason be subject to a new set of temptations. The temptation, for example, to judge others because it is easier to see their faults than one's own (7:1–5); the temptation to speak too openly, as

19. Luke 6:32–6.

though everyone was ready to receive these teachings (7:6); the temptation to despair, if the Father's gifts happen to be delayed (7:7–12); or the temptation to assume too readily that one is already saved (7:13–14). There is also the need to discriminate between true and false prophets, not being misled by the latter (7:15–23).

The City of God

The freedom to which we are called is not the freedom of mere self-control and contentment in this world; for that freedom becomes sin when it sets itself against the possibility of a *divine* freedom participated by men. To leave one's own "life" behind and take up the cross is to die to all anxiety about the self and its development, including "all those religious techniques that aim at the well-being of one's own 'I', 'depth-ego' or 'self.'"[20] This is also the reason why we are now (as a culture) in a worse state than paganism.

Jesus' claim is absolute: "No one comes to the Father except by me." This does not mean that the adherent of another religion cannot be saved, but it does mean that whether he knows it or not he can be saved *only by Jesus*. In the face of this claim, Balthasar argues, other religions will tend to dissolve or disintegrate, even in the process of trying to appropriate the more attractive aspects of Christianity ("socially engaged Buddhism," and so forth). The post-Christian society that rejects the claim of the Logos will tend to be totalitarian and militantly atheistic.

"In opposition to a 'flesh' that originates in Spirit and can become the Spirit's bearer—ultimately in the humble Incarnation of the divine Word—we see the implacable materialism that degrades matter to the mere raw material of its abstract, dis-incarnating power structures" (ibid., p. 445). The Christian revelation thus ultimately forces a concentration of worldly power into the hands of the Trinity of Hell (the Dragon, the Beast, and the Lying Spirit). In the words of Solovyev's fictional Antichrist: "World peace is assured forever. Every attempt to disturb it will instantly meet

20. Hans Urs von Balthasar, *Theo-Drama: Theological Dramatic Theory*, Vol. IV: The Action (San Francisco: Ignatius Press, 1994), p. 434.

with irresistible opposition; for from now on there is only a single central power on earth. . . . That power is mine" (cited ibid., p. 447).

At the end of time, a moment that perhaps draws near, the works of man will be revealed in a great judgment. The crisis is described in mythopoetic terms by John in the Book of Revelation. On the one hand we see the heavenly City built by God and man in harmony, the New Jerusalem, the liturgical city, descending from heaven as the centerpiece of the new creation. On the other, we see the great world city, called symbolically Babylon, a city build on exploitation and corruption of every kind, destined to be burned and thrown down.

> As she glorified herself and played the wanton, / so give her a like measure of torment and mourning./ Since in her heart she says, "A queen I sit, / I am no widow, mourning I shall never see,"/ so shall her plagues come in a single day, / patience and mourning and famine, / and she shall be burned with fire; / for mighty is the Lord God who judges her.[21]

Babylon is the city of impurity, in which men have lost themselves by serving themselves only, and their own greed. The City of God, by sublime contrast, is the city of the pure that see God "unveiled." It is the city of the Vision of God, in which "we shall be like him, because we shall see him as he is" (1 John 3:2).

> And I saw no temple in the city, for its temple is the Lord God the Almighty and the Lamb. And the city has no need of sun or moon to shine on it, for the glory of God gives it light, and its lamp is the Lamb. By its light will the nations walk, and the kings of the earth will bring their glory into it, and its gates will never be shut by day—and there will be no night there. They will bring into it the glory and the honor of the nations. But nothing unclean will ever enter it, nor anyone who does what is detestable or false, but only those who are written in the Lamb's book of life.[22]

This is the fruit of purity, in which those who are deemed worthy are filled with light, and all that is unclean will be purged away, and

---

21. Revelation 18:7–8.
22. Ibid., 21:22–27.

the tears of the mourners will cease forever. We glimpse this when we celebrate the Eucharist and receive Holy Communion. It is an image of the social world created by God and man working together—the City of the Peacemakers, the City of Mercy, the City of Beatitude.

A Divine Society

*The liturgy, reaching from God to man, and connecting man to the
fullness of the Godhead, is the action of the Trinity in the Church.
The Church in her liturgy partakes of the life of the divine society of
the three persons in God.* ⌒*Virgil Michel* [1]

In all human civilizations before our own, some form of religious
cult seems to have played a central role. The earliest temple composed of stones carved with stylized animal designs was found in
present-day Turkey at Göbekli Tepe. Situated at the northern end of
the Fertile Crescent, where agriculture originated and the first cities
were built, this ancient temple complex was built and rebuilt over
many generations starting 11,600 years ago—seven millennia before
the Great Pyramid, nine before Stonehenge, and long before human
beings gave up foraging for food and started to settle down. Intrigu-
ingly, it seems the temple was more sophisticated in its earlier
stages, and subsequent generations rebuilt it more crudely.

The discovery helps overturn the theory of the flamboyant
Stalinist archaeologist, V. Gordon Childe, that formal religion and
the rest of what we call civilization originated in the need to organize society, a need created by the invention of agriculture. (He
coined the phrase "Neolithic Revolution.") It seems more likely now
that civilization originated in the need and desire to worship—that
temples came first, and cities afterwards.[2]

All civilizations possess a temple. A universal sense of the sacred
is expressed by setting apart some particular place and time from
ordinary usage (sometimes with an outer and an inner precinct), in
order to represent the divine or eternal realm that is different from

---

1. Virgil Michel OSB, *The Liturgy of the Church According to the Roman Rite*
(New York: Macmillan, 1937), p. 40.
2. For more on Göbekli Tepe see *The National Geographic,* June 2011.

the world of the everyday. Linked to this is the idea of sacrifice—whether human, animal, or vegetable—by which some living creature is similarly "set aside" or consecrated for divine use. In this way the place, the temple, can be used to represent the divine realm, and the sacrifice can establish a link or a crossing-point, a bridge or doorway, between time and eternity.

There is one other essential element always found in the religious systems of mankind, and it is the man or woman set aside and consecrated to serve as mediator between the two realms—shaman, priest, or king—the one who performs the sacrifice, the purification, the atonement.

Appeasement of the gods, forgiveness of sins, or mediation with the powers that control the elements—there are many interpretations, many different religious systems. Widespread among ancient peoples is the idea that by means of such a sacrifice the priest or holy man is able to cross over and enter the other world to plead on behalf of the people, and return to teach or heal.

The same pattern is visible both in Ancient Egypt and in Ancient Israel, two very different cultures whose destinies and history have been intertwined ever since Joseph was sold into slavery by his brothers. The Pharaoh, it seems, was not merely a tyrant around whom all ritual revolved in order to emphasize his special importance, but as shaman, king, and initiate in one, served as a representative of everyman. The well-known Egyptian obsession with death (pyramids, mummification) was in fact an obsession rather with a ritual representation of the "crossing over" from one world to the next *in this life*; that is, the "dying before you die" affirmed by Plato and other ancient thinkers to be the goal of the philosophical and spiritual life. Or at least, so it was understood by the priestly caste who looked after the religious and cultural life of Egypt.[3]

Margaret Barker in her studies of the Hebrew Temple has shown how the different parts of the Temple represent the several Days of Creation. The Holy of Holies which contained the Ark of the

---

3. Here I am following the guidance not of the mainstream academic Egyptologists, but of R. A. Schwaller de Lubicz, John Anthony West, and Jeremy Naydler, and other writers I find more convincing on this topic.

Covenant and the glory of the divine Presence was the supreme
symbol of Day One, the day of super-celestial light.[4] It is from
behind the veil, embroidered with the colors blue, purple, crimson,
and white signifying the material cosmos and the "firmament" separating the waters above and below ("the holy from the most
holy"), that the world in which we dwell is projected by the Most
High God.[5] The High Priest of Israel, a son of Aaron but also in the
tradition of Melchizedek, represented in some traditions as a great
Angel, is the one who, on behalf of all the people, crosses this cosmic threshold and is "adopted" as the Son of God, becoming the
true King of the past, present, and future, alone permitted to enter
the world beyond time and to utter the sacred Name of God on the
Day of Atonement. He wears vestments of similar fabric and design
to the veil itself, implying his role as Mediator and Revealer.

All of this symbolism, present in the apocalyptic and mystical literature, is taken over, Barker argues, by Jesus Christ, who lives to
fulfill the prophecies and symbols of previous times and all religions. It is he who comes to be recognized as the true prophet,
priest, and king, the one who alone is able to ascend and descend
from heaven, as Jesus tells Nicodemus (John 3:13). The (inner?) veil
of the Temple is torn from top to bottom when Christ dies on the
Cross, meaning not only the end of the old order, but the joining of
heaven and earth, eternity and time, in him.

According to the Jewish Encyclopedia, the inner sanctuary of the
Temple, or the Holy of Holies, was a cubic cell measuring 10 ells or
just less than 40 feet on each side, and lined with gold. It was, then,
a golden cube, and within it were sacred objects such as the Altar,
the Throne, and (in the time of Solomon) the Ark of the Covenant.
Margaret Barker places great emphasis on the cubic shape, connecting it both with the cubic Kaaba of Islam (which is of comparable
size) and with the sacred decad/tetrad or *Tetraktys* of the Pythagore-
ans, not to mention the four letters of the Jewish Tetragrammaton
or sacred Name of God—a name that could be uttered only within

4. See, e.g., Margaret Barker, *The Great High Priest: The Temple Roots of Christian Theology* (London: T&T Clark International, 2003), pp. 185–7.
5. Ibid., pp. 202–217.

the sanctuary by the High Priest once a year. According to Barker (here reviving an ancient supposition of Eusebius and other Church Fathers regarding Plato) the secret teachings of Pythagoras were derived from the First Temple tradition via the Jewish exiles in Babylon.[6]

The inner sanctum of the Temple was lined with gold, but without windows for light. The light of Day One is "interior." Similarly, the cubic city that descends from heaven at the end of the Book of Revelation is lit by the Presence of the Lord. "And I saw no temple in the city, for its temple is the Lord God the Almighty and the Lamb. And the city has no need to sun or moon to shine upon it, for the glory of God is its light, and its lamp is the Lamb" (Rev. 21:22–3).

The Third Temple

The Temple of Solomon in Jerusalem was destroyed in 586 BC, when the Jewish people were exiled to Babylon. A later Babylonian king, Cyrus the Great, permitted the rebuilding of the Temple in the years leading up to 516 BC (Ezra 1:1–4, 2 Chron. 36:22–23). Later it was largely rebuilt by Herod, shortly before the time of Christ, before being destroyed again by the Romans in AD 70, in the final suppression of the Great Jewish Revolt. In a sense, the Jews have again been in exile ever since.

When the First Temple was destroyed much was lost, including many teachings. Most importantly, of course, the Ark of the Covenant disappeared, and along with it the *Shekinah* or divine presence that allegedly had filled the sanctuary like a shining cloud. The Second Temple was an inferior reconstruction, even after Herod's improvements.

When Jesus said, "Destroy this Temple, and in three days I will raise it up" (John 2:19), he was speaking less of Herod's Temple than of his body, and that was because his own flesh was indeed the Third Temple, and the greatest—the true dwelling-place of God on earth, soon to be destroyed by the Romans on the Cross and then raised from death on the third day. Christians subsequently built

---

6. Barker, *The Great High Priest*, pp. 262–93. I discuss this in more detail in *All Things Made New*, pp. 43–59.

---

churches, but these were to house the community gathered for worship around the Body of the Lord, miraculously multiplied in the Eucharist. Today, the Tabernacle in each Catholic Church is a kind of Holy of Holies because it houses the Body of Christ, though it is perhaps not always treated with the respect it deserves. Traditionally it occupied a central place behind the altar, recalling the ancient model of an inner sanctum, situated within the sanctuary where the priests are permitted to go, and separated by an iconostasis or rood screen from the nave where the congregation gather for the "work of the people" (the *ergon* of the *laos*), or formal worship.

All three Temples have this in common, that by their very existence they create a community, a social body, and a personal identity. Those who recognize the Temple and who participate, however remotely, in the worship that takes place there, by that fact acquire an identity. The human person is more than an individual particle, bound to others by exterior forces and willpower alone. The person is to a large extent constituted by relationships such as this—above all the relationship with God, defined as source and final goal. Worship is more than a hobby. This is what causes so much tension in a secular society, for which nothing but exterior forces and free choices can determine personal identity.

Church as Society

The Church is a society. She is not a perfect society, but she is the *only* society that bridges the gap between the moment of our Redemption and the moment of *Parousia* (Second Coming), when the perfect society, the society of saints, will finally be revealed. All other societies belong to an earlier stage of history, before everything changed. The Church is a bridge for those who are trying to get to the other side of a chasm that others are not even aware exists. The Church is a great ship ("nave" is from the Latin *navis*), an Ark, in which all who enter are transported in the direction of the rising sun through a flood that is drowning the world.

At the level of her individual members, she is a multitude, just as a single body is composed of a multitude of cells and organs, and a house is made up of many bricks. The tension between the One and the Many, the Body and the Multitude, is similar to the tension

33

between the Now and the Future, the Church of the present moment (ragged and incomplete, full of sinners far from completely purified) and the Church of the *eschaton* (the Last Day when the process will be complete, and every tear washed away: Rev. 21:4). The Church of the *eschaton* "subsists in" (*Lumen Gentium*, n.8) the incomplete Church of the present—the latter is the ship that takes us to the former.

If we lower our sights to focus on the Many, on the Church as institution, we are immediately dazed by the complexity that confronts us. This is the largest, most ancient corporation on earth, a vast body of more than a billion people spread among all continents and nations, divided between a multitude of cultures, administered through a profusion of offices. To find the hidden order in this complexity we might do well to start with the number twelve (the product of four, representing the four corners of the earth, and three, representing the Trinity). The Church is founded on the Twelve, the Apostles, who were in Christ's eyes the successors of the patriarchs who became the tribes of Israel. The Apostles, as the first bishops, are the original holders of the fullness of the priesthood given by Christ for the perpetuation of the Church. From there we can trace the multiplication into archbishops and cardinals, episcopal conferences, the Curia and the papacy—all the way to the parishes, the religious orders, and the laity. The whole structure rests upon the Twelve, as a plant might grow from twelve roots, but it grows and proliferates through time and circumstance.

There is a structure also *within* or *among* the Twelve, the "root system" of the Church (just as there was also among the tribes). In the Gospels we see three of the Twelve picked out as being especially close to our Lord—Peter, James, and John. It was these three who went with him to Mount Tabor and saw his glory revealed before the Passion. They witnessed him clothed with light and talking with Elijah and Moses. In the Garden of Gethsemane they went with him to pray but fell asleep. Of these three, one (Peter) was appointed by Jesus as the leader of the Apostles, the "rock" on which the Church would be built; that is, with the intention that he would represent the whole body. James, most closely related by blood to Jesus, became the Bishop of Jerusalem and represents the Church of the

Jews. John, the youngest and closest to his heart, the one who with Mary stands at the foot of the Cross, represents mysticism.

Other structures in the Church are less "essential" and more superficial (parish councils, bishops' conferences, etc.), though perhaps no less necessary. And of course much, if not most, of what goes on in the Church is not regulated and controlled by structures at all—I mean the life of the Spirit, who comes and goes as he wills among the People of God, stirring up charisms and sending prophets, mystics, and saints.

There is a connected mystery, too, about the role of women in the Church, ever since the Magdalen and her sisters became the first witnesses to the Resurrection. The life of the Church flows through these women and their successors, though the relationships connecting them are mostly invisible, and there are fewer formal, rocklike structures either to strengthen or to confine them.

The great Thomistic writer Matthias Scheeben warns us against taking too worldly a view. "Concerning the nature of the Church," he says, "the temptation might arise to form a notion that has regard only to externals, on the analogy of other societies that exist among men, and to account for its radical difference only by the fact that it is a religious community founded by God"—bound together for the purpose of common worship; offering a way to fulfill one's religious obligations, no doubt, and endowed with divine authority.[7] "But this circumstance would not make it supernatural and mysterious in its very nature." But the eyes of faith show us more than a society guided by Providence, or even an institution granted the authority to forgive sins.

> The Church is the body of the God-man; and all who enter it become members of the God-man so that, linked together in him and through him, they may share in the divine life and the divine glory of their head. Lastly, as seen by faith, the Church is more than a handmaid of God or of the God-man, a servant who would aid in bringing about a certain limited intimacy between God and man. As the mystical body of Christ, the Church is his true bride

7. M.J. Scheeben, *The Mysteries of Christianity* (London: Herder, 1946), pp. 540–41.

who, made fruitful by his divine power, has the destiny of bearing heavenly children to him and his heavenly Father, of nourishing these children with the substance and light of her bridegroom, and of conducting them beyond the whole range of created nature up to the very bosom of his heavenly Father.[8]

Church as Person

As for the purpose of all the day-to-day activities in the Church, the actions of bishops and priests, of committees and colleges and movements, it is simply to enable the mystical Church, the Church who subsists in the institution, the Church as corporate person, as Bride of Christ, to live and breathe through us and in us—much as the purpose of the ligaments and organs and bones and tissues of my body is to make it possible for me to exist as a personality, by virtue of the soul that permeates them.

The corporate person is the extended body of Christ, beginning with Mary in whose womb he lay and from whom he took all his physical substance, all his genetic material, and all his nourishment. This extended body of the Church, "one flesh" with Christ, is also metaphorically his "bride," for she comes to him on the Cross ("I will draw all people to myself," John 12:32) and unites herself with him through the Eucharist that contains the same sacrifice extended through time in sacramental form.

The balance between the corporate personality of the Church and her individual members is hard to maintain. If the Church were *not* the Church, not a supernatural organism, the problem could never be resolved. But Christ says: "where two or three are gathered together in my name, there am I in the midst of them" (Matt. 18:20)—he is both among them, and within them. Through this mystery of the One in the Many, through the Church, God creates in man "new depths which harmonize him with 'the depths of God,' and he projects man out of himself, right to the very end of the earth; he makes universal and spiritualizes, he personalizes and unifies."[9]

8. Ibid., pp. 541–2.
9. Henri de Lubac SJ, *Catholicism: Christ and the Common Destiny of Man* (San Francisco: Ignatius Press, 1988), p. 339.

In fact this projection is all *part of the Incarnation*, not something "grafted onto" the mission of Christ. It is part of the self-revelation of God—the revelation of the Trinity, and of man as the image and likeness of God. "By revealing the Father and by being revealed by him, Christ completes the revelation of man to himself."[10] This 1947 sentence of Henri de Lubac is echoed in (and no doubt influenced) the one from Vatican II that John Paul II loved to quote above all others: "Christ, the final Adam, by the revelation of the mystery of the Father and his love, fully reveals man to man himself and makes his supreme calling clear."[11] De Lubac writes:

> That image of God, the image of the Word, which the incarnate Word restores and gives back to its glory, is "I myself"; it is also the other, every other. It is that aspect of *me* in which I coincide with every other man, it is the hallmark of our common origin and the summons to our common destiny. It is our very unity in God.[12]

The Church makes human unity possible in the most complete sense. The link between the corporate and the individual is Christ, and in another sense the Holy Spirit, through whom Christ is made present in us. If this seems too individualistic, since the emphasis is on the individual Christ who is present in the many, rather than the many who are present in Christ, de Lubac has already explained that "True union does not tend to dissolve into one another the beings that it brings together, but to bring them to completion by means of one another."[13]

We need to hold on to the Trinity as the only possible basis for the unity of the one in the many and the many in the one. From the moment of the Annunciation and the conception of Christ, it is the Holy Spirit who constitutes the Son of God as the Person that he is. The same Spirit, sent by Christ, makes the members of the Church into Christ—or, as we might say, into Christ's Bride. As does Balthasar after him, de Lubac sees the three Persons in God as the basis

10. Ibid.
11. *Gaudium et Spes*, Constitution on the Church and the World, n. 22.
12. Henri de Lubac SJ, *Catholicism*, p. 340.
13. Ibid., p. 330.

for all diversity in creation, since the otherness of one creature from another is enfolded within a greater otherness in God: "It is impossible to imagine greater distinctions than those of this pure three-fold relationship, since it is these very distinctions that constitute them in their entirety," he writes. "And do they not arise in unity, the unity of the same Nature?"[14] "Union differentiates."[15]

The relationship of the Many to the One has been a fundamental question in philosophy since Plato. If we reject the nominalist idea that only the "many" or the "several" exist and that the "one" into which they are supposed to be integrated is merely a collection or category devised to contain them, we are left trying to make sense of some notion of metaphysical "participation." One may think of two circles in a Venn diagram. If A is entirely surrounded by B, it participates entirely in B. A has a share in B, without diminishing it. If A and B each overlaps the other but leaves some part of itself outside, then the participation is reciprocal (and perhaps there is another circle that enfolds both).

Thanks to the revelation of the Trinity, this notion became equally fundamental in theology. But Christianity transformed participation. In the Trinity, it becomes a mutual indwelling or coinherence—three circles, as it were, entirely overlapping each other.[16] Furthermore the Trinity is an act, rather than a thing. Thus for the Father, Son, or Spirit to participate in the Trinity means that each plays a part or has a role in relation to the others. This idea of "theo-drama" is extended to the whole creation, beginning with the Incarnation, the Church, and the sacraments. The entire saved cosmos depicted in the Book of Revelation is a complex pattern of dramatic participation. The human participates in the divine nature through

14. Ibid., p. 329.
15. Ibid., p. 331.
16. "In the deep and bright/essence of that exalted Light, three circles /appeared to me; they had three different colors,/but all of them were of the same dimension; /one circle seemed reflected by the second,/as rainbow is by rainbow, and the third/ seemed fire breathed equally by those two circles"—Dante Alighieri, *The Divine Comedy*, "Paradiso," Canto XXXIII, trans. Allen Mandelbaum (New York: Alfred A. Knopf, 1995), p. 540.

Christ; the multitude of Christians participate in the one Church; the bishops participate in the unity of the Church through their communion with the successor of Peter.

Eaten by Christ

The miracle of corporate unity that takes place in the Church must happen on the level of the body as well as the soul. It cannot be a social unity, or a spiritual one, without being also physical, since man in his proper personality is as much body as he is spirit. The Holy Spirit acts within the Church as the *soul of a body*, making it function as a unity, at the service of a personality. The cells of that body are essential to its life.

The incorporation of the physical body and therefore the entire person into this higher-order unity takes place through the Eucharist, which is why de Lubac adds to the unobjectionable phrase "the Church makes the Eucharist" the important corollary, "the Eucharist makes the Church."

It "makes" the Church because there would be no Church without the Mass: the Church is nothing other than the community gathered at a million altars to offer, consecrate, and receive the Bread of Life—a community that forms a body, a single corporate person,[17] because it is absorbed into Christ by eating and drinking him. The other sacraments play their part, of course. Baptism exists to prepare people to receive him in the Eucharist; Holy Orders exist to enable him to be offered on the altar.

What does it mean to be absorbed into Christ by eating and drinking him? The teaching is that, while normally to eat means to ingest something—to chew it, digest it, and so on—this cannot be true of the Eucharist, except of its appearances. Under those appearances, it is really and truly (in every particle) the risen and immortal Body and Blood, Soul and Divinity of Christ that we receive, incapable of being divided by our teeth or damaged by our

17. John Zizioulas talks of the "corporate personality" of Christ himself, but I think we are speaking of the personality of Ecclesia, of the Bride of Christ. For background see Paul McPartlan, *The Eucharist Makes the Church: Henri de Lubac and John Zizioulas in Dialogue* (Edinburgh: T&T Clark, 1993).

digestive juices. The appearances, then, are absorbed into our bodies, but the *reality* of what occurs is rather different.

With each particle of the host, the whole Christ is taken into our bodies (not chewed, not fragmented). If we are unbelieving, nothing more happens.[18] But consider what occurs if we offer ourselves in that moment to the one we are receiving under the appearances of bread and wine. In such a case, it is in truth he who will receive us into himself. It is he who "eats" us (in a higher sense of that word), and by whom we are absorbed. In this way we participate in his eternal life.[19]

Something just as strange takes place concerning time. The Mass is essentially a ritual reproduction of the Last Supper, which itself is an anticipation of the Passion on the Cross, which is in turn the temporal expression of the Wedding Feast of the Lamb described in the Book of Revelation—the eschatological banquet at the end of time. In other words, the Eucharist takes us back in time in order to take us forward, to the future. If we attend Mass, we are making ourselves present at the Cross *via* the Last Supper, and equally present at the end of time *via* the Cross that stands at time's center. Our *anamnesis* ("do this in memory of me") is a recapitulation of the whole of history, from the Passover to the New Jerusalem. In that act of participation we become citizens of the heavenly City, into which are poured all the treasures of time, all the adventures and dramas and victories and beauties that we had thought lost.

In these circumstances it is not possible to continue to speak about the present being real and the future merely imaginary. The

18. Except perhaps in the sense that St. Paul means when he warns that "any one who eats and drinks without discerning the body eats and drinks judgment upon himself. That is why many of you are weak and ill, and some have died" (1 Cor. 11:29–30).

19. The fact that the word translated "daily" in "give us this day our daily bread," *epi-ousios*, occurs here and only here in the Bible and nowhere else in ancient literature hints at the *newness* that the Lord brings, when he promises *Behold, I make all things new* (Rev. 21:5). One translation of this newly minted word would refer not only to the physical bread we need to live another day, but to the Lord himself in the Eucharist, who will nurture us for the *state of being* to come—the eighth day of creation.

Mass plunges us into a reality that exists at the end of time. Normal causality is reversed because that future reality transforms the present. The energy that comes into the world with the Resurrection and is available to us in the Mass flows backward through time. It flows from that (to us, future) point when time itself flows into eternity. It is as though by penetrating the wall of eternity, time itself has been opened to the influence of what lies on the other side.

That is one way of looking at it. There are others—for example, we might talk of the heavenly City as a "final cause" always mysteriously present to the human heart, or a "strange attractor" in the geometry of creation drawing all things to itself. However we conceive of it, the impact of the Eucharist celebrated and received in the Mass or Divine Liturgy does not leave the world unchanged—either the spiritual world or the world of creatures in general. If Christ in the Eucharist is generating the Church, he is also creating a "morphogenetic field" in which the pattern of love that we see in the Mass becomes an active force in society. It does not turn the world into a utopia, but it establishes new possibilities. It becomes easier to be good, since we should take with us from the Mass an understanding of self-sacrifice, and the energy of grace. In the Mass, we learn to give ourselves, and to receive God. That complete receptivity is precisely the basis of a loving relationship with our neighbor. Or put it this way: if we do *not* go out from the Mass and change the world for the better, we have little excuse for it.

William T. Cavanaugh has written about the effects of the Eucharist in the political and economic realm. Referring to the Letter to the Corinthians, he notes that for St. Paul the notion "body of Christ" was much more than a metaphor.

> So seriously did he take it that he believed that those Corinthians who were taking Eucharist without "discerning the body" were getting sick and dying (1 Cor. 11:27–32). The Christians at Corinth thought that the humiliation of the poor by the rich was unrelated to the celebration of the Lord's Supper. Paul told them otherwise. Here we see that the Eucharist not only produces unity but requires it. The Eucharist is not just a balm for the soul; it is a public act of the Church that disciplines the bodies of its members. Through the action of the Holy Spirit, the one body of Christ is

41

formed, in which the sufferings of others become my sufferings and simultaneously the sufferings of Christ himself (1 Cor. 12). The Eucharist produces a radical identification of three terms: Christ, those who suffer, and me (cf. Matt. 25:31–46).[20]

To heal the fragmentation of the world, to gather the scattered, to overcome the alienation between individuals and social groups, we need to act to create new structures and opportunities, from soup kitchens to cooperatives, from successful businesses to peace treaties. The secret to making such actions work is the unseen influence of a mystical body that already potentially incorporates everybody. In the Eucharist, we are helped to see the whole in every fragment, and Christ in every person.

Our Lady

In a sense the "institutional" Church, which seems so solid and real much of the time and to most people, is illusory in comparison with this divine society. You need to see through it—past all the imperfections and failures which, though real enough at their own level, will eventually pass away—and then the reality becomes visible. But the Church as divine society is entirely personal. That is what makes it real.

The Eucharist makes the Church, but the Eucharist is made by a priestly sacrifice, and that sacrifice is made possible by the *fiat* ("let it be") of the Virgin when she opens herself to the Word of God. Her assent to God's plan, a plan that may seem impossible in worldly terms, opens not just her but the whole world to the indwelling of the Holy Spirit. The Virgin becomes his vessel and perhaps even, in a way, his incarnation (according to St. Maximilian Kolbe). All else follows from this, or depends upon it. The Virgin is not the priest who calls down the Holy Spirit upon the altar; rather, *she is the altar itself.* She is that part of the earth that has been sanctified and set apart for the sacrifice, where the marriage of heaven and earth takes place.

---

20. William T. Cavanaugh, "The Body of Christ: The Eucharist and Politics," *Word & World*, Vol. 22:2 (Spring 2002), p. 176.

I have written about divine mercy, but Mary is mercy personified. Mercy is seen when heaven touches the earth.

> Mercy is the tranquility of His omnipotence and the sweetness of His omnipresence, the fruit of His eternity and the companion of His immensity, the chief satisfaction of His justice, the triumph of His wisdom, and the patient perseverance of His love. Wherever we go, there is mercy, the peaceful, active, broad, deep, endless mercy of our heavenly Father. If we work by day, we work in mercy's light, and we sleep at night in the lap of our Father's mercy. The courts of heaven gleam with its outpoured prolific beauty. Earth is covered with it, as the waters cover the bed of the stormy sea. Purgatory is as it were its own separate creation, and is lighted by its gentle moonlight, gleaming there soft and silvery through night and day. Even the realm of hopeless exile is less palpably dark than it would be, did not some excesses of mercy's light enter even there.[21]

The Church is the mercy of God. It begins with our Lady, like the first light of dawn, or the first breath of a newborn child. In that sense she is the heart of the Church, the heart of the Body of Christ. Around her are the others who represent important functions that the Body cannot survive without. Hans Urs von Balthasar famously writes about the relationship between Mary and Peter, the latter representing "office" in the Church, or what in secular terms is called power and authority. The particular charism of Peter is leadership, that of Mary/John subjective holiness, that of Paul/John theological insight, and so on. There is then, certainly, authority and power in the Church. No one can deny it. But the power of the office-holder in God's Church is inverted to become entirely service, to become humility. *The greatest among you shall be the least.* Thus in a sense Mary's "power" is even greater than Peter's, since it is the perfection of humility to which he can only aspire; and so "the Petrine universality is subject to the formative influence of the Marian, but not vice

---

21. Frederick William Faber, cited in John Saward, John Morrill, and Michael Tomko (eds), *Firmly I Believe and Truly: The Spiritual Tradition of Catholic England—An Anthology of Writings from 1483 to 1999* (Oxford University Press, 2011), p. 496.

versa."[22] She enables all things to be accomplished by the One who alone can bring them about, and all the other members of the Church receive their graces from her, participating in her glory.

At the Second Vatican Council the decision was taken to discuss the Mother of God only in the context of the Church—"Mariology" only in the context of ecclesiology. The crisis that followed, in which Mariology almost disappeared, is long over. The longer-term result was a deeper Mariology, and a deeper ecclesiology. Joseph Ratzinger points out:

> In contrast to the masculine, activistic-sociological *populous Dei* (People of God) approach, Church—ecclesia—is feminine. This fact opens a dimension of the mystery that points beyond sociology, a dimension wherein the real ground and unifying power of the reality Church first appears. Church is more than "people," more than structure and action: the Church contains the living mystery of maternity and of the bridal love that makes maternity possible. There can be ecclesial piety, love for the Church, only if this mystery exists. When the Church is no longer seen in any but a masculine, structural, purely theoretical way, what is most authentically ecclesial about *ecclesia* has been ignored—the center upon which the whole of biblical and patristic talk about the Church actually hinges.[23]

The Church, viewed through the lens of Mary, is no mere sociological structure, or mechanical instrument—which Ratzinger sees as in some sense a "masculine" conception (although this is unjust to masculinity properly understood). Thanks to Mary's presence at the heart of the Church, we cannot degrade the Church to a mere "it," a thing, or even a program of action. The Church rather means

---

22. H.U. von Balthasar, *The Office of Peter and the Structure of the Church* (San Francisco: Ignatius Press, 1986), p.206. Pope Francis has famously said on more than one occasion that because Mary is more important than the Apostles, this should be reflected in the roles played by women in the Church. Though she can never be a priest, and is not always a physical mother, woman always has the potential of spiritual motherhood, which can be expressed in a multitude of ways, some of them not invented yet.

23. Joseph Ratzinger, in Hans Urs von Balthasar and Joseph Cardinal Ratzinger, *Mary: The Church at the Source* (San Francisco: Ignatius Press, 2005), pp. 25–6.

"the creature's fusion with its Lord in spousal love, in which its hope for divinization is fulfilled by way of faith."[24] Mary serves as the seal both of creation and of the love that transcends everything created. She is the "pure heart" at the center that enables the Church to see God.

If this is true, the implications extend to sociology itself—a modern intellectual discipline dominated by a reductionist approach to everything human. The separation of the Church from all that lies outside is to some extent a false move, the result of the Enlightenment's attempt to disentangle nature from grace, the natural from the supernatural. The distinction may be valid, but not the separation. Whether or not they see themselves as belonging to a "Church," men are not isolated individuals but members of an organic body; and whether or not they believe in a "higher power" they depend on a relationship to their Creator and Redeemer.

Pillars of Wisdom

The divine society has seven pillars.[25] If we follow St. Augustine (who in this was followed by St. Thomas), these correspond to the first seven Beatitudes. Each of these in turn corresponds to one of the seven Gifts of the Holy Spirit. Then again, each also corresponds to one of the seven Petitions of the Our Father in which we implicitly pray for those self-same Gifts.

Our Father, hallowed be thy name. The Gift that enables us truly to hold the Father's name holy is called the *"Fear of the Lord,"* which is the "beginning of wisdom"—the respect due to God because he is all-powerful and all-holy. So when we pray this Petition, we are asking God to give us this Gift of Fear through the Holy Spirit. And the corresponding Beatitude is *Blessed are the poor in spirit, for theirs is the kingdom of heaven,* because the spiritually destitute have nothing, and they know they are nothing before the face of God, nothing

---

24. Ibid., p. 30.
25. "Wisdom has built her house, she has set up her seven pillars" (Prov. 9:1). Readers of this section will find a more detailed study of the relation of the Virtues to the Fruits of the Spirit in my *Fruits of the Spirit* (CTS, 2010), and of other correlations in my *Seven Sacraments*.

except what God chooses to make them. Face-to-face with our heavenly Father we are filled with awe and wonder—and, yes, that extreme form of respect we sometimes call fear.

Thy kingdom come. The first thing we ask of this God whose name we have hallowed is that his kingdom come among us, so that we may never be parted from him. The Gift associated with this petition is *Piety*, meaning religious devotion—such devotion that we place the kingdom first, and worry about nothing else (Matt. 6:33). *Blessed are the meek, for they shall inherit the earth.* Piety gives meekness and humility, and humility prepares the ground for the kingdom to be planted on earth.

Thy will be done, on earth as it is in heaven. This is how the kingdom comes—by our doing the will of the Father. The convergence of heaven and earth is brought about by the Gift of the Holy Spirit called "*Knowledge*." The person who knows the will of God and does it on earth has knowledge indeed, and in this lies his comfort, to console him for the loss of all that is taken from him in this life. *Blessed are those who mourn, for they shall be comforted.*

Give us this day our daily bread. Our strength to carry on in the world, doing the will of God and building his kingdom, is nourished by the Body of the Lord himself. This is food for the heart and soul, and associated with the Gift of *Fortitude* or courage. Those who have this gift and are strengthened by this food find their hunger for righteousness satisfied. Righteousness is re-established not least by the Christian who has the fortitude to stand firm and embody that righteousness for others, come what may (Matt. 5:10). *Blessed are those who hunger and thirst for righteousness, for they shall be satisfied.*

And forgive us our trespasses as we forgive those who trespass against us. The Gift of *Counsel* is the ability to discern the right from the wrong course of action. Through this gift we become aware of our own sins, our "trespasses," and our own need for forgiveness—a forgiveness that we cannot receive unless we extend it to others first. Only then will we obtain the mercy we ourselves need. *Blessed are the merciful, for they shall obtain mercy.*

And lead us not into temptation. With the Gift of *Understanding* we are able to know how to live as a Christian and to see temptations against virtue for what they are. This Gift is coupled with the Beatitude *Blessed are the pure in heart, for they shall see God*, because only such purity enables us to understand the nature of the Christian path—the Way that corresponds to the nature of God himself, and leads us to him. Understanding is like an ability to see the light.

But deliver us from evil. The final Petition corresponds to a plea for *Wisdom* as the Gift that crowns all the others, the final structural component that makes the house into a secure shelter, the union with God that removes us from the reach of evil forever. Only Wisdom enables us to make peace among men, and not just within ourselves. This is the perfection of Catholic social teaching. *Blessed are the peacemakers, for they shall be called sons of God.*

It is worth noting that the *Catechism of the Catholic Church* seems to adopt a different approach, expounding social teaching in relation to the Commandments rather than the Beatitudes. So where in the schema I have been developing is there room for the various virtues of Christian life, and the Commandments that encapsulate the natural law?

The Commandments are ten, but as we have seen they are divided into two groups of three and seven, conventionally called the two "tablets" of the Law, the first dealing with the ways we must express our love of God, and the second with the love of neighbor. It is the second tablet that the *Catechism* uses to teach Catholic social doctrine (2198). Thus all we need to do is take these seven Commandments and correlate them with the list of Beatitudes.

As for the virtues, there are also seven of these, divided into three *theological* virtues and four *cardinal* virtues. The cardinal virtues, known and discussed since pre-Christian antiquity, are the various good qualities that orient human beings in their moral life. They are the habitual patterns of behavior that define a person of good character the world over. Christians, of course, are no exception. But Christianity adds three more virtues, which it calls "theological" because their object is God. These are the habitual qualities that direct us towards and attach us to our maker: faith, hope, and love (or "charity"). In the following chart they are underlined.

Commandments	Virtues	Beatitudes
Fourth (parents)	Faith	Poor in spirit
Fifth (murder)	Temperance	Meek
Sixth (adultery)	Prudence	Mourn
Seventh (stealing)	Love	Hunger for Righteousness
Eighth (false witness)	Justice	Merciful
Ninth (neighbor's wife)	Hope	Pure in Heart
Tenth (neighbor's goods)	Fortitude	Peacemakers

These correlations supply ample fuel for meditation on the moral and spiritual foundations without which the kingdom cannot be built on rock, and the City of God will remain forever beyond our reach.

Catholic Social Doctrine

The Church cannot and must not take upon herself the political battle to bring about the most just society possible. She cannot and must not replace the State. Yet at the same time she cannot and must not remain on the sidelines in the fight for justice. She has to play her part through rational argument and she has to reawaken the spiritual energy without which justice, which always demands sacrifice, cannot prevail and prosper. ⁓Pope Benedict XVI[1]

The Gospel is quite clear. I am a bad person. Matthew 25:31–46 describes the Final Judgment, when the King will separate the sheep from the goats on the basis of whether they had, in life, fed the hungry, welcomed the stranger, clothed the naked, and visited those sick and in prison. I have done very little of this. I admit I have lived a fairly intellectual existence and a sheltered life, with little exposure to poverty, and virtually no attempt to engage with charities and organizations devoted to assisting the poor. I am not proud of this, since a conversion to Christianity might be expected to bring with it a determination to make the world a better place by living out the love of Christ.

Probably my story is not uncommon among Christians. We can see the rightness of doing good, but we seldom do it. If of an intellectual bent, we become more concerned with conversation, argument, apologetics, and philosophy. We postpone more radical action, or shelve it in order to look after our own family and immediate circle of friends—after all, that is a Christian duty too. But occasionally it may occur to us to wonder how different the world would be, how much healthier the Church, if we acted on our beliefs in the way the saints do, casting away our security and maybe

---

1. *Caritas in Veritate*, n. 28.

even our friends in order to serve those in desperate need, or defend life in some practical way. I took the name Francis at my confirmation, and was reminded of this at the election in 2013 of Pope Francis, who calls us to live our faith more authentically.

Pope Francis has been quick to remind us that (welfare state or no) the Christian Gospel still calls us to serve the poor and "wash each other's feet," responding to the needs of our neighbor—be he Samaritan or no—with compassion and care.

Christian theology begins with the Gospel; that is, with the simple but profound message that *perfect love* is the meaning and ultimate goal of existence, and that this love is revealed by being made incarnate in Jesus of Nazareth—that is, not simply taught but *lived* by him. What Christians call "love," therefore, is not simply a feeling or sentiment, whether of infatuation or sympathy. It is not reducible even to a high form of compassion or empathy. (It is therefore arguably distinct even from the notion of compassion or loving-kindness in Buddhism.)[2] Where feelings come and go, or vary in their intensity, love remains constant. It is rather an orientation or disposition of the will—a will that is not closed in upon itself, but able to receive from and give to another. To love is to open one's heart to others. When such a disposition expresses itself, it does so in acts of self-giving; that is, in the form of service.

Service of the Poor

Kindness, hospitality, and mercy have always been human virtues, and they are found everywhere, in all times, in every civilization. They rest on a fundamental ability to empathize with others, which is lacking only in certain exceptional individuals, and highly devel-

---

2. The distinction is explored by Henri de Lubac in *Aspects of Buddhism* (London: Sheed & Ward, 1953), as rooted in the fact that in Buddhism the neighbor cannot be loved "for himself," since the ego is illusory. Tenderness or compassion is directed rather towards his "moral or physical sufferings" (38). "Since in the depths of his being there is no ontological solidity deriving from a Creator; since he is nothing but a mass of component parts, with no inner unity, therefore there is nothing in the human being that can call for, or make possible, any ultimate love. Altruism of any kind, whatever its tinge, and however ardent it may be, can only be a procedure for getting rid of desire" (41).

oped in others. Christianity took these virtues and made them central—in a sense founded a religion upon them—by substituting them for the human and animal sacrifices that had always been thought necessary to appease the gods. Judaism had already spoken of this: "My sacrifice is a broken and contrite heart" (Ps. 51:17); "To obey is better than sacrifice, and to heed is better than the fat of rams" (1 Sam. 15:22); "For I desire steadfast love and not sacrifice, the knowledge of God rather than burnt offerings" (Hosea 6:6).

Christ replaced all *external* sacrifices with his own, and asked of his followers only that they join themselves to him in spirit. To do that they must have faith, but a living faith expresses itself in works, and the works that express the Christian faith are those of charity, mercy, and kindness.

The charity of the early Christians is well known, and in large part the rapid expansion of the faith may have been due to the fact that it appealed directly to the poor and those on the margins of Roman society. Christians shared their worldly goods with anyone who had need of them, and spoke of Christ when asked. If the radical abolition of any distinction between rich and poor in the earliest Church (Acts 4:32–37) could not be preserved, nevertheless *diaconia* or the "ministry of charity" became part of the fundamental structure of the Church and has remained so throughout two thousand years of history. The *diaconia* is one of the three essential elements of Christian existence and responsibility, the others being the proclamation of God's Word (*kerygma-martyria*), and the celebration of the sacraments of Christ's actual presence (*leitourgia*). This is discussed in some detail by Pope Benedict XVI in the second Part of his encyclical *Deus Caritas Est*, which is devoted to the *diaconia* in particular.[3]

Monasteries and religious orders, as well as individuals, have played an enormous role in this ministry of charity.

3. The first Part is devoted to *Caritas*. Cf. Werner G. Jeanrond, *A Theology of Love* (London: T&T Clark, 2010). For both Jews and Christians, the created order is good and charity is rewarded. For Christians, the poor are a form of sacrament in which Christ is present. See Gary A. Anderson, *Charity: The Place of the Poor in the Biblical Tradition* (New Haven: Yale University Press, 2013).

Bishops of the early Church were known as "Fathers of the Poor" and by their consecration oath were bound to show "mercy and kindness, in the name of the Lord, to the poor, the stranger, and all in want." In the first century, Pope St. Clement explained to the Corinthians that those who give to the poor, give as to Christ; in the third century the anonymous *Didascalia Apostolorum* lists the duties of a Christian towards the poor; in 370 St. Basil the Great, Bishop of Caesarea, built an entire village for the poor outside the city of Caesarea; and in the fifth century St. Theodosius opened two hospitals for the poor near Jerusalem. In the sixth century Pope Gregory the Great recorded that a quarter of the Church's income was devoted to the poor, while the Synod of Tours of 567 imposed on each parish the obligation of caring for the poor. The ninth century, during the reign of Charlemagne, saw a revival of the tradition that all Church property was the patrimony of the poor.[4]

The "social teaching" of the early Church was thus not a separate body of writings, but indistinguishable from the Scriptures, the homilies of the bishops and Church Fathers, and the daily actions of the Christians themselves, attempting to live a faith founded on the mercy of God. From the sixth century, St Benedict's Rule among others gave structure to the life of monks who were separating themselves from an increasingly prosperous existence in an established Church, and reviving the spirit of the early Christians through vows of poverty, chastity, and obedience. With the additional commitment to "stability" (staying in one place), many of these new monastic communities—especially after the fall of the Empire—became centers of civilization in the wilderness, but they were also places of hospitality and refuge, since the stranger in need was to be welcomed as Christ himself.[5]

4. Mark Turnham Elvins, *The Call to Hospitality: The Origins of the Hospitaller Vocation* (Leominster: Gracewing, 2013), Introduction. On the social *praxis* of the early Church see also Rodger Charles SJ, *Christian Social Witness and Teaching*, Vol. 1 (Leominster: Gracewing, 1998), pp. xiii–xiv.

5. Elvins describes how in the Middle Ages the monastery tended to take over the energy of the Christian life from the parishes. "In every district, alike on towering mountain and in lowly valley, arose monasteries [not solely Benedictine, of course] which formed centers of the organized religious life for the neighborhood,

Against this background, the "hospitaller" vocation developed at the end of the first millennium, prompted in part by the needs of the Crusades.[6] In 1072 the Hospital of St John was founded in Jerusalem, and soon after that a new religious Order, the Knights of St John, following the Benedictine Rule and later the Rule of St Augustine. The vocation of the Knights was specifically to serve the sick (of all faiths) as their lords. Maternity hospitals and field hospitals soon followed, and the Knights have spread and flourished up to the present day (a period of decline was followed by revival after 1879) as one of the largest charitable organizations in the world.

After the Reformation, however ("the result of the corruption in the Church which popes and bishops were too slow to check"[7]), many of the duties of charity began to be assumed by the State. Britain may serve as an example. "In pre-Reformation Britain the Church provided all the welfare, largely shelter and hospitality, for the sick and the poor,"[8] so that by the 1530s a population of less than 4 million was served by 1,500 monasteries and more than 750 religious hospitals or houses of hospitality, available free of charge to the homeless, the sick, the aged, and orphans. Monasteries and parishes were, in theory and often in practice, willing to support those in need.

With the dissolution of the monasteries and the suppression of much of Catholic civil society throughout England under the Tudors, this informal "welfare system" was swept away and the infirm and destitute found themselves living on the road. Elizabeth I was forced to enact a series of Poor Laws (1572, 1597, 1601) to get beggars and vagrants off the streets, or at least to keep them moving. The early Poor Laws simply prescribed punishments such as whipping or the stocks, or confined begging to certain defined

---

maintained schools, provided models for agriculture, industry, pisciculture, and forestry, sheltered the traveler, relieved the poor, reared the orphans, cared for the sick, and were havens of refuge for all who were weighted down by spiritual or corporeal misery. For centuries they were centers of all religious and cultural activity" (ibid., pp. 48–9).

6. See Elvins, *The Call to Hospitality.*
7. Rodger Charles SJ, *Christian Social Witness*, p. 1.
8. Ibid.

areas, until the Act of 1601 created a system of minimal relief based in parishes and paid for by taxation. The subsequent history of social welfare, right up to the creation of the National Health Service in Britain in the 1940s, is complex, not least because of the impact of wars, famines, and plagues; but it is arguable that, with the establishment of houses of correction and workhouses from Tudor times through to the reign of Victoria, the State-administered regime was always considerably harsher than the one that had preceded it.

The Modern Encyclical Tradition

The social encyclicals (teaching documents) of the Church in the modern period were conceived as a response by Pope Leo XIII to the social conditions of the nineteenth century brought about by the Industrial Revolution. These same conditions had undermined the common good of society and led to the revolutionary movements of 1848 and the development of communism. The same period saw the remnants of a functioning Catholic civil society of guilds and confraternities largely swept away in central Europe. This theory of Karl Marx (d. 1883) envisaged the inevitable development of a global society without nation states, governments, class divisions, or private property. Through the dialectic of class struggle, a "dictatorship of the bourgeoisie" would give way to a "dictatorship of the proletariat" (socialism) before achieving the communist utopia. In reality, of course, in those states where socialism held sway, utopia never arrived.

Seeing the injustice and discontent that nourished the growth of communism, the pope called in *Rerum Novarum* (1891)[9] for the amelioration of "the misery and wretchedness pressing so unjustly on the majority of the working class," and supported the rights of labor to form unions, but also affirmed the right to private property

---

9. *Rerum Novarum* itself was based on long tradition and on the work of thinkers such as Cardinal Manning of England and Bishop Wilhelm von Ketteler of Germany. More attention should be devoted to the Catholic social teaching of the nineteenth century, including the thought of Karl Adam Müller (d. 1829) who developed an influential response to the economic individualism of Adam Smith.

which was anathema to communism and most kinds of socialism. He spoke of the duties of both workers and employers to collaborate in building a prosperous and peaceful society. Pope Leo, in other words, opposed communism, while also opposing the more extreme forms of capitalism. Later popes built on the foundation laid by Leo, and tried to maintain this somewhat delicate balance—emphasizing the "universal destination of goods" or the "social mortgage," according to which the "*right to private property,* acquired or received in a just way, does not do away with the original gift of the earth to the whole of mankind. The *universal destination of goods* remains primordial, even if the promotion of the common good requires respect for the right to private property and its exercise" (*CCC*, n. 2403). The right to private property is subordinated to the right to common use.

St. Thomas Aquinas is acknowledging this principle when he argues that a poor man may help himself to a rich man's goods when in danger of starving. "In cases of need all things are common property, so that there would seem to be no sin in taking another's property, for need has made it common."[10] Clearly St. Thomas is talking of extreme cases, and other considerations come into play, but the principle is clear enough. Property of every sort—from land through to intellectual property—belongs absolutely only to God, and is "licensed" to us for the sake of the common good, to be the object of our labor, not to be hoarded or kept for the benefit of a few. The universal destination of goods therefore leads to a secondary principle: a *preferential option for the poor,* by which we try to compensate for the advantages possessed by the rich.[11]

This teaching is founded on an understanding of the "common good" that needs to be clearly explained. As D.C. Schindler puts it, "Genuine community can be founded only on the sort of good that can be shared, which means that it can be 'possessed' by more than

---

10. *Summa Theologiae,* II–II, Q 66, a 7. Thus "it is lawful for a man to succor his own need by means of another's property, by taking it either openly or secretly." (It might be advisable not to shout this from the rooftops.) I will return to the theme of justice in chapters 6 and 8.

11. I return to the theme of justice in Chapters 6 and 8.

one individual at the same time."[12] Think of it this way: a birthday cake can only be enjoyed by dividing it, but a birthday *party* is enjoyed by many simultaneously—and the more the merrier (within reason). Most social goods are of this type, but they cannot be understood as such if we approach them in the way Thomas Hobbes does, as individualists. They cannot even be understood in terms of a "social contract," as Schindler explains, since in that case we are looking not at a genuinely common good, but at a coincidence of individual goods. A contract simply specifies that I will receive my good if you receive yours.[13] Schindler argues that the common good of the *polis* is not a set of individual necessities (such as goods, services, and protection from harm) that the government is expected to provide or enable, nor is the common good the same as *public order*—simply allowing individuals to flourish through the equal exercise of freedom. The common good is genuinely *common*.

The common good unfolds in three main dimensions. *Solidarity* is the intrinsic relationship of the person to the family, the community, and the common good. It refers to the "horizontal" dimension of society, because the common good is that in which all share as equals, on the same level. *Subsidiarity*, on the other hand, involves the devolution of human freedom and responsibility to the lowest and most local level compatible with the common good. It pertains to the "vertical" dimension, because it serves the common good through an order that is hierarchical in nature. Finally, *sustainability* refers to the human responsibility for maintaining and cultivating the resources that have been entrusted to it. This applies to the dimension of "time." By neglecting the long-term social or environmental impact of a product, for example, we are ignoring a vital dimension of the common good.

---

12. D.C. Schindler, "Enriching the Good: Toward the Development of a Relational Anthropology," in *Communio* 37: 4 (Winter 2010), p. 647.

13. By contrast a *covenant* is a much "thicker" union, more akin to the unity between family members. It cannot be dissolved by the mere breaking of an agreement. See my *Catholic Social Teaching: A Way In* for a discussion of the importance of the contract in Catholic doctrine.

A Culture of Life

During the twentieth century, social conditions were again transformed. After two devastating world wars, the creation of the European Community and the United Nations, and the promulgation of a Universal Declaration of Human Rights—all in a period of relative prosperity—it was easy to assume that the complex economies of the West had entered a Golden Age. The assumption was strengthened by the euphoria that followed the defeat and collapse of communism in 1989. Things were not quite that simple. There were, for example, many important forms of poverty still unaddressed. Mother Teresa famously accused the affluent West of desperate spiritual poverty. Furthermore the fragility of the Western economies began to reveal itself in a series of economic crises. We began to suspect that the wealth of the industrial nations had been built on the exploitation of the third world, and the using up of natural resources that cannot be replaced.

The question of whether the Western economies still need radical reform came to the fore with the publication by Pope John Paul II of *Centesimus Annus* in 1991. That encyclical marked the hundredth anniversary of *Rerum Novarum*, and celebrated the downfall of communism in Eastern Europe, in which the pope from Poland had played a major role. It consolidated not only the pope's own previous social encyclicals but an entire century of social teaching. This teaching also included a theme I have not explored up to now, but which should be called central, especially for John Paul II—the teaching on the culture of life.

> It is necessary to go back to seeing the family as the *sanctuary of life.* The family is indeed sacred: it is the place in which life—the gift of God—can be properly welcomed and protected against the many attacks to which it is exposed, and can develop in accordance with what constitutes authentic human growth. In the face of the so-called culture of death, the family is the heart of the culture of life. (CA 39)

To this John Paul II was to devote yet another encyclical, *Evangelium Vitae* (The Gospel of Life, 1995).

It is often assumed that the abolition of slavery in the nineteenth century was a turning point in Western civilization, marking a definitive moral advance. But while certain obvious forms of slavery on which the colonial powers depended were abolished at that time,[14] others remain and even thrive to the present day, as campaigners and activists such as the missionary priest Shay Cullen constantly remind us. Sex slavery and prostitution in particular, including the systematic abuse of children, has flourished alongside worldwide internet access, which also explains the ubiquity of pornography (with all the exploitation that implies) among young men of the rising generation even in the West. Whatever moral advances we may have made are offset by the growing prevalence even today of slavery, abortion, and pornography—not to mention the steadily increasing pressure for freely available abortion and euthanasia.

This is all part of the context that John Paul II chose to identify as the "culture of death," opposed to the "culture of life" represented by the Church.[15] In one sense the conflict between these is hardly new. The pope himself quotes one of the earliest non-biblical Christian texts, the Didache, to this effect:

There are two ways, a way of life and a way of death; there is a great difference between them. . . . In accordance with the precept of the teaching: you shall not kill . . . you shall not put a child to death by abortion nor kill it once it is born. . . . The way of death is this: . . . they show no compassion for the poor, they do not suffer with the suffering, they do not acknowledge their Creator, they kill their children and by abortion cause God's creatures to perish; they drive away the needy, oppress the suffering, they are advocates of the rich and unjust judges of the poor; they are filled with every sin. May you be able to stay ever apart, o children, from all these sins![16]

John Paul II, however, made this the center of his attention and devoted much effort to understanding and combatting the mental-

14. No doubt partly because the development of technology was making human slaves redundant anyway.

15. For a study of the way our culture has come to stifle its conscience, a process reflected in literature and biography, see Edward Short, *Culture and Abortion* (Leominster: Gracewing, 2013).

16. Cited in Pope John Paul II, *Evangelium Vitae*, n. 54.

ity behind the culture of death. He showed that it is rooted in the attempt to reduce man to an isolated individual, entirely visible and subordinated to the desire and the will of others.[17]

The century of social teaching initiated by Leo XIII thus culminated in the teaching of John Paul II—but not in *Centesimus Annus* alone. The pope's social doctrine cannot be separated from his teaching on the culture of life, on philosophy (*Fides et Ratio*) and on moral theology (in *Veritatis Splendor*). It is these documents, and others too numerous to list here, that filled out in great detail the theological and philosophical principles underlying the culture of life. And none of these principles (solidarity and subsidiarity included) are more important than that of Personalism. It is the intrinsic and constitutive relationship to God, uniquely possessed by man (but through which the whole world of creation is joined to its Creator), that gives him his inalienable dignity, a dignity that is unfolded in the doctrine of human rights succinctly summarized in *Centesimus Annus* (n. 47):

> Among the most important of these rights, mention must be made of the right to life, an integral part of which is the right of the child to develop in the mother's womb from the moment of conception; the right to live in a united family and in a moral environment conducive to the growth of the child's personality; the right to develop one's intelligence and freedom in seeking and knowing the truth; the right to share in the work which makes wise use of the earth's material resources, and to derive from that work the means to support oneself and one's dependents; and the right freely to establish a family, to have and to rear children through the responsible exercise of one's sexuality. In a certain sense, the source and synthesis of these rights is religious freedom, understood as the right to live in the truth of one's faith and in conformity with one's transcendent dignity as a person.

17. The appalling crimes of Dr. Kermit Gosnell, the Philadelphia abortionist sentenced in 2013 for brutally killing embryonic children born alive, demonstrate the result of this mentality. Man becomes mere matter—biological tissue—to be exterminated when unwanted, or traded and experimented upon for the sake of material gain. Murder becomes commerce: the culture of death at its most gruesome.

Caritas in Veritate

The eight-year pontificate of Benedict XVI, who was by background a theologian and founding member of the *Communio* school, began in 2005, although as Cardinal Ratzinger he had been a close collaborator of Pope John Paul II from 1981 as Prefect of the Congregation for the Doctrine of the Faith. Benedict's main social encyclical, *Caritas in Veritate* ("Charity in Truth," 2009), was published in the wake of the great economic crisis that engulfed the world economies after 2007. I want to focus on this encyclical in some detail because it marks a watershed in the history of Catholic social teaching.[18]

Closely related to the pope's two previous encyclical letters, on *Love* and on *Hope*, *Caritas in Veritate* starts from the fact that "God is love." Love or charity is the heart of the Church's social doctrine and is applicable to everyone, Christian or not. But what gives meaning and value to charity, saving it from sentimentality, is truth. Love is not merely a mood or a feeling, but *"Logos,"* intelligible order. This is what gives the encyclical its teeth, in line with the pope's appeal elsewhere to the need for us to broaden our concept of reason, rather than confining it to purely material concerns (n. 31). In chapter 5 he describes the deepest foundation of human solidarity and subsidiarity, namely the nature of the human creature as spiritual, and therefore as "defined through interpersonal relations" (n. 53), in the image of the Trinity (n. 54), and only growing to maturity by living these relations properly.

God is One, but also Three—three persons in one undivided substance. The Trinity is the basis for diversity-within-communion at every level of creation, and man (that is, the human being, or humanity) is made in its image and likeness. This mystery is

---

18. The encyclical had been intended for publication on the anniversary of Paul VI's *Populorum Progressio* (1967), but was delayed in order to take full account of the crisis. See the helpful symposium of articles on the encyclical in *Communio*, 37:4 (Winter 2010). For a range of responses to this encyclical see Daniel K. Finn (ed.), *The Moral Dynamics of Economic Life: An Extension and Critique of* Caritas in Veritate (Oxford University Press, 2013).

inexhaustible. The pope calls for the social sciences to work with metaphysics and theology in order to do justice to "man's transcendent dignity" as a social and therefore relational creature. In particular, he says, we need *"a deeper critical evaluation of the category of relation"* (n. 53) in order to elucidate the image of God in man and its implications for our social existence. Connected with this emphasis on wisdom and metaphysics is an insistence that God and theology cannot be excluded from the public realm (cultural, social, economic, political) without damaging or seriously distorting human development (n. 56).

At a practical level, in response to the new circumstances—"global interrelations, the damaging effects on the real economy of badly managed and largely speculative financial dealing, large-scale migration of peoples, often provoked by some particular circumstance and then given insufficient attention, the unregulated exploitation of the earth's resources" (n. 21)—the pope advocates a form of sustainable and holistic development that takes account of all the dimensions of the human person and remains open to the transcendent.

In chapter 4 he examines several threats to the integrity of human development. One of these is the proliferation of rights detached from duties, which takes place when rights are no longer understood as rooted in the nature and authentic needs of the person. Another is the impoverishment of sexuality and the imposition of materialistic ideas and policies with regard to the family. Human development on every level will be thwarted by continued attacks on marriage, the unborn, and the elderly. He mentions also the excessive centralization of certain development programs, which take little account of the need for subsidiarity and effective local management.

Finally, he stresses the enormous range of duties that arise from our relationship to the *environment,* which is bound up with our relationship to the poor and towards future generations. Nature is a gift of the Creator, containing an inbuilt order that we must respect. And once more, stewardship of the environment cannot be separated from respect for human life, sexuality, and the family—as the pope puts it in section 51, the Church must "defend not only earth, water and air as gifts of creation that belong to everyone. She must above all protect mankind from self-destruction. There is need for what might be called a human ecology, correctly understood."

Human ecology is bound up with a sense of the dignity of the human person, particularly "the right to life and to a natural death." For "the book of nature is one and indivisible: it takes in not only the environment but also life, sexuality, marriage, the family, social relations" (n.51). The theme of human ecology was to be taken up again from the beginning of the pontificate of Pope Francis.[19] We will return to it in the following chapter.

Justice and Love

Another important idea that runs through the encyclical is the inseparability of justice and charity (n.6). Giving and forgiving both transcend justice, but they also complete it. This idea is developed further in chapter 3, which establishes the priority of the "*gratuitous*" (including the notion of truth itself as a gift, because it is not something we can produce but transcends us, is "greater than we are") over the contractual arrangements of the market (nn. 34–5). With these remarks the pope deliberately overturns the model of *homo economicus*—the "self-interested individual" who plays a central role in textbook economic theory.

Justice is more than fairness. Traditionally there are two kinds of justice. Distributive justice is about *bestowal*, or the relationship of the community to the individual, and the way the community divides property between its members. Commutative justice is

---

19. "We are losing our attitude of wonder, of contemplation, of listening to creation and thus we no longer manage to interpret in it what Benedict XVI calls 'the rhythm of the love-story between God and man.' Why does this happen? Why do we think and live horizontally? We have drifted away from God, we no longer read his signs. However, 'cultivating and caring' do not only entail the relationship between us and the environment, between man and creation. They also concern human relations. The popes have spoken of a human ecology, closely connected with environmental ecology. We are living in a time of crisis; we see it in the environment, but above all we see it in men and women. The human person is in danger: this much is certain—the human person is in danger today, hence the urgent need for human ecology! And the peril is grave, because the cause of the problem is not superficial but deeply rooted. It is not merely a question of economics but of ethics and anthropology." (From the General Audience of June 5, 2013, slightly corrected for grammar.)

about *exchange* between individuals.[20] In both cases, justice is about ensuring that the individual receives a fair amount ("his due"), either from his fellows or from the community. But, as Benedict shows, there is much more to the story than this.

Economic life depends on three "logics": not only the straightforward logic of contractual exchange, but also that of political justice (a more complex balancing act), and that of unconditional gift (on which the fraternal bonds of society depend). The human act of giving, and the kindness, mercy, or generosity it represents, is certainly as important as, and probably more basic than, justice itself. Without it there would be no society. Flowing from this is a call to create space within the market for economic entities aiming at a higher goal than pure profit. The "principle of gratuitousness" is not to be confined to civil society or delegated to the State. It is to be fully integrated within the market through the presence (alongside profit-oriented private enterprise and various types of public enterprise, and hybridizing with them) of commercial entities based on mutualist principles and pursuing social ends; for example, by taking account of the interests of all the stakeholders—all those who have a stake or interest in the company, including the customers and the workers—and not just the shareholders (nn. 38, 40).

Justice consists in giving to everyone what is due to them, what they have a right to, what "belongs" to them. The question is: what

20. "In a climate of mutual trust, the *market* is the economic institution that permits encounter between persons, inasmuch as they are economic subjects who make use of contracts to regulate their relations as they exchange goods and services of equivalent value between them, in order to satisfy their needs and desires. The market is subject to the principles of so-called *commutative justice*, which regulates the relations of giving and receiving between parties to a transaction. But the social doctrine of the Church has unceasingly highlighted the importance of *distributive justice* and *social justice* for the market economy, not only because it belongs within a broader social and political context, but also because of the wider network of relations within which it operates. In fact, if the market is governed solely by the principle of the equivalence in value of exchanged goods, it cannot produce the social cohesion that it requires in order to function well. *Without internal forms of solidarity and mutual trust, the market cannot completely fulfill its proper economic function.* And today it is this trust which has ceased to exist, and the loss of trust is a grave loss" (n. 35). See also *CCC*, n. 2411.

is due? And how do we know what is due? Free-market conservatives prioritize an understanding of freedom based on the assumption that all moral obligations stem from individual acts of will. In a
contract, each party voluntarily binds itself to do or give something
in exchange for something else. In a market-dominated society,
therefore, the contract becomes the basic paradigm for all human
relationships. Opposed to this is the traditional understanding that
obligations (i.e. duties and rights as the twin aspects of responsibility) are often *prior* to acts of will, because they flow from the relationships constitutive of our identity as creatures in society,
creatures who are called to self-fulfillment through love; that is,
self-reception and self-gift.

Obligations such as the duty to pay one's workers a just family
wage,[21] or to allow time for worship, or to preserve human life, are
rooted in our constitutive relation to God, not in any decision to
grant those rights in return for some advantage to myself. As the
pope says, "if the only basis of human rights is to be found in the
deliberations of an assembly of citizens, those rights can be changed
at any time" (n. 43). Human rights are based on the needs of each
person to fulfill himself according to his nature—that is, what is due
to us as persons—and on the duty of others to permit that fulfillment.

The failure to see this is linked to a failure to admit the "natural
desire for God" (as distinct from a natural "capacity" for God)
taught by Aquinas. If human nature has to be made to desire God by
a supernatural influence upon it, it must have a natural fulfillment
outside God. In fact, our need for God would then be the result of an

21. Allan Carlson argues that despite many statements on the importance of the
family in the recent magisterium, encyclicals after *Rerum Novarum* have down-
played the notion that a just wage is a "family wage," sufficient to enable one bread-
winner to support spouse and children. See A. Carlson, "Family, the Economy, and
Distributism," in *Communio*, 37:4 (Winter 2010), pp. 634–42. Nevertheless, John
Paul II still insists in *Centesimus Annus* that a "workman's wages should be sufficient to enable him to support himself, his wife and his children" (n. 8). The teaching is picked up and reiterated in the *Compendium of the Social Doctrine of the
Church* (n. 250). Without a family wage, both spouses must work, and as a result
the family structure comes under impossible strain.

act of will (in the first place, God's), rather than being due to the nature of the human being. In history, the assumption of a natural order separated from the supernatural order proved to be the first step in claiming the autonomy of the natural and the total irrelevance of the supernatural (and thus of theology) to anything in the "real world"—a truly secular order, a *novus ordo saeclorum*. Instead, Benedict believes, man's relation to God, and the basic rights that flow from this, is part of what constitutes us as human beings.

In *Caritas in Veritate* the pope insists that justice is "inseparable from charity" (n. 6). Charity "demands justice," in the sense of demanding "recognition and respect for the legitimate rights of individuals and peoples," as a first step. For, he says, "I cannot 'give' what is mine to the other, without first giving him what pertains to him in justice. If we love others with charity, then first of all we are just towards them." (Note the pope's emphasis on "legitimate" rights, which is clarified in chapter 4, n. 43, of the encyclical—as we have to teach our children, not everything we want is a right.) But there is also a sense in which *justice demands charity*, for the pope adds elsewhere: "today it is clear that without gratuitousness, there can be no justice in the first place" (n. 38). And, of course, charity "transcends" justice, since it calls us to go further than what may be fair, into the realm of beneficence and liberality.

De Lubac's understanding of nature and grace helps us to understand this point. If justice is giving what is due to another in the integrity of their humanity, it must ultimately mean that we will be giving them more than they have any right to *expect*. I have no natural right to the vision of God, yet I am called to that vision nevertheless. In a sense we can only do "justice" to the integrity of their humanity by loving them (and that is perhaps why at Matthew 5:40 Jesus says, "if any one would sue you and take your coat, let him have your cloak as well"). There is no purely natural man whose "due" is determined solely by his natural needs. For in fact our natural needs include the need for love, which is supernatural.[22]

---

22. The desire and need for infinity is present in the human heart, but it cannot be fulfilled without a further free gift from God—the sharing of his divine nature with us. On the natural desire for God according to Aquinas there is a large literature.

The Religion of Money

Let us think this through in the simplest terms possible. In *Caritas in Veritate*, Pope Benedict tells us that, "if the market is governed solely by the principle of the equivalence in value of exchanged goods, it cannot produce the social cohesion that it requires in order to function well. *Without internal forms of solidarity and mutual trust, the market cannot completely fulfill its proper economic function*" (n. 35). That trust has today been severely undermined. (Trust is itself a manifestation of gratuity, because two people who trust each other have given something of themselves, not merely property, in exchange, thus making themselves vulnerable. Trust implies risk to the person.) He adds that "in *commercial relationships* the *principle of gratuitousness* and the logic of gift as an expression of fraternity can and must *find their place within normal economic activity*" (n. 36).

So what do we make of the market, and of the pope's warning?

There are two main ways in which to exchange or share tangible goods: it may be done either as a gift, or as a transaction. In a transaction—corresponding to contract-style relationships in law involving commodities—one thing is given in return for another. This may be a kind of barter, where I give you my sheep in return for your goats, or it may involve money. Money was invented for situations where I don't happen to want your goats, or anything else that you have at the moment, but I might want something later. We establish currency as a medium of exchange. Money is therefore a symbol of the spirit of love within the market: it connects everything together and enables it to flow. That explains why it can so easily become a false god.

"You cannot serve both God and money" (Matt. 6:24). Pope Francis often speaks of the modern "idol" of money—especially money that appears to be produced by itself, through speculation, rather than through labor. The danger is one to which the modern

---

See David L. Schindler's Introduction to Henri de Lubac, *The Mystery of the Supernatural* (New York: Crossroad, 1998). Cf. *Summa Contra Gentiles*, Bk 3, Part 1, Ch. 25, which concludes in part that "man naturally desires, as his ultimate end, to know the first cause," which is God.

world is particularly susceptible. The nominalist philosophers from Ockham to Hobbes dispensed with the notion of there being an intrinsic or real value in things or people, leading by default to the substitution of a purely artificial monetary value achieved by negotiation. From using a monetary value to compare things with each other, it was a short step to seeing money as a good in itself, a repository containing *in potentia* all the things it could buy (that is, in the modern view, everything!)—an idol indeed. In a sense this was an inversion of the old realism, attributing ultimate reality to something lower on the ontological scale than material things.[23]

Money may indeed have begun as a sacred thing. The word is derived from the goddess Juno Moneta in Rome, Juno being one of the Roman "Trinity" along with Jupiter and Athena, and she was also the mother of the muses, responsible for divine protection of the arts and sciences. Later the concept was secularized and eventually turned into a demonic mockery of the sacred. In the modern world, the concept of unlimited economic growth—a purely quantitative idea—has taken the place of any religious conception of human flourishing. Our society is based on this idea of growth as a continually expanding cycle of expectation (which supplies the motivation to drive the economy forward), with trade leading to income, and income leading to consumption and investment. Expansion is made possible by improvements in technology making possible cheaper production (machines replacing slaves and eventually workers) combined with supposedly unlimited natural resources (natural energies released by advancing technology), and the stimulation of consumption by advertising and other means. The only alternative to growth is thought to be decline—the fear of which so dominates our lives at present, and leads to the bailout of failing banks and even governments by those with more credibility.

Growth of this sort requires money itself to become a form of

---

23. For the nature and history of money see Philip Goodchild, *The Theology of Money* (Duke University Press, 2009), also D.C. Schindler, "Why Socrates Didn't Charge: Plato and the Metaphysics of Money," *Communio: International Catholic Review* 36:3 (Fall 2009), pp. 394–426, and other articles in the same issue by Giorgio Buccellati, Wendell Berry, and Mark Shiffman.

loan. Coinage is replaced by credit. Philip Goodchild writes that money is now "essentially credit, a belief system, in which we participate in practice so long as we treat money as valuable. This means that money is also debt. Every time we handle money, we handle someone else's debt or obligation."

> Prior to the modern world, the economic sphere was bounded by the finitude of the production of value through human labor, on the one hand, and the finitude of money in circulation, on the other. In the modern world, however, the finitude of production has been partially overcome by harnessing energy stored in fossil fuels and the elements. At the same time, the finitude of currency has been overcome by treating signs of monetary value as themselves valuable, ensuring the value of newly created money by issuing it in the form of loans, attached to debts. Rates of production and rates of interest escape finitude by compound growth. Production for the sake of profit replaces production for the sake of use.[24]

In this way, he says, "money as a supreme value and transcendent obligation shapes the conduct of our lives and institutions. Debt has replaced God as the guarantee for human cooperation, and our modern globalized world is driven by the religion of money."

In the first address of his pontificate concerned with the global financial crisis, Pope Francis stated that the "worship of the golden calf of old (cf. Exod. 32:15–34) has found a new and heartless image in the cult of money and the dictatorship of an economy which is faceless and lacking any truly humane goal."[25] He continued: "A new, invisible and at times virtual, tyranny is established, one which unilaterally and irremediably imposes its own laws and rules. Moreover, indebtedness and credit distance countries from their real economy and citizens from their real buying power. Added to this, as if it were needed, is widespread corruption and selfish fiscal evasion, which have taken on worldwide dimensions. The will to power and of possession has become limitless."

24. Goodchild, *The Theology of Money*, p. 11.

25. Pope Francis, Address for the New Non-Resident Ambassadors to the Holy See: Kyrgyzstan, Antigua and Barbuda, Luxembourg, and Botswana, 16 May 2013 (translation by Vatican Radio).

Logic of the Market

Lacking a well-defined community of faith, and under the influence of an individualist anthropology that defines human beings as units of production and consumption, modernity has turned the market—the field of transactions enabled by the lending and spending of money—into the primary means of social interaction. It is in this sense that the "logic of the market" has come to dominate and permeate our society and ways of thinking. Commodity exchange takes the place of gift-exchange—even within the family. The pope is trying to draw attention to this danger, and remind us that the market is not everything. In fact we have to find a way of reintegrating the "logic of gift" within the market.

One way is through the use of small loans (the Grameen Bank and other forms of microcredit). A loan is not quite a gift, and not quite a transaction. It lies on a spectrum between the two. If I lend you capital without interest, and without necessarily hoping to be paid back unless things go very well for you, it virtually amounts to a gift. You could say it is a kind of "temporary" gift. To insist on return within a set period of time, and to ask for a percentage on top, makes it more like a transaction again, and it turns money from being a medium of exchange into a commodity in its own right. This is the old argument against usury, or charging for the use of money.[26] Microcredit and credit unions (member-owned financial cooperatives) can be a way of rehumanizing the banking system, by lending within the context of already-established friendships and communities.

Another way is by defining more carefully what can and cannot be bought and sold, and under what conditions. Throughout history there have always been limits, determined by the prevailing culture. There are limits even today. Not everything is for sale. We do not think it right to buy and sell human beings, for example. But

---

26. On usury and indeed the whole question of a gift economy, see Lewis Hyde, *The Gift: How the Creative Spirit Transforms the World* (Edinburgh: Canongate, 2006). Originally interest could be taken only on loans to people outside the family or tribe. Thanks to the rise of individualism, the "magic circle" of belonging shrank and the "spirit of gratuity" evaporated from society (p. 118). See also Thomas Storck, "Is Usury Still a Sin?" *Communio: International Catholic Review* 36:3 (Fall 2009), pp. 447–74, also available online at www.secondspring.co.uk/economy.

people sell their bodies for sex, or rent out their wombs for surrogacy. Antarctica may not be for sale, but the native peoples who regarded other lands as being for use not ownership have long since been dispossessed of them. Is it right to sell pornography, or weapons of mass destruction, or to take out patents on a genetic code? What kinds of information are to be made freely available (the makers of Wikipedia and open-source software have one view, governments might take another).[27] May we sell clean air and water, when they become scarce? Such questions force us to realize that there is nothing absolute about private property. Its definition and limits are dependent on negotiation and shaped by tradition and politics.

A third way is simply by giving, even if we give away what has previously been purchased. "Sell what you have and give to the poor." That still remains the most direct way to affirm a freedom that transcends the logic of the market.[28]

Those in the Distributist, Green, and "alternative economics" movements were not slow in noting that the encyclical opens the door to the development of "economic entities" that act on principles other than pure profit, or which treat profit merely as a means to a social end, including cooperatives, credit unions, micro-finance, and the "economy of communion" (see n. 46).[29] In section 39 Pope Benedict writes that the redistribution of wealth by the State is today

27. In fact the internet has opened up new ways of introducing gratuity into the marketplace through mass collaboration (freecycle, linux, skype, wikis, etc.). See www.macrowikinomics.com.

28. Power over our own destiny has been confused with the power to choose and re-choose endlessly, with no permanent commitment and in abstraction from all the narratives that give a meaning to our lives. The state of life founded on poverty, chastity, and obedience still stands as an alternative, a reminder of our humanity and an image of real freedom. These points will be explored later.

29. "Economy of Communion" is the name given to a particular business model developed by the Focolare movement after a visit by Chiara Lubich to Brazil in 1991. Chiara was disturbed to find a whole ring of shanty towns in a circle surrounding the main cities, *favelas*, where people lived in abject poverty, "a crown of thorns" around the city. Those involved with the Focolare in Brazil included not only professionals and the middle class but many of the poor. To help meet the material needs of the local community, Chiara proposed that for-profit businesses could generate additional jobs and voluntarily share profits in three parts: 1) for direct aid to those in need, 2) for educational programs that foster "a culture of giving" and 3)

"evidently insufficient to satisfy the demands of a fully humane economy." He proposes something more radical: "labor receives assets (in the form of stake-holdings) and hires capital (not vice-versa), while capital itself comes in part from worker and community-supported credit unions rather than exclusively from shareholder-driven retail banks." Furthermore, "the world economy needs to switch from short-term financial speculation to long-term investment in the real economy, social development and environmental sustainability."

John Milbank, in an essay on gratuity in the economy ("Liberality versus Liberalism") that is worth reading as a whole, almost as a commentary on the encyclical although it was first published three years earlier, writes: "Things like the economy of fair-traded food-items may not sound dramatic or decisive and indeed they remain pathetically marginal and often compromised, but nevertheless the extension of such gift-exchange bit by bit is the sure way forward rather than revolution, government action alone, or else capitalistic solutions. . . . [W]e need a different sort of market: a re-subordination of money transaction to a new mode of universal gift-exchange. This requires that in every economic exchange of labor or commodity there is always a negotiation of ethical value at issue."[30]

End of an Era

Pope Benedict's encyclical hopes that new "hybrid" forms of commercial behavior will emerge in the marketplace in the future (n. 38). It insists that the "weakest members of society should be helped to defend themselves against usury" (n. 65),[31] and that use of technol-

---

for continued business development. EoC businesses commit themselves to building sound relationships with employees, customers, regulatory agencies, the general public, and the environment. These new relationships include those who receive aid, who are active participants in the project. Sharing one's needs with dignity and sincerity is appreciated as a contribution to increase the life of communion, and many renounce the help just as soon as they reach a bare minimum of economic independence. The Focolare movement has millions of members, and nearly 1,000 companies are by now associated with the EoC. See www.edc-online.org.

30. J. Milbank, *The Future of Love: Essays in Political Theology* (London: SCM Press, 2009), pp. 252–3.

31. Pope Benedict is referring to usury in the sense of charging excessive interest, which is a sin keeping many developing nations in extreme poverty.

ogy be subordinated to the "holistic meaning" of the human (n. 70).

In sum, *Caritas in Veritate* laid the foundations of a new era in Catholic social teaching. It took Catholic social teaching to a new level by basing it explicitly on the theology of the Trinity. On this basis it introduced a new principle, that of "gratuitousness" and "reciprocal gift," enabling us to break the "hegemony of the binary model of market-plus-State" (nn. 38, 39, 41). In other words, we do not have to choose between letting our lives be controlled by big government or big business (or by a shady collusion of the two, such as the "market-state" emerging in Europe). The old debate with the neocons has been left behind.

An important collection of essays by Adrian Pabst makes a plea for a "civil economy," meaning a market economy that is firmly embedded in the mediating institutions of civil society, beginning with the family.[32] The word "civil" evokes the network of social relations that depend on virtues and universal principles (principles often ignored by the largest institutions).

Economics as a human activity is not ethically neutral, and must be structured and governed in an ethical manner; that is, in accordance with the highest ends of man. Economics and politics are not to be separated, because justice must enter into the economy from the outset, and justice is made perfect only in "giving and forgiving."

The radical implications of this principle for the market economy will need time to unfold. They will unfold in an era of growing instability and enormous peril. We can no longer pretend that the world is in a stable (or steadily improving) state and that change can be managed. The rate of social change is itself accelerating, driven by technological innovation. The availability of new weapons, of new means of transport and communication, and the destruction of irreplaceable natural resources, leading to political conflict over land, water, and energy, means a time of crisis to which we can see no end. How many of our social structures and personal comforts will survive a time of growing unemployment, mass migration, drought, plague, and war? The ecological crisis is only

---

32. A. Pabst, *The Crisis of Global Capitalism: Pope Benedict XVI's Social Encyclical and the Future of Political Economy* (Eugene, OR: Cascade Books, 2011).

one element in what may come to be seen as the end of an age, a transition to a new period of civilization, at present only visible though the smoke on the other side of a chasm of fire.

Back in 1998, a decade before the crisis of 2008 revealed that Western economies were increasingly basing themselves on debts that could never be paid back,[33] a well-placed observer of the global scene, Edward Luttwak, wrote a book about the triumph of "turbo-capitalism"—economic growth based on globalization, deregulation, and technological change, linked to growing unemployment for the unskilled and poverty for the global "losers." At that time, turbo-capitalism seemed unstoppable, yet Luttwak pointed out that it contained the seeds of its own destruction, not least in the creation of dangerous levels of disaffection creating social instability and feeding global terrorism.

> Allowing turbo-capitalism to convert all institutions—from hospitals and publishing houses to long-distance races—into profit-maximizing enterprises, deforms or even perverts their essential content, while improving their economic performance.... This, after all, is the turbo-capitalist reversal: societies serve economies, not the other way around. When all capital is allocated efficiently to whatever entities earn the highest returns, there is none to spare for institutions that do unprofitable things because of felt moral obligations or moralistic pretensions, professional ethics or professional conceits, high ideas or mere habit.[34]

Luttwak describes this as the great dilemma of our times, and our governments have no solution to it, other than to let it run its course, hoping that new technology will continually come to the rescue. Of course, Luttwak writes,

33. In order to keep the economy moving it became necessary to offer enormous amounts of credit, creating a burden of debt that could not realistically be returned—a fact that was concealed as long as possible by the packaging and selling of these debts in various complex forms, like a shell game in which the trick is to deceive the eye.

34. E. Luttwak, *Turbo-Capitalism: Winners and Losers in the Global Economy* (London: Weidenfeld & Nicolson, 1998), p. 236. The obsession with maximizing profit to shareholders is only one of the reasons things went wrong, short-termism and simple failure of governance being two of the others.

As compared to the slavery of the defunct communist economies, dispiriting bureaucratic socialism and the grotesque failures of nationalist economics, turbo-capitalism is materially altogether superior, and morally at least not inferior, in spite of its corrosive effects on society, families and culture itself. Yet to accept its empire over every aspect of life, from art to sport in addition to all forms of business, cannot be the culminating achievement of human existence. Turbo-capitalism, too, shall pass.[35]

Indeed it shall, and we have seen the signs of its fragility since these words were written.[36] Those who oppose it tend to place their trust in localism, the development of clean energy, organic farming, and the redistribution of power and wealth. Some argue that rising population and the aspirations of developing peoples will prevent such solutions. Trusting in the resilience of planet earth and the ingenuity of mankind, they propose more use of nuclear power, exploitation of shale deposits, and genetically engineered crops to keep civilization going—perhaps combined with schemes for the offsetting of carbon emissions—until the global population levels out.

An alternative that actually works will have to be built on very different foundations. Human development, Benedict concludes in his encyclical, depends on our *"rising above a materialistic vision of human events"* to include the spiritual dimension, the "beyond" that technology cannot give (n. 77), in a "humanism open to the Absolute" (n. 78). In other words, we must become aware of our constitutive relation to the transcendent, our "calling" towards God for the common good of all, in love and truth.

---

35. Ibid., p. 237.

36. The *New Statesman* (March, 27, 2013) commented soberly but accurately: "Europe remains in crisis and the banking system is largely unreformed. In Britain, where the banks were bailed out at a great cost to the nation, wages are flat or falling, unemployment remains very high, and the old welfare model is unraveling. Institutional trust is at an all-time low. . . . With its emphasis on abstract individualism, liberalism, the great driver of social emancipation and economic prosperity, now feels inadequate to this new age of insecurity." In the United States, where economic liberalism remains more confident, the problems are just as real. But the undermining of families and the destruction and manipulation of unborn human life in the developed world represent a crisis deeper than economic.

The Rise of the Machines

The only sort of inner life allowed by the Technician would be a modest and moderate form of introspection, directed by the doctor and tending to produce an optimistic frame of mind by eliminating—by plucking out the very roots of—any desire that could not be fulfilled in this world. Fools! You don't care a tinker's curse for the inner life, yet it is nevertheless through the inner life and in it that certain real values have been transmitted to us without which liberty would be nothing but an empty word. You don't care a tinker's curse for the said values either? So be it. ⁓Georges Bernanos[1]

When every landscape is bordered by roads or marched across by pylons, when every riverbed is strewn with plastic and metallic waste, when even the wildest environment is carefully managed by ecological experts for its own protection, we are sealed on every side by the artificial: by our own image projected onto nature. But the self turned in upon itself is living in a coffin, and a civilization that worships the self is what John Paul II termed a "culture of death."

In such a culture, the real is what can be measured. Human life has no value but the going market rate, and if we animals have any purpose on earth it is to maximize our pleasure while prolonging our existence. We are here to consume—or to be entertained. As one pundit said, "We have moved from a world in which we define ourselves by work to one where we define ourselves—and, in many ways, discover our meaning—through consumption: leisure, expenditure on material goods and other things outside work."[2]

That is as much as to say, we eat in McDonalds or Pizza Hut, we

---

1. Bernanos, *Tradition of Freedom* (London: Denis Dobson, 1950), p. 156.
2. *RSA Journal* (July 1997). For a penetrating critique of the modern world and the effects of consumerism see Romano Guardini, *Letters from Lake Como: Explorations in Technology and the Human Race* (Grand Rapids: Eerdmans, 1994).

drink Coke or Pepsi, and we decorate our apartments with exquisite taste. Our range of choice among ice creams exceeds the wildest indulgent dreams of a Nero or Caligula. But apart from all that, we have no vocation, and no power to determine our destiny.

We have spawned this culture together. It comes from Europe, from divisions and hatreds created before America was a nation. The responsibility for it lies not with Americans but with Christians. In a sense you could say it was the fault of Christ. Faith in Jesus gave a radically new impetus to history. It disrupted the slow breathing, the cyclic rise and fall of civilizations that lived in an uneasy harmony with the forces of the cosmos, recognizing in nature a fixed and eternal wisdom. Christianity injected a brand new idea: that the Creator of all might have stepped through the magic mirror and into our world, becoming man. In so doing he gave to history a real center and a shape, a middle and an end.

It was Jesus who raised the stakes. We are now playing for eternal life. He brought a new freedom. In sacramental union—that is, in loving union—with him we can achieve a destiny higher than fate and change the course of nature. To quote Christopher Dawson: "Eternity had entered into time and henceforward the singular and the temporal had acquired an eternal significance. The closed circle of time had been broken and a ladder had been let down from heaven to earth, by which mankind can escape from the 'sorrowful wheel' which had cast its shadow over Greek and Indian thought, and go forward in newness of life to a new world."[3]

The dynamism of the Christian faith created Western civilization, as historians like Dawson, Pierre Duhem, and Stanley Jaki have shown. But from the outset there was a flaw, a failure in the human response to the Incarnation. As the new civilization grew, that flaw was revealed ever more clearly. A jagged crack widened, engulfing both East and West, splitting nature from grace, so that Christendom was cut off from its very source of life. The worst, the old saying goes, is the corruption of the best. If that is so, then the culture of life corrupted is the culture of death. Cut off from the vine we

---

3. *Religion and the Modern State*, p. 80.

can do less than nothing; severed from the One who alone can hold together the forces of grace and imagination released by the Incarnation we are in a worse state than ever the pagans were.

The Battle of the Logos

Let us trace it back, this jagged crack in the soul of Christendom, as near as we can to its earliest point. Three men are sleeping in a garden. Peter, James, and John could not keep awake, and so failed to pray with their Master. This much we know from the Gospel account. But what, exactly, would their prayers have achieved? Judas repented a little too late: perhaps he would have been saved if his brothers had reached out to him in prayer. Jesus died on the Cross; Jerusalem fell. Of course, individual Jews as well as Gentiles did convert, so that out of the wreckage of Israel and Rome a Christian Empire, a Christendom could arise. But already a deadly separation had opened up between the earthly and the heavenly city, which had been united on earth in the Body of Christ. If Jerusalem had become the center of the new faith, it might have drawn all nations and peoples to itself. Instead, the vengeful ghost of a monotheism never fully integrated with Christianity was able to emerge from the deserts of the South to become the scourge and the terror of Europe in the Middle Ages. The foundations of secular modernity were laid in the struggle with Islam, when the Christian crusaders, attempting to recapture the Holy City by force of arms, succeeded by their brutality, diverted towards Constantinople, only in sealing the division between Eastern and Western Christendom.

All though the subsequent fragmentation of Europe, the collapse of the economic and social framework of feudalism, the rise of the merchant classes and the nation state, "philosophic reason" advanced at the expense of the contemplative intellect. The Protestant Reformation destroyed the dream of a united Christendom in the West, and in the confusion the humanists of the Renaissance were able to forge a new unifying culture across the Catholic-Protestant divide by opening the way to a new paganism and secularization of knowledge. Hilaire Belloc once wrote that if it had not been for the Reformation, the energies of the Renaissance would have fuelled a Golden Age. The colossal nudes of Michelangelo are certainly impressive, but in them we see that it is man rather than God who has begun to take center stage.

We are living in an era of voluntarism; a period in which religion has been dying because it has been reduced to an act of the will, and thought has been subordinated to sentiment. The conversion of culture that is called for is a profound one, because part of the problem of our culture is that religious faith is assumed by both believers and non-believers to be a purely human act. Of course, faith is an "infused theological virtue," a divinely inspired habit, and to that extent certainly also a matter of the will. But the created human will has been misunderstood in modernity as primarily *active and generative*. The deepest Christian tradition, by contrast, understands the will as primarily *receptive*—and that means turned towards the truth. A will turned in upon itself, upon the self, cannot give thanks, cannot receive grace. Such a will can believe only with *blind faith*. What we must affirm, against the false Gnosticism of atheistic reason, against even the rules of the club of professional philosophers and theologians, is the reality of a *seeing faith*.

The first volume of Hans Urs von Balthasar's series *The Glory of the Lord* is precisely a defense of this concept of *seeing faith*, and even of what we might call "Christian Gnosis" (following the great Alexandrians, Clement and Origen, rather than the heretics dubbed "Gnostics" by Irenaeus and others).[4] I won't try to summarize it here, but simply acknowledge it as part of the background to this concluding section. The healing of our souls and of our society will only come with an *opening of vision*. But the vision we are talking about—the blossoming of the spiritual senses—depends on *purity*, or rather purity of heart, as we saw at the beginning. What I mean by purity is openness to truth. It has to do with being like a mirror, and we recall that a mirror is only able to reflect when it is turned outward. Folded in on itself it can see only reflections of reflections, and ultimately, locked in darkness, it sees nothing at all. The struggle for purity is thus the struggle for light, the struggle to let nothing get in the way of the light except things that the light wishes to reveal.

The conversion of culture, then, implies a *conversion to purity* in

4. See especially Balthasar, *The Glory of the Lord*, Vol. I, pp. 136–41.

order to be able to see the truth. Yet we know the remarkable degree to which our culture dedicates its creative energy to the corruption of innocence and the pollution of the imagination. This is a culture dead set against asceticism. "Not for nothing does Holy Scripture name 'concupiscence of the eyes' among the three powers which constitute the world that 'lieth in the power of evil (1 John 2:16; 5:19)," writes the Thomist philosopher Josef Pieper:

> It reaches the extremes of its destructive and eradicating power when it builds itself a world according to its own image and likeness: when it surrounds itself with the restlessness of a perpetual moving picture of meaningless shows, and with the literally deafening noise of impressions and sensations breathlessly rushing past the windows of the senses. Behind the flimsy pomp of its facade dwells absolute nothingness; it is a world of, at most, ephemeral creations, which often within less than a quarter hour become stale and discarded, like a newspaper or magazine swiftly scanned or merely perused; a world which, to the piercing eye of the healthy mind untouched by its contagion, appears like the amusement quarter of a big city in the hard brightness of a winter morning: desperately bare, disconsolate and ghostly. The destructiveness of this disorder which originates from, and grows upon, obsessive addiction, lies in the fact that it stifles man's primitive power of perceiving reality; that it makes man incapable not only of coming to himself but also of reaching reality and truth.[5]

The stage is set, if this is true, for a titanic struggle. The errors of modernity are spiritually based, and will not be rooted out easily. But should we be surprised at this? The "Battle of the Logos" was foreseen in the Book of Revelation. The Battle is described in the most graphic way in the Book of Revelation (19:11–21), where the Word of God, clad in robes dipped in blood, rides out to war, his eyes like a flame of fire. "From his mouth issues a sharp sword with which to smite the nations, and he will rule them with a rod of iron; he will tread the winepress of the fury of the wrath of God the Almighty." The Founder of Christianity, after all, is on record as saying he came not to bring peace but a sword (Matt. 10:34–6). The

---

5. *Josef Pieper: An Anthology* (San Francisco: Ignatius Press, 1989), pp. 86–7.

sword is an instrument of division, of opposition. Sword implies Battle.

According to the reading of Hans Urs von Balthasar in the fourth volume of *Theo-Drama*, the Battle is made necessary by the sin that God must expose and even, in a sense, *deliberately provoke*, in order finally to overcome. "Christ's utter Yes to God and to the world," he writes, "drives the utter No—the demonic, anti-Christian No—out of its hiding place. 'If I had not come and spoken to them, they would not have sin; . . . but now they have seen and hated both me and my Father.'"[6] In the very act of gathering us to himself through history, Christ scatters his flock. In the act of bringing peace, he provokes war.

In a period of rapidly evolving technology and the social changes that inevitably flow from this, the "globalization of solidarity" (Pope John Paul II) is becoming ever more urgent. But Christians are confused about the role of technological development in this process. While there are plenty of critics of capitalism, this is less true of technology—the advance of technology being more obviously responsible for the "successes" of capitalism than an economic system based on selfishness and greed. In the 1960s, the Second Vatican Council adopted, in *Gaudium et Spes*, a generally optimistic view that "mankind's triumphs are signs of God's greatness and the fruit of his sublime plan" (n. 34), and that worldly progress may lead to "the better ordering of human society" (n. 39). The hope has often been expressed in Church documents since that time that moral and scientific progress will proceed hand in hand. Yet the Council was also aware of the ambiguity of worldly progress (see *Gaudium et Spes* sections 54–7); and it is clear that in fact there is much cause for concern. What once looked like hope now appears to have been wishful thinking.[7]

The next phase in the development of Catholic social teaching— from Pope Francis onwards—will have to include some attempt to

---

6. *Theo-Drama*, IV, p. 427, citing John 15:24.

7. For a detailed analysis of *Gaudium et Spes*, please see papers in *Communio: International Catholic Review* 23:4 (Spring 1996) by Walter Kasper, Pedro Morandé, and David L. Schindler.

analyze the social and ethical issues raised by recent technological developments and their applications. That in turn will necessarily involve renewed attention not only to anthropology and ethics, but also to eschatology, and the theology of history.

Ecological Conversion

We have seen that one of the key developments in the social teaching of John Paul II was to recognize the importance of human technological development on the environment, prompted by the huge secular "Green" movement that had been gathering popular momentum since the time of the Council. Whatever its faults, Rachel Carson's book *Silent Spring* (1962) had drawn the world's awareness to the often irreparable damage being done to the natural world by pesticides and other forms of pollution. The emerging science of ecology demonstrated the interconnectedness of all life on earth. Photographs of the earth from space sent back by the Apollo astronauts served as icons to raise awareness of the fragility of what came to be known as the earthly "ecosystem." Just as the Church had belatedly acknowledged the new problems raised by industrial society in the nineteenth century, so in the second half of the twentieth the environmental crisis became an important element in papal teaching.

It was mentioned (along with the threat of nuclear war) in sections 8 and 15 of John Paul II's first encyclical, *Redemptor Hominis* (1978), but its fullest statement came in the 1990 Message for the World Day of Peace, *Peace with God the Creator; Peace with All Creation.* On the basis of the "integrity of creation" the pope argues that "Simplicity, moderation, and discipline, as well as a spirit of sacrifice, must become part of everyday life" (n. 13). This amounts to "a genuine conversion in ways of thought and behavior."

The same teaching was then picked up in the pope's social encyclicals—the main vehicle for his teaching on faith and morals—such as *Sollicitudo Rei Socialis* (1987), *Centesimus Annus* (1991), and *Evangelium Vitae* (1995)—and from there entered into the *Catechism of the Catholic Church* and the *Compendium of Social Doctrine.* In SRS he insisted that "one cannot use with impunity the different categories of beings, whether living or inanimate—animals, plants, the natural elements—simply as one wishes, according to one's own economic needs" (n. 34), while in CA (n. 38) and EV (n. 42) he introduced the term "human ecology" to refer to the intimate relationship between the welfare of humanity (which he linked to the wellbeing of the family) and that of the environment, based on the interdependence of all life on earth.[8]

In a General Audience of 2001, near the end of his life, John Paul II expressed his disappointment with the response to these calls of responsible stewardship (our "ecological vocation," as he called it in a talk given at Castel Gondolfo on August 25, 2002), and the need for "ecological conversion."

This close relationship between environmental ecology and the moral or human ecology of the family also became one of the hallmarks of Pope Benedict XVI's teaching. He even set a good example by installing solar panels in the Vatican and planting trees in Hungary, attempting to make the Vatican the first carbon-neutral state in the world. Like his predecessor he was at loggerheads with environmentalists who see human populations as a plague upon the planet.

Morality requires us to judge means as well as ends. There are many possible ways to reduce a population, ranging from genocide to migration, and to reduce the number of births per household, from natural family planning to abortion. The Church teaches "responsible parenthood," encouraging parents to judge carefully how many children they might reasonably seek to have in their particular circumstances, only using morally licit methods, such as abstaining from sexual relations at times when conception is likely,

---

8. More should be said about the treatment of animals, who tend to be neglected in treatments of Catholic social teaching (including this one, I regret to say). In farming and the cosmetics industry, not to mention commonly in scientific experimentation, they are cruelly mistreated as machines without feeling or dignity. Such mistreatment thrives in obscurity and ignorance, and indeed most people never see the conditions in which such animals are kept and the ways they are exploited. Although she affirms that animals may be "used" by man and should not be treated as "persons," the Church also condemns cruelty to animals in the *Catechism of the Catholic Church* (n. 2416), as follows: "*Animals* are God's creatures. He surrounds them with his providential care. By their mere existence they bless him and give him glory. Thus men owe them kindness. We should recall the gentleness with which saints like St. Francis of Assisi or St. Philip Neri treated animals."

not methods that involve abortion, or forms of contraception that harm the healthy functioning of the body.

Man is called to be the wise steward of creation. The Church must defend earth, water, and air as "gifts of creation that belong to everyone," and help to prevent mankind from destroying itself (CV, n. 51). These sentiments have established themselves as part of the common sense of our age, especially among the young. At the same time, we must respect and defend the diversity of human culture, not indiscriminately but prudently, and not assume that every human community on the face of the planet must necessarily be aspiring to exactly the same "Western" lifestyle, with its addiction to electronics and pharmaceuticals.

This means, among other things, that authentic human development is best served not merely by technology—we will look at that temptation below—but by *appropriate* technology (CV, n. 27). The term is associated with the Catholic social thinker and Green movement pioneer E.F. Schumacher. It refers to technology that does not require infidelity to the "human"—technology that can serve human development without destroying what is of value in a culture. The impetus for the idea seems originally to have come from Gandhi's advocacy of sewing machines, spinning wheels, and bicycles—in other words, relatively simple technologies that nevertheless can make a huge difference to productivity at the local level, empowering the poor, and requiring fewer resources to produce and maintain.

The idea of appropriate technology could perhaps be given a wider application, but it tends to be referred to in connection with the needs of the developing world, where capital is scarce and self-sufficiency is the immediate goal. One example will suffice. In Africa, there has been a lot of talk about sand dams. The decentralized storage of water is an important strategy in semi-arid and arid regions outside the reach of perennial rivers, springs, deep groundwater, or other conventional water sources. Building small concrete dams backfilled with sand in seasonal rivers is an ancient method of storing water that is now being used extensively in Kenya and elsewhere to support local farming communities. As water becomes an increasingly scarce resource in many parts of the world, this relatively cheap solution is becoming more important. Similarly, the development of simple grazing plans for livestock in the world's vast endangered grasslands can help to prevent desertification. This is a field in which Catholic charities and missionary orders should be heavily involved.

A New World Order

If the Church were to throw herself behind sustainability and appropriate technology in the developing world it would be an excellent thing. But whether even such a shift would change the direction of human history is questionable. As technology, as we say, "advances" (towards what?), it creates a new situation—a new balance between the world we receive as gift and the world we build to our own specifications. For the first time in human history, more people are living in urban than rural surroundings. And it is city-dwellers who create the greatest negative impact on the environment.

Human history is, of course, made up of transitions. It is dynamic, although until recently the changes tended to take place over great periods of time. Civilizations such as those of Egypt or China existed for millennia without changing beyond recognition. But in the last few centuries the pace has quickened. According to numerous surveys of cultural history,[9] the crucial "passage to modernity" took place in the late thirteenth or early fourteenth century through to the seventeenth, bringing an end to a civilization that was still in approximate continuity with every ancient and traditional civilization known to us. The transition was driven by thinkers such as Ockham, Bacon, and Descartes. The Reformation and Enlightenment are associated with many triumphs of the human spirit, many further achievements and discoveries (the Industrial Revolution, the Age of Discovery, the Atomic Age, etc.), but each of these contributed to the further acceleration of technological and social change on a planetary scale.

---

9. Louis Dupré, *Passage to Modernity: An Essay in the Hermeneutics of Nature and Culture* (Yale University Press, 1993). See also Balthasar, *Theo-Drama*, pp. 457–64; Glenn W. Olsen, *The Turn to Transcendence: The Role of Religion in the Twenty-First Century* (Washington, DC: CUA Press, 2010).

By the nineteenth century, a new myth began to dominate the European imagination, helping to cut us off from our own past: the Myth of Progress. All previous ages were seen as primitive and undeveloped; our own as superior and destined to inherit the earth. The myth was fuelled by the obvious advance of technology and the global dominance of the colonial powers. Technological progress was real enough, and on this depended the exploitation of natural resources and the creation of economic wealth for which capitalism inevitably took all the credit. Moral and social progress towards a more just and kindly order was perhaps less real, for while the new information media made it possible for human consciences to be stung by events far away from home, it also enabled the easy manipulation of human feeling at the expense of independent thought.

Modernity gave rise to three other great forces or "big ideas" in particular: *democracy* (the sovereignty of the people), *nationalism* (the sovereignty of states) and *rationalism* (the sovereignty of reason). In a way each of these was a manifestation of the rising tide of *individualism*, involving dissolution into ever-smaller units of the traditions that had previously bound people together, culminating in a conception of society determined by the will of the individual. But this was only the beginning. It was the phase that followed that laid the foundations of the urbanization of culture.

Nationalism requires the support of industrial might, and "industry" in the modern sense is the rationalized organization of labor to serve production, trade, and war. Postmodernity was a simply a continuation and intensification of this logic. By 1970 it had permeated most Western societies to the core. This transition was from the previous concern with democracy, nationalism, and rationalism towards *consumerism* (political choices reduced to consumer choices), *globalization* (transnationals, the "international community," the worldwide web), and *relativism* (truth replaced by doctrines of convenience).

To illustrate: for a time it had made sense for the United States to see itself as a "melting pot" in which refugees from many cultural and ethnic traditions could willingly be absorbed. Their new loyalty would be to the nation that gave them a home. In the historical phase that followed, however, this was less and less the case. Subcul-

85

tures would no longer submit to a national ethos; they could not be assimilated in the old way.

The End of Nations

Increasingly, it is being suggested that the era of nationalism itself may now be coming to an end—at least in some parts of the world. The most serious problems facing mankind are either too big or too small for nations to hope to tackle. In *A Turning Point for Europe?* Cardinal Ratzinger spoke of nationalism as a modern heresy, a form of tribalism that spread across Europe in the nineteenth century, no doubt of temporary duration.[10] Perhaps the more effective unit of human organization is no longer the nation, but (as it has been in the past but now on a larger scale) the city.[11]

Nations, which are created to a large extent by a process of histor-

10. J. Ratzinger, *A Turning Point for Europe? The Church in the Modern World—Assessment and Forecast* (San Francisco: Ignatius Press, 1994), pp. 120–123. He goes on to argue that this heresy will become a thing of the past only if we renounce our belief in progress, recognize the priority of ethics over politics, and reclaim the idea of God (pp. 135–142). A more positive view of nations is this. The identity of a nation is an aspect of the common good of its people—what they know, will, feel, and love writ large; what they won't do, and what they will. It is the past (memory) and the future (imagination). It is the stories it tells about itself, the ideals it aspires to. Deeper than all this it is a mission. As in the case of my personal identity, I am what I am given to do. I am unfinished; I must become what I am. Thus we find our identity when we hear a call, the summons to be a self. This is why a nation has a patron saint. Often, that saint expresses the particular character and mission of the nation, at least in some symbolic way. England should be asking St. George, what dragon must we conquer?

11. Benjamin Barber, *If Mayors Ruled the World: Why They Should, and Why They Already Do* (Yale University Press, 2013). An example proposed by Barber is that 80% of all energy is used in cities, and 80% of global carbon emissions come from cities of more than 50,000 people. Where nations regularly fail to sign energy and carbon agreements, cities can take the lead and work together much more effectively. The campaign against international terrorism may also benefit from collaboration between cities. Paradoxically, the intensity of national feeling may grow as its rational basis disappears. Nationalism remains a strong force, and may be expected to become more violent the more it comes under threat. Another unit of social organization that is a strong candidate for replacing the nation in power and influence is the corporation. On this topic, see Michael Black, "The Crisis of the Corporation" online at www.secondspring.co.uk/economy/articles.html.

ical accident and political fortune, are not the most natural way of governing large groups of people or creating deep-rooted solidarity. This is obvious in the case of the nations of the Middle East and Africa established by the influence of European powers. Cultural, economic, and geographical *regions* would seem a more appropriate basis for such solidarity, and cities are best placed to take the leadership of these regions. Global governance through UN representatives meeting in New York is demonstrably ineffective, whereas collaboration between cities with similar or connected problems generates an international network that may actually work.

Urbanization has other implications. In the new phase of human civilization, technology no longer serves the nation; it aims to serve the individual. We have moved from the crudities of mass production to a more sophisticated technological process that allows the appearance of consumer choice and products customized for individual needs and taste. The retail economy is driven by the search for the non-standard item that will serve (for a few days!) as a status symbol. All of this is at best a pathetic imitation, and at worst a demonic mockery, of the true individuality achieved through the traditional crafts in the period before modern industry made them economically unviable. (More of that later.)

Instead of simply draining people and resources from the countryside, the city now spills over and absorbs the country. The ultimate aim of industrial civilization is nearing fulfillment: the actual replacement of the natural world by a manufactured world entirely designed by man. The postmodern manufactured world is, however, not merely a world of physical artifacts dominating the countryside and the skyline (factories, pylons, skyscrapers); in this latter stage of our culture the manufactured world increasingly exists in cyberspace. It is a world of information (and of supposed information, in the sense of propaganda)—that is, of virtual reality.

The city (and the "virtual" city located in cyberspace) is not the only candidate to replace the nation as the dominant power in our civilization. Another is the *corporation*, that mysterious entity through which most human business is now conducted. Invested with an identity in law amounting to that of a person, the existence of the corporation is based on a spirit that unites its members, and mutual submission in that spirit for the sake of a common good. The corporation was originally a religious idea, in fact it derives from the Jewish notion of the covenant and was transferred *via* St. Paul to the Christian Church, before, in the Middle Ages, it was used as the model for the corporations that ran universities and guilds.[12]

Whatever the powers in charge, whether city, corporation, secret cabal, or some new kind of community formed over the internet, postmodern culture is decentered, in the sense that it is even less bound to tradition than its predecessor was. The past, with all its riches, is either filtered through the technology that presents it to view, or eliminated and forgotten altogether. On the other hand, this "decentering" goes hand in hand with a centering elsewhere: for example, in the liberal ideology of consumption. This explains how our society can be both so *individualistic* and so *conformist*. This simultaneous decentering or detaching from tradition and recentering in an alternative liberal tradition (that vaunts its freedom precisely from tradition) is already characteristic of modernity.

The political categories of Left and Right originated in the French National Assembly as the nation state began to define itself in contradistinction to the *ancien régime*, but have become increasingly difficult to apply. At our more advanced stage of modernity, politics are determined by a range of other concerns, particularly a growing anxiety about security. It is likely, for example, that before long a great many instruments of mass destruction will be in the hands of individuals and rogue states. The instability that this creates is becoming the major political concern on the planet in the present century, cutting across all party political lines. The battle over the freedom of the internet is typical of the new world order. The demand for control (in the interests of security, peace, unity, or ecology) will gradually override concerns for freedom, privacy, and

12. See Michael Black, "The Crisis of the Corporation," in *Second Spring* (Issue 17, Spring 2013). It is worth noting that the only corporations that survive and flourish over a long period of time are those which treat their enterprises as "living work communities"—i.e., humanistically rather than as purely economic machines, valuing human talent above money and capital. See Arie de Geus, *The Living Company: Growth. Learning, and Longevity in Business* (London: Nicholas Brealey, 1999).

local autonomy. The growing power and sophistication of our technology requires ever-more sophisticated safety measures.

In this way the new technological mass culture inevitably penetrates every nook and cranny, erodes every pocket of resistance.

The Christian Response

At the time of *Rerum Novarum*, at the height of the Victorian period, the Church could presuppose the existence of a certain cultural framework. She assumed a community still to some extent rooted through an agricultural economy in the natural environment, and a common belief in the dignity of human nature, the same in all human beings. Thanks to the vestiges of pre-modern civilization, in other words, she was able to appeal to a natural moral law and attack specific injustices. But once the logic of modernity has finally eroded even the vestiges of pre-modernity, the Church must go further. She has no alternative but to give a whole new religious inspiration to the culture. That is why Pope John Paul II made the "new evangelization" the theme of his pontificate, and why his social encyclicals have to be read merely as a part of a wider cultural critique—the critique of the "culture of death" advanced by *Veritatis Splendor* (1993), *Evangelium Vitae* (1995), and *Fides et Ratio* (1998)—and why Benedict XVI re-launched the new evangelization.

Whereas the target of *Rerum Novarum* had to be the injustices brought about by industrial capitalism (and the socialist reaction to capitalism), the target of the new cultural critique must be—in addition to these specific injustices—something much more subtle and pervasive: our consumerist, technologically driven way of life, the logic that expresses itself in this way of life, and the spiritual disorder that lies behind it. The tyranny of mechanism is the projection of a mentality that reduces all of nature, including human nature, to something merely mechanical.

In fact this is one place where Catholic social teaching meets the "new feminism" called for by Pope John Paul II in 1995,[13] since this

---

13. "In transforming culture so that it supports life, women occupy a place, in thought and action, which is unique and decisive. It depends on them to promote a

"tyranny of mechanism" is due to a certain distortion of what might be called the "masculine genius" (a point we will pick up again at the end of chapter 9). Hans Urs von Balthasar makes the connection as follows: "Under the guise of equality and equalization of the sexes, the goal is being pursued to masculinize the entire civilization, which even now is marked by male technological rationality. By further putting the sexual sphere at the disposal of every technological manipulation, the person-centered height and depth of sexual differentiation is lost."[14]

The lifestyle of the affluent West does still, to be sure, generate specific inequalities of wealth and patterns of exploitation across the planet, much as the early stages of capitalism generated great hardship and injustice in the West. These injustices continue to cry out to heaven: they need to be denounced and opposed, just as before. The lifestyle of postmodernity, however, has lifted a mask and revealed the "death of God" and the reduction of knowledge to power that lies at the very core of the modern project—much deeper than these important, but relatively superficial, injustices. When in the medieval civilization (for all its faults) work, art, study, and political life were perceived as belonging to a religiously based or sanctioned order, these things were nevertheless still (in principle) oriented towards the divine, even if society was divided as to how this orientation was to be expressed.

But the practically atheistic or secularized society of modernity, which is shaped from within no longer by a religious tradition but by other forces altogether (and this applies whether or not a large number of citizens attend churches on a regular basis), can have no

---

'new feminism' which rejects the temptation of imitating models of 'male domination,' in order to acknowledge and affirm the true genius of women in every aspect of the life of society, and overcome all discrimination, violence, and exploitation"—John Paul II, *Evangelium Vitae* (1995), n. 99. The new feminism will be treated in more depth by Léonie Caldecott in a forthcoming book.

14. H.U. von Balthasar, "How Weighty is the Argument from 'Uninterrupted Tradition' to Justify the Male Priesthood?" in Helmut Moll (ed.), *The Church and Women* (San Francisco: Ignatius Press, 1988), p. 159. Balthasar makes the point that discussion of these points should be purified of all classical, patristic, and medieval antifeminism, which of course is not always easy in practice.

official religion, no thanksgiving to God on behalf of the society as a whole. Such official religious ceremonies that remain are emptied of real content; they become purely conventional, if not meaningless, and are likely to be abolished in the name of efficiency. Thus modernity entails, ultimately, an injustice that transcends the occasional or accidental exploitation of man by man—a more fundamental injustice against not only the image of God in man, but God himself.[15]

Lest this seem to be simply a plea for a return to an older sacral society, I should add that the roots of the modern (dis)order lie far back in time, and that medieval society was marked not only by "faults," as I have just hinted, but by deep flaws and problems of its own. This should not distract us from the seriousness of our situation. An attack on God is an attack on the cosmos, and *vice versa*. One of the most important victims of the historical process is a sense of the integrity of the world as a gift of God formed by divine wisdom. Respect for the "integrity of creation" is inseparably linked to a sense of the transcendent, and of the Absolute. A concern with poverty and injustice is also reinforced by this awareness of the sacred, and thus of our responsibility towards the divine image in the world.

Not Neutral

Against this background, the critique of technology developed by Benedict XVI in *Caritas in Veritate* makes a lot of sense. Controversies over abortion in the late twentieth century presaged even more bitter and profound disputes over genetic engineering in the twenty-first. When the British government licensed the cloning of human embryos for the purpose of medical experimentation, and at the same time the sale of abortifacients to children without parental permission, parts of the Catholic community recognized that a new threshold had been crossed. It seemed to some that humankind was now in the business of inventing *new sins* for the first time in history. Only by examining the (implicit) anthropology

---

15. Furthermore, the injustice against God that is bound up with the abandonment of religion in turn leads to the further abuse of man, who is now systematically stripped of his transcendent dignity.

of our society, its operative assumptions and theories concerning human nature and its destiny, could Catholic thought make a contribution to resolving the ethical issues raised by modern technology. A merely moralistic response to technological developments— a list of rights and wrongs—was insufficient.

The problem lies deeper, in an anthropology assumed in the technology and in modernity itself. Technology is far from morally neutral, as it is frequently assumed to be in both popular and scholarly writings on this subject. "The medium is the message" (McLuhan), and a technology is not simply a technique that may be employed for good or ill purposes. It carries within its very structure a value system and a worldview—perhaps even a metaphysics and a theology.[16]

In *Caritas in Veritate* Pope Benedict addresses the question of technology, which has been of concern to philosophers since Heidegger.[17] On the one hand, he writes, "Technology enables us to exercise dominion over matter, to reduce risks, to save labor, to improve our conditions of life" (n. 69). On the other hand, it can become "an ideological power that threatens to confine us within an *a priori* that holds us back from encountering being and truth. Were that to happen, we would all know, evaluate, and make decisions about our life situations from within a technocratic cultural perspective to which we would structurally belong, without ever being able to discover a meaning that is not of our own making" (n. 70).

The idea of technology as *ideological power* is extremely important, and needs a bit of unpacking. It may be helpful to look at what some of the more extreme critics of technology have said on this point. Despite the fact that Pope Benedict does not refer to them by name, he may well have had them in mind, and if not, they at least clarify the meaning of such a statement. The "bluff" in the title of

16. See David L. Schindler, "George Grant and Modernity's Technological Ontology," in *Ordering Love: Liberal Societies and the Memory of God* (Grand Rapids: Eerdmans, 2011), pp. 277-87.

17. Martin Heidegger, *The Question Concerning Technology and Other Essays* (New York: Harper & Row, 1977). For Heidegger "Cybernetics is the metaphysics of the atomic age." See Jean-Pierre Dupuy, *The Mark of the Sacred* (Stanford University Press, 2013), p. 55.

Jacques Ellul's book *The Technological Bluff,* for example, refers to the widespread and growing conviction that technology is the answer to every problem (unemployment, pollution, poverty, war, depression, inequality).[18] Many of the most perceptive critics of this syndrome seem to come from France. Michel Henry sums up this line of thought in the most vivid terms:

> Technology is alchemy; it is the self-fulfillment of nature in place of the self-fulfillment of the life that we are. It is barbarism, the new barbarism of our time, in place of culture. Inasmuch as it puts the prescriptions and regulations of life out of play, it is not simply barbarism in its most extreme and inhumane form that has ever been known—it is sheer madness.[19]

Benedict's language is necessarily more moderate, though its implications may be every bit as radical once they have been thought through. His critique rests on a profound Christian anthropology, a sense that we receive our own existence from God, that truth is a "given," and that our true freedom lies in respect for the "call of being" (n. 70). Like Ellul, he argues that we have come to rely on "automatic or impersonal forces" to improve our lot, but this is a mistake. "When technology is allowed to take over, the result is confusion between ends and means, such that the sole criterion for action in business is thought to be the maximization of profit, in politics the consolidation of power, and in science the findings of research" (n. 71).

There must be "moral consistency" between ends and means. That is to say, technology must be at the service not of our desires and intentions, but of truth, and in particular the truth of the human person who is made for love. Benedict presumably agrees that technology is hardly ever morally "neutral" in the way we assume when we say, casually, that everything depends on the way you choose to use it (the same computer can be used to write a mas-

18. J. Ellul, *The Technological Bluff* (Grand Rapids: Eerdmans, 1990).

19. M. Henry, *Barbarism* (London: Continuum, 2012), p. 52. Henry claims that the slide into insanity began when Galileo eliminated subjective perceptions or "secondary qualities" from the domain of reality, simply on the grounds that they were not measurable.

terpiece, design a bomb, or view pornography). Adrian Walker puts his finger on the problem here when he points out that this faith in the neutrality of technology merely expresses

> the essence of technology itself—the conviction that the [human] transformation of nature is uncircumscribed by any moral standard given in the nature of things apart from human will. The belief that technology is a set of neutral instruments, like technology itself, is of a piece with the typically modern conviction that there is no moral order in physical nature, just brute matter whose only meaning *we* put into it through our transformative making and doing.[20]

A given piece of technology should be judged not just according to the end it is being used for, but the ends implicit in the technology itself as "means." A computer, says Walker, processes information, which seems harmless enough, but this means that it carries within it the idea that meaning can be broken down into packets of electrical signals; thus necessarily treating a whole as if it were what Aristotle called a "heap" (*soros*).

Telephone, television, and the internet, for example, change our sense of space and time, and have a variety of effects on the relationships within the family and the wider social community. Some of these effects will be humanly beneficial, others less so, but an assessment of the technology is not possible without paying attention to the overall pattern of these effects, and to the purpose or function of the technology in relation to the purpose of human life itself. In what respect is a given tool actually serving the true end of man?[21]

In other words, technology always has purposes of its own, or (if you prefer) an implicit logic that we accept when we buy into the machine for our own purposes. Technology represents an entire world-view, an organizing myth for our culture, and increasingly it

20. A. Walker, "Not Neutral: Technology and the 'Theology of the Body,'" *Second Spring* 7, p. 29.

21. For a view of the potentially catastrophic effects of over-reliance on technology in education see S. Caldecott, *Beauty in the Word*. For a more general critique applied to the whole civilization see E.M. Forster's science-fiction novella, *The Machine Stops* (1909).

is coming to shape the way we view and experience our own bodies and those of our children.

Up until now, the Church has tended to go along with the general view that technological progress is benign and in any case irresistible. Christians must simply make the best of it. Every new invention may be used for good or ill: the Church should simply discourage its use for ill. If technologies in themselves are *not* morally or culturally neutral after all, then this policy needs to be re-examined. The crisis over human cloning is likely to force such a re-examination in any case, for now even now many scientists and technicians are asking: "are some kinds of knowledge so terrible they should not be pursued?"

Transhumanism

This question was phrased in the *Newsweek* "Issues 2001" special edition, which drew attention particularly to a widely-quoted paper by Bill Joy, the cofounder and chief scientist of Sun Microsystems, in the April 2000 issue of *Wired* magazine. This paper was influential and alarming because it came from a man at the cutting edge of the present technological revolution. He wrote: "we are on the cusp of the further perfection of extreme evil," through the "empowerment of extreme individuals," and the "pursuit of unrestricted and undirected growth through science and technology," especially through robotics, genetic engineering, and nanotechnology.

In his article, Bill Joy went on to evoke a truly apocalyptic scenario: the prospect that (if we do not first destroy ourselves) our technology itself, soon to be self-replicating, may dispense with human beings altogether.

> By 2030, we are likely to be able to build machines, in quantity, a million times as powerful as the personal computers of today. . . . As this enormous computing power is combined with the manipulative advances of the physical sciences and the new, deep understandings in genetics, enormous transformative power is being unleashed. These combinations open up the opportunity to completely redesign the world, for better or worse: the replicating and evolving processes that have been confined to the natural world are about to become realms of human endeavor.

There is in fact a powerful "transhumanist" movement of people who believe man is about to take control of his own evolution, or that he is about to cede his place to a *homo superior* or "posthuman" of his own construction. We see already the widespread use of performance-enhancing drugs and prosthetics. It is a small step from present forms of medical intervention to the incorporation of genetic modifications or improvements that can be passed on through human reproduction, or replicated commercially in artificial wombs. Among the modifications suggested are gills to enable human beings to adapt to an undersea environment, or more radical changes to enable life on other planets or in permanent space stations.

Naturally the rapid development of information technology and computing suggests other scenarios, such as the incorporation of a direct and permanent connection to the internet within the human brain itself, and the creation of artificial intelligence that will appear to be conscious and creative. Robots, androids, and cyborgs were once the stuff of science fiction, but the children who grew up on these tales are now being employed to make them a reality. It is widely assumed, as Joy notes, that once an artificial—or artificially enhanced—intelligence has been created that is capable of self-replication, the speed of evolution will increase even more rapidly, leading to futures we can barely imagine.

Joy believes that the new technologies are being developed less by governments than by corporate enterprise. However, the possibility that such technologies might be employed by the State for coercive social engineering or military purposes also seems extremely likely.

Common sense, and the experience we have already accumulated of human interference with the environment, suggest that such developments will not only give rise to new forms (and new extremes) of wealth and poverty, but pose a risk to the biosphere itself that cannot be easily quantified. Joy would prefer to err on the side of caution. "The only realistic alternative I see is relinquishment: to limit development of the technologies that are too dangerous, by limiting our pursuit of certain kinds of knowledge." He looks to his grandmother and to the Dalai Lama for examples of "common sense," and takes hope from the unilateral US abandonment of the development of biological weapons, which "stemmed from the realization that while it would take an enormous effort to create these terrible weapons, they could from then on easily be duplicated and fall into the hands of rogue nations or groups." However, verifying relinquishment will require transparency amounting to the loss of privacy, the invention of new forms of protection for intellectual property, and the adoption by scientists and engineers of "a strong code of ethical conduct" akin to the Hippocratic Oath.

It is hard to imagine attempts to ban certain technologies, or at least to prevent them from falling into private hands (out of fear of "unacceptable risk" and public outcry), being more than partially and temporarily effective. After all, some at least of the new technologies being developed will have very clear and direct benefits, and it is easy to cry "Luddite!" However, it is not the case that research is currently being driven by sheer curiosity (or the desire to benefit mankind) along an inevitable path. Scientific endeavor always runs along certain channels, created by political and commercial pressures, by social and metaphysical assumptions, by the availability of funding and desire for fame, and by the manifold "spirit of the age." Rather than ask how we might repress certain types of research, we might therefore consider how to redirect some of those creative energies—to make them, perhaps, even *more* unambiguously beneficial to mankind. Bill Joy himself touches on this when he suggests we might "rethink our utopian choices"—the dreams that define our direction.

Adventure of Transcendence

Our relation to the absolute, the spiritual dimension of man, is in the end what sets the limits of both Market and State. Humanity is not itself part of the Market. This is what Catholic teaching means by the "dignity" of the human person. Our existence is beyond price. Nor can the person be subsumed by politics or commerce, forced to act against its conscience, or deprived of its most important freedoms. We have come to a line in the sand, across which neither totalitarianism nor liberalism must be allowed to pass.

We have earlier glimpsed where these limits come from. They are not merely imposed by an act of will. They are based on reality, on truth. The culture of life is founded on the recognition of *objective form*, the existence not just of individual human beings but of a human nature in which all these individuals participate and which is what connects us to our Creator. That is, human life—also other life, but certainly human—is no mere flux of particles or flow of information, to be shaped and manipulated by those that have the power to do so. There is an inner dimension in man that we cannot measure directly, but which we grasp in an act of imaginative perception or intuition.

This is the spiritual element, the presence in us of something that transcends time and death, something that gives our decisions and personality a dignity that matter alone does not possess, on which our spiritual life depends. "Beyond the limits of experimental methods, beyond the boundaries of the sphere which some call meta-analysis, wherever the perception of the senses no longer suffices or where neither the perception of the senses alone nor scientific verification is possible, begins the *adventure of transcendence*."[22]

We become aware of the limits of the Market and the State as we become aware of this "beyond" that is in us. The first sin, described in Genesis as the eating of a forbidden fruit from the Tree of the Knowledge of Good and Evil, was the transgression of a limit, the limit of created nature. This inherent "limitation" is the fact that we cannot decide good and evil for ourselves, but only conform to or reject a good that already exists (in God).[23] Our conscience, therefore, is not the power of deciding but the power of discerning. It is a gift of the Holy Spirit that enables us to remember the fullness of goodness in the Father. It is the Son who reveals this goodness, but the Spirit is the awakener of memory, the memory of what has been revealed (John 14:26).

Whenever Market or State overstep their limits, it is because the voice of the Spirit has been silenced by a desire for money or power (or else sheer curiosity—the desire to do something just because we can, to find out what will happen), which are substitutes for the

---

22. Pope Benedict XVI, Address to the Participants at the 12th General Assembly of the Pontifical Academy for Life and Congress on "The Human Embryo in the Pre-Implantation Phase" (February 27, 2006). My emphasis.
23. Pope John Paul II, *Dominum et Vivificantem*, n. 36.

true good. Consumerism begins with the Tree of Knowledge. The same is true of political tyranny, which begins with alienation from God, giving rise to a fear of others, against whom we then try to protect ourselves.[24]

Thus when a pope speaks of the new idolatry, this is based on his sensitive awareness of what is happening to man in our age—the dissolution of the divine image, so that the individual human being inevitably becomes the victim of a new cult, in a world where power has become all-important and is concentrated in the hands of a few. According to this new cult or tyranny, man himself can be bought and sold, customized for the purchaser. And when the pope speaks about the sins of gossip and slander and the spreading of misinformation, as he has on many occasions, he is not merely indulging a whim, but bringing into the light an important dimension of Catholic social teaching—important because it concerns the way we treat each other.

A culture of life is not simply one in which abortion is banned, and provision made for unwanted children and their mothers; nor is it a culture in which the elderly are supported and comforted through the last stages of life instead of being quietly killed. It is those things, surely; but it is also a culture in which all human beings are welcomed and treated with kindness and respect.

What goals are we setting for ourselves? Men might have been standing on Mars by now, if the drive to conquer space had not evaporated after the United States beat Soviet Russia to the Moon. Funding went in other directions. Similarly, the direction of current research can be changed by legislation and investment that sets other priorities, priorities more in tune with our true purpose on this earth and with the dignity of the human person.

It is a vital aspect of this dignity to which we now turn. It is essential that we reclaim our humanity in the face of the Machine, and to do this we must understand the human body as more than a machine.

---

24. "But the Lord God called to the man, and said to him, 'Where are you?' And he said, 'I heard the sound of thee in the garden, and I was afraid, because I was naked; and I hid myself'" (Gen. 3:9–10).

The Mystery of Gender

Thus in this dimension, a primordial sacrament *is constituted, understood as a* sign that efficaciously transmits in the visible world the invisible mystery hidden in God from eternity. *And this is the mystery of Truth and Love, the mystery of divine life, in which man really participates. In the history of man, it is original innocence that begins this participation and is also the source of original happiness. The sacrament, as a visible sign, is constituted with man, inasmuch as he is a "body," through his "visible" masculinity and femininity. The body, in fact, and only the body, is capable of making visible what is invisible: the spiritual and the divine. It has been created to transfer into the visible reality of the world the mystery hidden from eternity in God, and thus to be a sign of it.*
　～John Paul II, February 20, 1980, General Audience[1]

John Paul's reflections on what he sometimes called "the gospel of the body" unfolded through a famous series of talks he gave at his Wednesday audiences in St Peter's Square, but his teaching was also developed in numerous other speeches and addresses, encyclical letters and exhortations on marriage, women, and the Blessed Virgin Mary. It has become increasingly clear that these meditations have the potential to transform our understanding, not only of human sexuality and ethics, but of human nature and the foundations of human society. In what follows I want to try to indicate as succinctly as possible a few of the key points in these reflections, especially those that relate human gender to the divine image.

Three Books of Revelation

Before we can follow what the pope is saying about the "gospel of

---

1. John Paul II, *Man and Woman He Created Them: A Theology of the Body* (Boston: Pauline, 2006), p. 203. (Further page references to this book will be given in parentheses after the quotation.)

the body" we need to understand his method. It is based on a reading of reality as symbolic, as *meaningful*, which when applied to ourselves he calls the "language of the body." In line with the traditional understanding of all religious peoples, not just Christians, he interprets the whole world as a book of symbols expressing invisible realities.

Most religious traditions tell us that there are essentially two revelations of the divine nature accessible to man, namely the revelation in nature (which we can call the *cosmic* revelation), and a revelation in human words that constitutes the sacred scriptures of that tradition. Each of these two "books" illuminates the other, for the language of the sacred scriptures depends on images and metaphors drawn from the book of nature, while the scriptures teach us how to penetrate the language of nature to a deeper level of meaning. In the quotation above, for example, the pope talks about the body as a "sign."

For Christians, however, there is a third "book" or revelation. This is the Incarnation of God himself within the world, as a human being. Here nature and human language both converge on a single Word that is God expressing himself directly in the language of the flesh. Thus Jesus Christ raises holy scripture to a new degree, just as he raises human nature to a new degree. By expressing divinity in human nature, Jesus enables us to read the two other books at a deeper level, seeing in them the "mystery hidden from eternity in God" which is the mystery of God's own interior life, into which we ourselves are invited through his death and resurrection and as the body of the Church. This makes the difference between a "sign" and a "sacrament"—a sacrament being an "efficacious" sign, or one that can *bring about* what it represents. In fact the pope speaks of the "sacrament of redemption" referring to the Incarnation itself, together with the sacrifice of the Cross.

The pope develops his reflections not just theologically, but philosophically, using a phenomenological approach that pays close attention to actual lived experience (phenomenology is a method of reflection upon the "phenomena" or the world as it presents itself to consciousness). The two approaches come together in the form of a commentary on selected passages of Holy Scripture, so that divine revelation is used to illuminate experience and *vice versa*. By employing this technique he develops an analysis of the human condition as such, the condition of being a person, which is also always a condition of being either male or female. For the human person is not just a spirit, but a lived body, and the gender of that body must be read symbolically as telling us something about the life of God.

The pope in fact talks about the "spousal" or "nuptial" meaning of the body, which he says is "not something merely conceptual" but concerns a "way of living the body" in its masculinity and femininity, an *"inner dimension . . .* that stands at the root of all facts that constitute man's history" (pp. 255–6). This nuptial meaning has been limited, violated, and deformed over time and by modern culture, until we have almost lost the power of "seeing" it, but it is still there to be discovered with the help of grace, like a spark deep within the human heart. The "language of the body," therefore, must be recovered, and that is what the pope seeks to do. But as he says, correctly reading this "language" results not so much in a set of statements as in a "way of living" and therefore a culture (the culture of life).

Being a Person

"Christ, the final Adam, by the revelation of the mystery of the Father and his love, fully reveals man to man himself and makes his supreme calling clear" (*Gaudium et Spes*, n. 22). In this sentence from the Second Vatican Council, which John Paul II quotes in each of his encyclicals, the Christian revelation is described as the "mystery of the Father and his love." Essentially, it is the unfolding of that mystery summed up by St. John in the New Testament in the three words, "God is love" (1 John 4).

St. John does not simply mean that God loves, or that he is to be identified with the emotion of love. He means that he *is Love*. He is generating or overflowing love, i.e., the Father. He is receiving and faithful love, giving in return, i.e., the Son. He is love given and received, i.e. the Holy Spirit. The sentence "God is love" implies that God is a Trinity of Persons. But how does this revelation of the Trinity "reveal man to himself"? We are beings made by God in his image. This means that we can become eternally happy like him only by participating in that love. We too, in our own way, "are love," or must become so. This is the gospel of the human person.

The divine Trinitarian love enables us to understand the intrinsic relatedness we ourselves possess in our heart to others, as persons called to communion. We recognize that the love which connects us to each other constitutes our destiny. It is what we are made for. In the words of *Gaudium et Spes* (n. 24), "man, who is the only creature on earth which God willed for itself, cannot fully find himself except through a sincere gift of himself." This means that one person can only achieve fulfillment by pouring itself out for another, just as the Father and the Son give everything of themselves to the other in the Holy Spirit. Christ teaches that "He who finds his life will lose it, and he who loses his life for my sake will find it" (Matt. 10:39).

Following this line of thought, Pope John Paul II went beyond the Boethian definition of the person as an "individual substance of a rational nature" to argue that a necessary part of what it means to be a person is to be in a loving relationship—beginning, of course, with our relationship to God our maker. Without the experience of love, the self remains incomplete and imperfect. Love (in the sense of reciprocal self-gift) is necessary for the completion of one's own creation.

Gender is the *inextinguishable sign* of this calling to self-gift, this being-made-for-another. We cannot even exist as human beings without it, for we are always either male or female. The biblical starting point for the pope's reflection on this is God's saying, "It is not good that the man should be alone" (Gen. 2:18). God brings the animals to Adam but none of them can answer his need for love, which is the condition of being a person. Man only finds a true companion in his solitude when he meets Woman, formed out of his own substance but with a distinct soul and feminine nature. "This at last is bone of my bones and flesh of my flesh," he cries (Gen. 2:23), joyfully perceiving this gift that fills the void in his heart, and the two of them cleave together. (His cry is the first Eucharist, in the original sense of the word *eucharistia* as "thanksgiving," offered by Adam as priest of creation.)

Purity and Lust

The words of a Victorian poet capture an aspect of the human experience the pope is referring to when he speaks of the reciprocal "interpenetrating" love of the married couple, the archetype of which is glimpsed in Eden.

> Who, except, perhaps, Hegel, has ever noted, except by way of poetical metaphor, the surprising fact, simply natural and of general experience, of the double and reciprocal consciousness of love; that marvelous state in which each of two persons in distinct bodies perceives sensibly all that the other feels in regard to him or herself, although their feelings are of the most opposite characters; and this so completely, each discerning and enjoying the distinct desire and felicity of the other, that you might say that in each was the fullness of both sexes. To note one such human fact as this is to exalt life to fuller consciousness, and to do more for true science than to discover a thousand new suns.[2]

The pope comments a great deal on the fact that at first, in their original state of innocence, the man and woman were naked and not ashamed, but that shame (along with the need for clothing) awoke for the first time after they had broken the divine commandment. He talks about the experience of shame as due to "disunion in the body" (p. 348)—the disruption of the union that previously existed in the "one flesh" of man and woman together, and in the heart of each. The change that we see taking place in them tells us much about the nature of their union.

The reason they were not at first ashamed of being naked in each other's presence is related to the reason we are not ashamed of being naked when we are alone with ourselves. Each was "within" the other. This was due to the completeness of the self-gift of Adam and Eve. The pope describes it as the "reciprocal interpenetration of the 'I' of the human person" (p. 202). Later in a comment on Ephesians 5:28 he writes, "Through love, the wife's 'I' becomes, so to speak, the husband's 'I.' The body is the expression of this 'I,' it is the basis of its identity" (p. 611). Innocence and purity made it impossible for

---

2. Coventry Patmore, *The Rod, The Root, and the Flower* (London: Bell & Sons, 1923), p. 105.

either of them to reduce the other to a mere "object": they saw the body of the other not as an *object* for themselves but as the expression of a *subject*, another person in their full integrity, but a person who was experienced *from within the unity of love*.

Thus purity is "a requirement of love" (p. 325), for it is the dimension of innocence enabling us truly to "know" each other (and ourselves) in self-gift. It is a fruit of the Holy Spirit dwelling within the person as in a temple, and is grounded in the gift of the Spirit known as "piety," meaning reverence for the gifts of God (pp. 352–3). It is "the glory of the human body before God" and "the glory of God in the human body, through which masculinity and femininity are manifested" (p. 353). It is the condition under which the true beauty of the human person can be revealed. In a way, the teaching on purity brings to a focus the pope's whole teaching on the gendered body as integral to the human person made in the image and likeness of God, and (in that image) made to know God in knowing the Other as the gift of God. In fact he says himself that "The link of purity with love, and the link of the same purity in love with piety as gift of the Holy Spirit, is a little known guiding thread of the theology of the body, but nevertheless deserves particularly deep study" (p. 353).

As we shall see this "guiding thread" will lead us also to a deeper understanding of how gender and purity play a crucial role in the creation of a Christian social order.

Control of Desire

The Fall changed the way we view each other and the world. Instead of seeing with God's eyes all things as "good"—the primordial divine affirmation repeated, significantly, precisely seven times during the creation account in Genesis—man now sees only from his own limited perspective. He "looks [in order] to desire," as the pope says in his commentary on Matthew 5:28. The primordial sin lies in setting human desires free to determine human decisions. Desires have their place in a healthy spiritual life, but they should not be in control. As soon as we have chosen to obey one of them, instead of acting in the light of the broader picture and all the other factors of which we are aware, it grows psychologically stronger in us, and we become enslaved to it.

In fact, the pope has an interesting discourse on "insatiability" where he explains how sexual desire becomes unbalanced after the Fall because man and woman were unable any longer to live what he calls their "original beatifying conjugal union of persons" (p. 251), the mutual transparency and delight that each took in the other, making each the "I" of the other. Since they were no longer perfectly united,[3] and yet perfect union is what they still desired, they tried to achieve it through continually renewing a sexual contact that could never satisfy completely.

This is why God tells Eve in Genesis 3:16, "Your desire shall be for your husband, but he will dominate you." The pope writes, "From the moment in which the man *'dominates'* her, *the communion of persons*—which consists in the spiritual unity of the two subjects who gave themselves to each other—*is replaced by a different mutual relationship*, namely, by a relationship *of possession* of the other as an object of one's own desire" (p. 254).

The possibility of true or complete self-gift—either to another human being in marriage or to God in celibacy—depends on perfect self-possession. We cannot give what we do not own. "The satisfaction of the passions is, in fact, one thing; quite another is the joy a person finds in possessing himself more fully, since in this way he can also become more fully a true gift for another person," the pope says (p. 359). Concupiscence or lust "limits and restricts self-mastery from within, and thereby *in some sense makes the interior freedom of the gift impossible*" (p. 260). For sin shatters our being into fragments, setting us against ourselves. In a state of sin, having lost my integrity, I am no longer unified enough to be able to give myself *as a whole* to another. I can only give parts of myself. It also affects the way I see the world, because the mirror of consciousness in which I see all things is disturbed and shattered, so that I see only fragmentary views of the whole—views of it in relation to the fulfillment of my own desires.

---

3. Strictly speaking, the original union was not "perfect"—a word that more properly applies to the eschatological end of man—but rather "untroubled." It was the sin they had committed that revealed their imperfection, and thus awoke their desire for something better.

It is only by receiving Christ's threefold victory over concupiscence that we can regain the gift of reverence for God's gift, and along with it our *simplicity, lucid clarity,* and *interior joy* in the experience of the body. Concupiscence is traditionally defined as desire of the flesh, desire of the eyes, and the pride of life, following 1 John 2:16 (that is to say, lust experienced in the body, the soul, and the spirit of man). It is present in the temptation of Eve when she saw that the tree was "good for food," and that it was "a delight to the eyes," and was "to be desired to make one wise" (Gen. 3:6). This threefold concupiscence is defeated by Christ in the wilderness, when he refuses to turn stones into bread, when he refuses to impress men with his power, and when he refuses to worship the ruler of this world (Matt. 4:1–11, Luke 4:1–13). After this the devil "leaves him for a time," only to return to wrestle with him in the garden of Gethsemane, where the triple victory is confirmed (Mark 14:32–42, Matt. 26:36–46).

In his exhortation on the consecrated life, the pope identifies this threefold victory over concupiscence with the three so-called "evangelical counsels" of poverty, chastity, and obedience, described elsewhere in this book as the three "dimensions of freedom":

> Evangelical chastity helps us to transform in our interior life everything that has its sources in the lust of the flesh; evangelical poverty, everything that finds its source in the lust of the eyes; and evangelical obedience enables us to transform in a radical way that which in the human heart arises from the pride of life.... The evangelical counsels in their essential purpose aim at "the renewal of creation": "the world," thanks to them, is to be subjected to man and given to him in such a way that man himself may be perfectly given to God.[4]

The Trinitarian Image

But why is it that the *image* of God—God who is in himself three Persons, not two—ends up being made of just *two* elements (the male and the female)? By probing this matter we arrive at a more theological understanding of the union of love that constituted the

---

4. John Paul II, *Redemptionis Donum* (1984), n. 9.

primordial sacrament of marriage. For in fact marriage was never a matter of the human couple alone. There were three involved from the beginning—two visible, one invisible by nature. Adam experienced Eve not just as something randomly encountered in his environment, but as the gift of God brought forth from his own body. He was united with Eve in a union of one flesh *through the presence of the Creator God* who "is love."

It was therefore in God, not just in themselves, that Adam and Eve found each other and were united to form an image of the Trinity. Furthermore it was in their mutual loving submission to the will of God, as he walked with them in the garden, that the two remained (for a while) in their original state of innocence, and they were intended in that state to become fruitful and multiply. As a matter of fact their submission to God was prior to any submission they made to each other. It was only when they rejected God's will, fleeing God's presence and hiding their bodies from each other for the first time, that this unity of grace was shattered.

In order for two persons to become one, yet without one of them absorbing the other, they must become three. There is an intuition of this in Plato's *Timaeus*, where "it's impossible for any two things to form a proper structure without the presence of a third thing; there has to be some bond to mediate between the two of them and bring them together" (31c). This is perhaps one of the most subtle and difficult points in the pope's analysis of the relation between the sexes. It is the deepest foundation on which to understand the Church's critique of contraception in *Humanae Vitae* (a detailed commentary on the 1968 encyclical is found in the final part of the pope's book). The following is my own attempt to understand it, and to put it in my own words.

Nuptial or covenantal love, the kind of love that unites *two persons in one flesh* is necessarily Trinitarian, rather than dualistic. The union of marriage is a union of two sexes, each of which needs the other in order to reproduce biologically. This complementarity for the sake of reproduction is what makes it possible for the couple to image the Trinity *as a couple*, and thus to be united not just in friendship, as any two people may be, but in a sacramental marriage—something that is not possible for a same-sex couple, no matter how loving and faithful they may be. What determines the biological difference between the sexes is their role in reproduction. It is this complementarity that enables them to represent something very specific in the Trinity, namely the proceeding of the Holy Spirit from the Father and Son—the union of two Persons in a Third.[5]

Not that Father and Son are male and female to each other. The ladder of analogy works in the other direction: things in the world may be likened to God, from whom they derive, but God remains always beyond, always greater (*semper maior*). The marriage of man and woman resembles that between Christ and his Church, not the other way around (Eph. 5:21–33). The marriage of Christ and his Church resembles that of divine and human natures in the Person of the Son. That hypostatic union resembles the union of Persons in the Trinity, where there is no question of several natures, but only one. At each level, the analogy is based on a more intense kind of union above and beyond it. The mutual indwelling of man and woman in sexual love is therefore a biological reflection, albeit a remote one, of the indwelling of the divine Persons in one another.

Inscribed within the nature of the conjugal act, expressed in the language of the body itself, is an indwelling not just of the body but of the *person* of the man with the *person* of the woman. This merging in love (without dissolution) is an image of the Trinity because it involves the presence of a Third, representing all the newness and otherness and difference of each from each that is being given and accepted in that act of union.

This Third is, firstly, God himself, who is the Giver of each to the other. But the presence of that mysterious Third may also reveal itself through the conception of a child, which is always an act of God as well as the joint act of the man and his wife. The use of contraception is a way of rejecting that unpredictable, life-giving presence of God. However harmless it may appear at first, it falsifies the

---

5. For the Orthodox the Holy Spirit does not proceed from the Son, and this leads them to see the analogy rather differently. For Paul Evdokimov, whose book *Woman and the Salvation of the World* (Crestwood, NY: SVS Press, 1997) contains a Christian anthropology that bears comparison with that of John Paul II, there is an ontic affinity between masculinity and the Son, and femininity and the Spirit, this uni-duality expressing the Father, who is "the third Person of every love" (p. 27).

symbolic properties of the conjugal act, and attacks the supernatural essence of the sacrament of marriage. Like intercourse outside marriage, it destroys the full potential of sex to bring about that union which is its real purpose in God's plan for creation.

The Virgin's Secret

Despite the Trinitarian image in procreation I have just described, gender itself is not entirely determined by the need for physical reproduction. There is a still deeper reason for it. Bearing in mind the words of Jesus that those who are resurrected have neither wives nor husbands (Mark 12:25, Luke 20:34–5), the pope writes that "Marriage and procreation do not definitively determine the original and fundamental meaning of being a body nor of being, as a body, male and female. Marriage and procreation only give concrete reality to that meaning in the dimension of history" (p. 399).

Here the "dimension of history" refers to that state of existence in which we, along with the whole creation, are subject to suffering and death. In our final state after the resurrection, death has no hold over us, as St. Paul tells us (1 Cor. 14:42). The same seems to have been the case before our expulsion from Eden, i.e. before it was determined the man should be subject to death. Since according to modern science entropy and death are an essential element of the world we know, this must mean that we did once (and will one day again) exist in a very different state. Of course, it is hard if not impossible to imagine how some other state of matter would affect our experience of gender. But the pope may want to leave room for St. Gregory of Nyssa's suggestion that physical intercourse was only necessary to achieve reproduction after we had been expelled from Eden and clothed with the "skins of animals" (Gen. 3:21), in which case it is conceivable that procreation in Eden might have taken some other form.

This is a delicate question, because it is often assumed that John Paul II agrees with St. Augustine and with St. Thomas that sexual reproduction would have taken place in Eden (if we had not fallen from grace) in much the same way as it does now. But there seems to be no passage where the pope affirms this view unambiguously. On the contrary, he is very clear that man's knowledge of the "generative" as distinct from the "spousal" meaning of his body is revealed to us only after the Fall, after the beginning of history, and that it is linked to the revelation of the "horizon of death" (pp. 205, 216–17). It is the form man's generativity takes under the conditions of historical time. The *beauty and goodness* of this form is not in doubt. (No one who has read the pope's book can doubt his appreciation of it.) But how the full depth of the meaning in masculinity and femininity—including fatherhood and motherhood—would have or could have been revealed in the original state he wisely does not speculate, only reminding us that Mary of Nazareth, too, questioned how she could become a mother without having "known" man in the sense of Genesis 4:1–2.

The poet Coventry Patmore, a (several times) happily married man, draws on his own experience in support of St. Augustine's view that St. Joseph was truly married to Mary despite her virginity, in a union that points towards the virginal quality intended for marriage in the original state.

> Every true Lover has perceived, at least in a few moments of his life, that the fullest fruition of love is without the loss of virginity. Lover and Mistress become sensibly one flesh in the instant that they confess to one another a full and mutual complacency of intellect, will, affection, and sense, with the promise of inviolable faith. *That* is the moment of fruition, and all that follows is, as St. Thomas Aquinas says, "an accidental perfection of marriage"; for such consent breeds indefinite and abiding increase of life between the lovers; which life is none the less real and substantial because it does not manifest itself in a separated entity.[6]

The Deepest Meaning of Gender

If the need to reproduce physically has only conditioned the form gender takes for us *in this world*, the real source of gender must lie deeper. It lies not in the generative but in the spousal meaning of the body, which will ultimately find fulfillment in the virginal state of the world to come, when the direct vision of God will subsume all human "intersubjectivity" along with the relations that consti-

---

6. *The Rod, the Root, and the Flower*, p. 150.

tute the cosmos itself (pp. 395–6). The spousal and gendered body is an image of the Trinity, we might say, because of the nature of woman as "gift" for man. In the Trinity, the Spirit is Gift both given and received, and unites Father and Son in the act of giving (John Paul II describes the Holy Spirit in his encyclical *Dominum et Vivificantem* as "Person-Gift"). In the creation, woman is brought to man precisely as "gift," crowning the gift of creation in general, which has been made "for him."[7] Gender is therefore a participation in the Trinity even in the virginal state.

Adam represents the Son, the Receiver of the Father's Gift, and Eve the Holy Spirit, or that which the Father gives. She is the breath of life, the living essence ("rib," which the pope tells us on page 160 means "life" in Sumerian, and on page 552 "seems to indicate the heart") of the man, taken out of him and returned in the one form in which he can find himself in his own solitude—that is, in the form of another person to whom he can give himself. In the form, in a sense, of his own love now revealed to him in the person of another. The nature of woman, then, or the deepest meaning of her gender, is *to be Gift* for man, to manifest the Spirit, just as the deepest nature of man is to be the *Receiver of the Gift*, and to manifest the Son to her.

Femininity in its totality, at its deepest level, is the essence of humanity made visible to itself, as the definitive beauty and glory of creation (p. 584). Similarly the essence of masculinity consists in the loving response to this gift which awakens Woman to her own self. Both man and woman therefore *find themselves in the gift of self*, reciprocally accepted and welcomed. This is the ontological moment that the pope identifies with the words "they were naked and not ashamed" (Gen. 2:25). It is regained and even transcended in the moment of the Annunciation, when the Virgin Mary's unreserved self-gift (*fiat*) makes of her the Gift of creation *par excellence*, a Gift first of all to her own Son, conceived in the very moment that he receives a Mother.

Christ came to set us free, to make possible a renewed integrity and purity of vision. He did this, in a sense, by inscribing the sacra-

---

7. See *Man and Woman*, pp. 178–85 and especially pp. 180, 196–8.

ment of marriage into the substance of creation through his Cross
(p. 529). For the redemption that was achieved on the Cross was a
marriage feast, as the Church tells us, in which Christ was united in
one flesh with the Church even as his body and soul were separated
in death. Our salvation is brought about through the shedding of
Christ's blood, in which he gave himself entirely for us, and through
the love uniting us with him, which is poured into our hearts by the
Holy Spirit. That same act—sacrifice, marriage feast, consummation—is translated into liturgical or sacramental form and present
throughout the Church in the Mass.

Nuptiality affects all of us, whether we are married or not. While
I may never be anyone's spouse, I am always a son or daughter, a sister or brother (pp. 524, 566). In such ways and combinations of
ways, I necessarily participate in the (cosmic) relationship of one
gender to another. Each of us is a part of that man or woman who
has existed with and for the other since the beginning. Similarly, in
the redemption, each of us who receive baptism become a part of
the new Adam and the new Eve—or rather, in the new Adam *though*
the new Eve. So it is not that, individually, we need to be married in
order to be saved, but we do need to play our part in the marriage
between Christ and his Church in order to be saved (whether as married people or as single).[8]

Each of us, of course, is only a tiny fragment of humanity and of
the Church. Both men and women, all of us together and throughout history, make up *Ecclesia*, and as such are united to the divine
Bridegroom as fragments of an overall "feminine" to his "masculine." To be feminine is the basic human condition, but in that fem-

---

8. The call to celibacy also has to be understood in terms of the nuptial relation
between Christ and the Church. The celibate (male or female) is called to become a
living image of the Church as Bride of Christ. This state of life is based on the fact
that both male and female, as creatures, are "feminine" (receptive) in relation to
Christ. In the case of marriage, male and female are collaborating in becoming an
image, not of the Church in her relation to Christ, but of the Church and Christ in
relationship to each other. This is based on the fact that male and female differ
from each other sufficiently to represent the complementarity between creator and
creature, redeemer and redeemed—only faintly, but enough to be the basis for a
sacramental representation.

inine reality of the Church both genders are manifested, since both
are ultimately contained in Christ just as both were contained in
Adam before God drew Eve from his side and presented her to him.
As all men and women descend from Eve after that separation, so
we are the gift the Son receives from the Father and which he offers
up to his Father on the Cross. The Church is the world transformed
into Woman, which means into Gift—Gift for the Son, and Gift of
the Son to the Father.

The Great Task

This vision of man in God and God in man lies behind the Church's
insistence that the family is the first and vital cell of society, where
each of us learns what it means to love and to be a person. *"Enlight-
ened by the radiance of the biblical message, the Church considers the
family as the first natural society, with underived rights that are
proper to it, and places it at the center of social life."*[9] The family has
priority over the rest of civil society and over the State, which actually exist for the sake of the family. The implication being that a
*"society built on a family scale is the best guarantee against drifting off
course into individualism or collectivism, because within the family
the person is always at the center of attention as an end and never as a
means."*[10]

In the light of this constant teaching of the Church about the
importance of the family, which assumes the family is based on the
marriage of a man and a woman, the seriousness of the contemporary debate over the possibility of gay "marriage" is evident. In fact
in the modern world the Church has lost this particular battle—
with consequences that no doubt will soon be revealed.[11]

No one has done more for the traditional family than Pope John
Paul II, but his teaching on this subject is never isolated. He never

9. Pontifical Council for Justice and Peace, *Compendium of the Social Doctrine
of the Church* (2004), n. 211.
10. Ibid., n. 213.
11. On this point see *Compendium* nn. 224 on gender identity and 228 on the
legal recognition of unions between homosexual persons, which implies a "radical
transformation" of the concept of marriage itself, "with grave detriment to the
common good." See Appendix.

loses sight of the bigger picture. In his Apostolic Exhortation *Familiaris Consortio*, for example, he writes:

> The great task that has to be faced today for the renewal of society is that of recapturing the ultimate meaning of life and its fundamental values. Only an awareness of the primacy of these values enables man to use the immense possibilities given him by science in such a way as to bring about the true advancement of the human person in his or her whole truth, in his or her freedom and dignity. Science is called to ally itself with wisdom.[12]

This is the "great task" of the new evangelization, and the task involves an alliance between science and wisdom—the idea of which was explored further in the same pope's encyclical *Fides et Ratio*. But the key to this alliance is the human person, who must be fully understood. Man is both the one who understands, and the one who must be understood. All fields of investigation lead back to him, as the observer who must make sense of his discoveries.

And this is what the "theology or gospel of the body" is all about, for the person can only be understood in the light of relationship—especially the primordial relationship between man, woman, and God revealed "mythologically" in Genesis and actually in Christ. Therefore what we have been thinking about in this chapter is not a sideshow but the foundation of the whole of Catholic social teaching. It is about the way the society of man can be made in the image and likeness of the society of God, which is the Trinity.

12. Pope John Paul II, *Familiaris Consortio* (On the Role of the Christian Family in the Modern World, 1981), n. 8.

A Theology of Freedom

He who can merely choose between arbitrary options is not yet free. Only he who takes the measure of his action from within and need obey no external constraint is free. Therefore, he is free who has become one with his essence, one with the truth itself. For he who is one with the truth no longer acts according to external necessities and constraints; essence, willing, and acting have coincided in him.
⟶Joseph Cardinal Ratzinger[1]

Why should we not do whatever we want? The question of freedom is bound up with the question of law and of morality. At the root of the modern debate lies David Hume's claim (widely accepted by Enlightenment thinkers after him) that an "ought" cannot be derived from an "is"—or in other words that facts must be kept separate from values. In that case, where do the "oughts" come from? How can we know what we should or should not do?

One set of arguments conclude that the morality of an act can be judged by the desirability or otherwise of the outcome (consequentialism, utilitarianism). The difficulty with this is that, on the one hand we cannot necessarily *know* the outcome of a given act. After all, how far ahead are we intending to look? On the other hand, there is also a problem in judging the desirability of the outcome.

Another set of arguments derive our moral duties from *rules* which themselves need to be justified or accounted for (they might, for example, be deemed necessary for the survival or good order of society).

The answer of the Catholic tradition is usually expressed in terms of "natural law" or "virtues," but these exist in a number of variants. For example, in the voluntarist tradition one might argue that good

1. Ratzinger, "Freedom and Liberation: The Anthropological Vision of the Instruction 'Libertatis Conscientia,'" *Communio* 14 (Spring 1987), pp. 55–72.

can be judged according to conformity with a set of laws arbitrarily determined by God as supreme lawgiver—an obvious example being the Ten Commandments. According to this argument, being all-powerful, God can determine what is right or wrong, and our place is simply to obey or be punished. In theory, God could decree murder or torture to be a morally good act. But there is another, more authentically Catholic tradition called realism, in which the laws set by God's will are not arbitrary but in conformity with his own nature or (to put it another way) with his Wisdom, such that even God could not change them. This is the tradition of which Thomas Aquinas is the most important representative.[2]

Benedict XVI spoke of the natural law problem in one of the most important addresses of his pontificate: to the German Bundestag on September 22, 2011. "How do we recognize what is right?" he asked. "Unlike other great religions, Christianity has never proposed a revealed body of law to the State and to society, that is to say a juridical order derived from revelation. Instead, it has pointed to nature and reason as the true sources of law"—both rooted in the creative reason of God. He spoke of the supposed gulf between "is" and "ought" as based on a purely functionalist conception of nature and a positivist conception of reason that excludes ethics and religion from the outset. But this, he said, entails a narrowing of reason and a confinement of the human world to a "concrete bunker with no windows." "And yet we cannot hide from ourselves the fact that even in this artificial world, we are still covertly drawing upon God's raw materials, which we refashion into our own products. The windows must be flung open again, we must see the wide world, the sky and the earth once more and learn to make proper use of all this." We must not forget that nature is created and speaks of its Creator. We must develop a "listening heart."

---

2. The main break in the tradition—from a theory of natural law to one of natural rights, or one which subordinates the former to the latter—came with Hobbes and Locke. Rights are no longer derived from duties but the reverse, beginning with the right to self-preservation, and the only executor of the "law of nature" is man himself. Human nature has no *telos* other than that which we give ourselves. This according to Ernest L. Fortin, "On the Presumed Medieval Origin of Individual Rights," *Communio* 26:1 (Spring 1999), pp. 55–79.

Rethinking Natural Law

It is sometimes said that Catholics lack a language in which to speak to the secular world about secularism, or in which to begin a discussion of faith and morals—and this inspires the attempt to develop an account of the natural law compatible with liberal notions of rationality.[3] But perhaps the common language we are looking for lies elsewhere, in the universal human experience of religious hunger and mystical insight. It is the language of *spirituality* that we need—a language that transcends secular materialism just as it also transcends religious moralism.

In *The Radiance of Being* I tried to show that our existence itself is relational, based in the relationship of God with himself. The very root of being is love. I claimed that cosmic existence culminates in human personality, through which it is taken up into the intimate and eternal relations of the Trinity. The whole world, knowingly or unknowingly, is in the process of being saved from death in the Holy Spirit, by "becoming Church" (becoming, that is, the extended body of Christ). This reconnects the natural sciences to theology by way of metaphysics. It also transforms the idea of a "natural moral law" by integrating it within a covenantal ethics centered on the call to holiness—a spirituality.

These insights are the result of a long development of doctrine, and have been argued over for centuries. Boethius's definition of "person" as "an individual substance of a rational nature"—widely adopted by Latin theologians throughout the Middle Ages—was crucially silent on the importance of relationship. Within the more Aristotelian framework of a later scholasticism, it was all too easy to think of "substance" as a nature existing in itself, obedient to a set of laws that could in theory be studied without reference to the Creator who originally implanted them. Applied to non-human substances, this set the scene for the development of modern science in

---

3. Olsen, *The Turn to Transcendence*, p. 296. On this problem—and the various attempts to develop an alternative, theologically-founded approach in recent years, see Tracey Rowland, "Natural Law: From Neo-Thomism to Nuptial Mysticism," *Communio: International Catholic Review* 35:3 (Fall 2008), pp. 374–396, and other articles in the same issue.

complete independence of the humanities. Applied to *human* substances, it meant that the doctrine of natural law came to be applied to man with scant reference to Christ—as though morally correct behavior did not depend on the supernatural call to love. As a result, ethics became detached from theology, and the theory of natural law became vulnerable to many of the criticisms directed at it by modem philosophers.

But Boethius himself was a Christian Neo-Platonist, and for him the human substance was *not* self-subsistent but entirely relational. As the recipient of being man exists and grows perfect only by participation in divine relationality; that is, in the "ecstatic self-giving" of the Trinity.[4] As far as ethics is concerned, the only way forward from here is to ground the natural law in the concrete and universal norm of love. Persons exist only in relation to each other and to God, and they are centered in him rather than in themselves. Our "integral human fulfillment," our ultimate happiness, lies not on any natural level, but in the supernatural life of the Trinity, and in response to a specific and unique call from God.

For St. Thomas, centuries later, God's nature is identified with Eternal Law, in which the natural law participates. The Eternal Law is the same as divine reason—an intelligible order of things that pre-exists in God. In other words, the Eternal Law is love (St. Thomas indeed calls love the "form" or inner essence of all the virtues). The shape or pattern or *original* of this love is the Trinity. And since everything that exists bears the image of God its creator, and since God is perfectly free (though in him freedom and necessity coincide), certain creatures will bear an image of that freedom, and they too will be fulfilled only in love. Those creatures are able to take responsibility for their actions. A stone follows the laws of nature without choice, and an animal acts from instinct, whereas a rational being such as a man is able to conceive alternative courses of action and judge between them.[5]

4. Adrian Pabst, *Metaphysics: The Creation of Hierarchy* (Grand Rapids: Eerdmans, 2012), pp. 131–8.

5. The freedom of man in performing certain actions consists in being a necessary if not sufficient cause (in the sense of *efficient* cause) of those actions, so that the action would not have taken place without my bringing it about. St. Augustine's

Catholic ethical traditions such as this are teleological, in that they envisage human nature, indeed all creation, as existing for an end (*telos*), which is in God. The end is that state or form in which the creature achieves perfection or completion. (The Beatitudes are the description of the human creature on the way to this end.) So one answer to the question, "Where do the *oughts* come from?" is that they simply define what needs to be done in order to achieve this (super)natural goal. Any deliberately willed act is morally good or evil depending on whether it serves that purpose, or helps to achieve it.[6] Furthermore, creatures exist in community, and human beings exist in society, so that the law that is in them, reflecting the Eternal Law, is for the sake not just of the individual, but of the society, and therefore the common good.

The problem with the usual conception of natural law (which conceives it as a reflection in the creature of Eternal Law) is that it is based on a false understanding of "nature" as something separate from God. Furthermore it gives the impression that moral obligation or values can simply and easily be "read off" the face of nature as she presents herself to us, regardless of our religious faith. But it is faith, not anything purely "natural," that enables us to grasp our

---

treatment of this phenomenon is examined in Ludger Hoelscher, *The Reality of the Mind: St Augustine's Philosophical Arguments for the Human Soul as Spiritual Substance* (London and New York: Routledge & Kegan Paul, 1986), p. 117. Hoelscher's book follows Augustine's proof that the body and soul constitute different substances, anticipating Descartes, but leave as a mystery the exact means by which they are bound together (p. 220). This union is to be found on another level of the human composite, that of the "spirit" (discussed in *The Radiance of Being*), rather than in, say, the physical organ (the pineal gland) proposed by Descartes.

6. Thus John Finnis argues for a version of natural law morality based on the idea that there are seven self-evident human goods: 1) human life (health and procreation); 2) knowledge and aesthetic appreciation; 3) skilled performance; 4) self-integration; 5) authenticity/practical reasonableness; 6) justice and friendship; and 7) religion/holiness. This enables him to make a case for the natural law without reference to belief in God. The self-evidence of these goods is not universally accepted. For example, Servais Pinckaers OP speaks rather of the "five natural inclinations" in human nature that establish the natural law in our hearts, which is based on a yearning for perfection and completion: the inclination to the good, to preserve being, to marry, to know the truth, and to live in society (*Morality: The Catholic View*, South Bend: St Augustine's Press, 2001, pp. 96–109).

end in God—and, indeed, to "see" things in this light. Faith reaches out beyond nature to final cause, beatitude, and eschatological fulfillment. At the same time faith itself is "evolving" through the events of salvation history (the covenant between God and man) or through the events of Church history to reach beyond its present (still imperfect) state in us. The Holy Spirit is "guiding us into all truth" (John 16:13), but we are not there yet.

For John Paul II the human body is a "sign." Indeed the theology of the body seems to fit naturally into a kind of Catholic semiotics, according to which everything in the world is a sign or symbol or sacrament of something else. A law of analogy links everything that exists, because each and everything participates in being *per se*. The old argument about whether the supreme reality resides in being or in truth or in the good is resolved by Christianity in the realization that the supreme reality is love, which is the highest truth and the highest good rolled into one. This gives a grounding for Catholic ethics, anchoring it in the transcendent and avoiding the pitfalls of idealism.

Natural law is an interpretation of certain facts, no more. Facts do not transform into moral obligations without interpretation. Interpretations rest on certain assumptions. We may have reasons for our assumptions about the ends of human nature and the nature of human perfection, but those reasons are derived in a complex and subtle way, even if we also trust in an authority guided by the Spirit that endorses certain interim conclusions. In fact it is only from within the Spirit of love that we can both grasp a fuller truth and persuade others of it, love being the anticipation or foretaste of the true end of man's existence, and also the basis for any community within which coherent thought is possible.

How does this transform our view of natural law? We cannot drop the term, for apart from anything else, it is "the only valid bulwark against the arbitrary power or the deception of ideological manipulation."[7] But we should be more cautious in using it, remembering

7. Pope Benedict XVI, "Address to the Participants of the International Congress on Natural Moral Law" (2007). Not everyone would agree with this. Alasdair MacIntyre, David Schindler, and others view the Catholic use of natural law and

that "knowledge of this law inscribed on the heart of man increases with the progress of the moral conscience."[8]

The Eye of the Heart

It is also possible to give the concept of "natural law" a more Platonic interpretation, as Pope Benedict did, to avoid some of the pitfalls I have mentioned. The Spirit's "guiding into truth" might be viewed as a process of assisted *anamnesis* or recalling of the good and the true that are one with our original nature. The whole of moral development is a process of remembering and conforming oneself to this state of being, which is a pure expression of love, the light beyond all other lights. The advent of Jesus Christ is the revelation, for those who have forgotten it, of human perfection, and his death and resurrection make possible our human existence in the Trinity.[9]

In an interview with Eugenio Scalfari, published in *La Repubblica* on October 1, 2013, Pope Francis was asked, "Your Holiness, is there is a single vision of the Good? And who decides what it is?" He replied, simply, "Each of us has a vision of good and of evil. We have to encourage people to move towards what they think is Good." Scalfari pushes him: "The conscience is autonomous, you said, and everyone must obey his conscience. I think that's one of the most courageous steps taken by a pope." Francis responds, "And I repeat

---

"rights" rhetoric by the New Natural Law school of Finnis and others as conceding too much to the modern secular worldview; that is, by abstracting in advance from the infrastructure provided by a religious tradition or narrative, and accepting the idea of autonomous self-fulfillment. See Tracey Rowland, *Culture and the Thomist Tradition After Vatican II* (London: Routledge, 2003), Ch. 7.

8. Ibid. For Thomists "conscience" refers to a judgment of practical reason, i.e. a judgment in particular circumstances about how to act, in the light of *synderesis* or the ability to know (or skill of knowing) what should or should not be done in general. It is the latter that overcomes the gap between "is" and "ought." See, e.g., Eric D'Arcy, *Conscience and Its Right to Freedom* (London: Sheed & Ward, 1961).

9. See Joseph Ratzinger, "Conscience and Truth," *Communio* 37:3 (Fall 2010), p. 535. Romano Guardini had written: "It can be historically proved that the word 'conscience' and its meaning are connected with the ultimate layers of religious consciousness, with the 'Ground of the soul' and the 'spiritual spark'" (*Conscience*, p. 72).

it here. Everyone has his own idea of good and evil and must choose to follow the good and fight evil as he conceives them."

The "subjectivity" of the pope's reply puzzled some, but what he said was perfectly in line with the rest of Catholic teaching. It did not aim to be a complete or systematic teaching on conscience, which can be found in the *Catechism of the Catholic Church* to which the pope adheres. It was certainly not an "authoritative" statement, of the kind that emerge when a pope is called up to speak from the "chair of St Peter" to resolve some matter in dispute for the whole Church. It was a conversation, an interview, a friendly engagement. It was one of the things that Pope Francis does best.

In particular, it did not mention our responsibility to develop and educate this "vision" or "idea" of good and evil that we may have. We do not just pick it off the shelf, or let another (whether it be a parent or a teacher or a newspaper) determine it for us. The Church's teaching on morality is part of that process of self-education—that is, assuming we give any credibility to the Church as an authority for us, then we will need to take her teaching into account as we work through the arguments and concerns in our own minds, rationally. (She is one factor, but an important one.)

The statement is right, and corresponds to what John Henry Newman wrote in his famous *Letter to the Duke of Norfolk*, in stating that we can only fight evil and follow the good according to *our own best idea of what these are*. Even if we are going to make mistakes, because we have not yet fully understood everything, we have to do the best we can in the given moment with what we have available to us.

I take it that one lesson of the Genesis account of the Fall and the taking of the Fruit concerns this very question, for the Serpent tells the couple that "God knows that when you eat of it your eyes will be opened, and you will be like God, knowing good and evil" (3:5). This raises a host of questions, not least what is supposed to be *wrong* with "knowing good and evil"? Is it not precisely *necessary* if we are to be able to work out for ourselves what is right and what is wrong?

The answer seems to lie in the difference between knowing good, and knowing good and evil, and knowing evil. God wants us to know the good, not to know evil. We often assume we can only know the good if we have a choice between them, and know them both equally. But that is not right. If we know them equally, we are changed by both, and our knowing of the good is changed and spoiled. In the end, if we know both, we will know only evil. On the contrary, if we know the good, by adhering to God, the evil becomes irrelevant to us.[10]

But what is the good? What makes it part of the world? What kind of thing? It is any kind of thing, provided it will fulfill and complete us. It is what we are drawn towards because we want to become fully what we were made to be. We see our fulfillment in the "good," and we are attracted by the radiance—the "beauty"—that connects us with it, like a pathway across the water.

Aquinas and others have seen Beauty as an aspect of the Good, and these ideas are certainly very closely interwoven, but they are not identical. Beauty is the *radiance* of the Good and the True, and that radiance of being is another aspect of Love, which is the self-giving act at the heart of all existence, especially the existence of God. It is the dynamic act, the verb not the noun, that reaches out and across the differences between things and unites them, or gives them the savor of one another. That is how the angels communicate, according to St. Denys—by the giving of light. God himself dwells in light, *inaccessible light* (1 Tim. 6:16). It is inaccessible because it is his gift to himself; and at the same time it has become accessible, because he has given us this very self in his Son.

We know evil by suffering it. We know the good by being drawn to its beauty and ultimately by sharing it. And as for conscience, that is the self-knowledge, the eye of the heart, the memory of the breath of God (Gen. 2:7), by which we recognize the good *as good*—as containing that promise for us. No wonder we must each have "our own vision of good and evil." No one else can do our seeing for us.

Dimensions of Freedom
The restrictions on our behavior imposed by moral principles should not be thought of as restrictions on freedom, any more than

---

10. God knows evil only "indirectly," according to Aquinas: not by any privation in himself, but by knowing the good of which evil is the privation. We do not need to know evil in any other way.

the rules of chess are considered obstacles to the playing of a game. Freedom is not simply an ability to choose, as a chess player might choose to move his knight to any space on the board. It is in the ability to choose according to the reality and needs of the game, as a knight might make a move two spaces forward and one to the side.

Was Jesus free? Pope Benedict threw light on this question in his commentary on Jesus's prayer on the Mount of Olives in his book *Jesus of Nazareth*. Discussing the response of St. Maximus the Confessor to the heresy of monotheletism (the belief that Christ can have had only one will), he explains that in Jesus, who has two natures, there must also be two wills, a natural and a divine will. "And this is possible without annihilating the specifically human element, because the human will, as created by God, is ordered to the divine will. In becoming attuned to the divine will, it experiences its fulfillment, not its annihilation."[11] For human beings, consenting to God's will is their opportunity to become more fully themselves.

The key to "integral liberation" is therefore the discovery of a new principle of action.[12] Maximillian Kolbe was never freer than when he was offering his own life for a fellow prisoner in Auschwitz—an action founded on the interior freedom that came from a love of God's will. An authentic liberation theology starts, then, from the notion of freedom as liberation from sin—liberation from the "false self" created by the closure of the human will upon itself. Only on this basis would it be prepared to "judge a prevalent and all-intrusive culture" (*VS*, n. 88), with its "serious forms of social and economic justice and political corruption affecting entire peoples and nations" (*VS*, n. 98).

11. *Jesus of Nazareth*, p. 160.

12. In *Centesimus Annus* John Paul II calls for a recovery of the Christian imagination in politics. He writes: "The crisis of Marxism does not rid the world of the situations of injustice and oppression which Marxism itself exploited and on which it fed. To those who are searching today for a new and authentic theory and praxis of liberation, the Church offers not only her social doctrine and, in general, her teaching about the human person redeemed in Christ, but also her concrete commitment and material assistance in the struggle against marginalization and suffering" (n. 26). We must move beyond all that was "short-lived" in the attempts to find "an impossible compromise between Marxism and Christianity," towards "an authentic theology of integral human liberation."

Freedom has been distorted by individualism. For the individualist, cut off from his neighbor (Charles Taylor refers to the "buffered self"), freedom consists in the power of choice unconstrained by any relations to others. We turn in upon ourselves to the extent we sever these relationships. In reality, however, freedom corresponds to communion, to relationship, and therefore to the truth of our being, which despite what we may like to imagine is received from others and fulfilled through others.

In our own Western culture, we have to learn to see through the veneer of economic prosperity to the spiritual poverty within, to the profound alienation of those who sell their labor as a commodity, and of those ensnared in the web of false needs created by consumerism (*CA*, n. 41). We must perceive more clearly the collective selfishness and lack of respect for life that lie behind the pillaging of our environment, the arms trade, and the wars that continually undermine human development.

Human liberation is founded on the ability to give and receive—that is, to love—in the likeness of the Trinitarian God. As stated previously, the form of this giving and receiving, and thus of a spirituality that can support a civilization of love, is indicated in the three "evangelical counsels" of poverty, chastity, and obedience. For the function of the counsels is to emancipate our spirit from dependence on earthly things, so that we may more freely contemplate God, love him, and fulfill his will.

One might also recall the instruction of St. Francis de Sales to a lay woman: "Strive then, Philothea, to practice these three virtues well, according to your state; without placing you in the state of perfection they will nevertheless bring you to perfection itself, for we are all bound to practice them, though not all in the same way."[13] Slightly later in the seventeenth century, Augustine Baker OSB in

---

13. Francis de Sales, *Introduction to the Devout Life* (London: Burns & Oates, 1956), p. 121. For Balthasar's own thinking on the counsels, see (in addition to works already cited) "Are There Lay People in the Church?" in *New Elucidations* and "Towards a Theology of the Secular Institute" in *Explorations in Theology*, Vol. II: Spouse of the Word (San Francisco: Ignatius Press, 1991). Cf. Libero Gerosa, "Secular Institutes, Lay Associations, and Ecclesial Movements in the Theology of Hans Urs von Balthasar," *Communio* 17 (Fall 1990), pp. 342–61.

his book *Sancta Sophia* gave "instructions profitable to seculars" wherein he spoke of the "obligation" of a devout person to "imitate" the duties of religious life, including the counsels.

The counsels indeed may be said to define the form the Cross in the spiritual life of the Christian, whether that life lived in a religious, lay or priestly state. They are intimately connected with the infused virtues of faith, hope, and love. The ascetical spirit of the counsels opens up *three dimensions of freedom* in the human subject; the life of grace supplies the positive content corresponding to each subjective disposition to receptivity. The counsels corresponding to the archetypal Christian attitude exemplified at the Annunciation; that is, Mary's *fiat voluntas tua* (faith, love, obedience), her virginity (hope, love, chastity), and even her marriage to Joseph (hope, love, poverty). The latter, indeed, according to the tradition, is entered into as a conscious act of self-dispossession and self-oblation in order to prepare the way of the future Messiah.

Liberation of the Heart

The counsels, then, are nothing less than the "form of Christian holiness," and the means by which we may learn to obey the two "great commandments" enjoined by both Old and New Testaments: the love of God and love of neighbor. This twofold love requires an interior freedom that comes only by detaching ourselves from our possessions, our passions, and our self-will.

Poverty in itself, of course, as mere deprivation of possessions or even of the means to sustain life, is hardly "liberating." Indeed, as Christians we are obliged to respond to material need with compassion, by sharing whatever we possess. What does liberate is the "poverty of spirit" that is closely entwined with humility and the hope of the kingdom (Luke 6:20). To be poor in spirit is compatible with great wealth, but only on two conditions; firstly that we are genuinely prepared to embrace exterior poverty the moment this is asked of us, and secondly that our possessions are at the service of the common good. "None of you can be my disciple without giving up all that he owns" (Luke 14:33). It is possible to be rich yet interiorly detached, just as it is possible to be poor yet envious.

The love of "Lady Poverty" is, of course, quite incompatible with the habitual, self-centered pursuit of wealth and comfort, for "You cannot serve both God and Mammon" (Luke 16:13). The discipline of fasting should therefore be mentioned here as an important but often neglected element in the spiritual life. It has direct, as yet almost unexplored, social implications. Olivier Clément summarizes the teaching of the early Fathers as follows:

> Fasting prevents us from identifying ourselves with the world in order merely to possess it, and enables us to see the world in a light coming from elsewhere. Thus every creature, every thing, becomes an object of contemplation. Fasting puts between ourselves and the world a wondering and respectful distance. It enables us to hunger for God as well, and to welcome our bodily hunger as an echo, the "sighing" of creation. And so for the Fathers fasting from food is inseparable from prayer and almsgiving, from the loving relationship re-established with God, and from spontaneous, inventive sharing with one's neighbor.[14]

If spiritual poverty betokens the subordination of desire for such things as food and security to our desire for God, then *chastity* applies the same principle to our natural desire for companionship and human love. As embodied creatures, of course, we are constantly pressed towards some physical expression of love. The evangelical counsel reminds us not to become the slaves of impulse—it is a necessary virtue even in marriage, for the marriage vow places the body of each spouse at the service of the other in an exclusive and indissoluble relationship to one person. In other words, the complete continence required of the religious is only a raising of the chastity required of the married state to another level: both are a gift of the body (including the possibility of fertility) to another than the self; in the case of the religious this gift is to God and the Church, in view of that state in which "there will be no giving in marriage" because all will be "one body" in God.

In whatever state of life, the opportunity for any physical expression of love must be regarded as a grace. If we seize it as though by right, we are forcing God out of the center of things to the periphery. If we are prepared at all times to respond to God's initiative, if

14. *The Roots of Christian Mysticism* (New York: New City, 1993) p. 141.

even our most decisive actions are formed in this secret dimension of receptivity, patience, and gratitude, then our physical relationships and even our bodies themselves will be redeemed, and transformed by that redemption. "Hope shimmers at all times as a light of grace from God, bending over men as an unfathomable freedom not yet understood."[15]

Chastity pertains particularly to that "purity of heart" that makes possible the vision of God (Matt. 5:8)—that beatific vision which is the consummation of our "nuptial" relationship with God in Christ. This is the true freedom we hope for, since "The one who sees is free, and time and space belong to him."[16] "Creation itself will be set free" (Rom. 8:21), for it participates "in the light that falls on him," and he "cannot take hold of anything for himself alone that is not equally meant for everything created." The whole of creation—"the wide earth, the intimacy of a home, the familiarity of a landscape . . . in all its beauty and wildness, in its captivity"—shares his hope, his "dream of freedom, access to the Creator, to his presence and his love."[17] The "scope" of chastity, as a virtue and as a way of life, is therefore more than social; it is nothing less than cosmic.

As for *obedience*, since the Second World War this has tended to be viewed entirely in a negative light, as the very antithesis of freedom. It has become clear that we must always ask: obedience to whom? In what spirit? Only once an initial discrimination has been made does it become possible to see that a certain kind of obedience might still be a means of liberation. The key, again, is provided by St. Francis, whose second Admonition deserves to be quoted in full (though the italics are mine):

> The Lord said to Adam: Eat of every tree; do not eat of the tree of knowledge of good and evil. He was able to eat of every tree of paradise since he did not sin as long as he did not go against obedience. For the person eats of the tree of the knowledge of good who *appropriates to himself his own will* and thus exalts himself

---

15. Adrienne von Speyr, *The Victory of Love: A Meditation on Romans 8* (San Francisco: Ignatius Press, 1990), p. 65.

16. Ibid.

17. Ibid., 66.

over the good things which the Lord says and does in him; and thus, through the suggestion of the devil and the transgression of the command, what he eats becomes for him the fruit of the knowledge of evil. Therefore it is necessary that he bear the punishment.[18]

The essential point is that *we are not God*. Authentic human freedom is the freedom of a creature living by grace. The state in which we are created is a state of obedience to God, which is identical with the very highest state of human freedom. In a sense, I *am* my will; I do not *possess* my will, for I belong to the God who makes me what I am. The obedience of the counsels is first of all this obedience to God, an obedience whose positive content is supplied by the virtue of faith in God's word. It requires to be manifested in obedience to men, but in the third Admonition St. Francis again gets the balance right: "'He who wishes to save his life must lose it' (Luke 9:24). That person leaves everything he possesses and loses his body who surrenders his whole self to obedience at the hands of his prelate. And whatever he does and says which he knows is not contrary to the prelate's will, provided what he does is good, is true obedience. . . . But if the prelate should command something contrary to his conscience, although he does not obey him, still he should not abandon him. . . ."[19]

Self-surrender to God in obedience, so far from being contrary to freedom, is the highest use and expression of freedom. "Only one who stands outside love, who identifies freedom with egocentric self-determination, can regard this loving surrender of freedom as a deprivation of freedom."[20] Freedom is belonging and participation.[21]

The purifying effects of the ascesis of the counsels do not remain simply interior. The kingdom "within" is also the kingdom "in our

---

18. Francis and Clare of Assisi, *Francis and Clare: The Complete Works*, Classics of Western Spirituality (Mahwah, NJ: Paulist, 1986), p. 27.

19. Ibid., pp. 27–8.

20. Speyr, *The Victory of Love*, p. 60.

21. See Thomas Rourke, "Fundamental Politics: What We Must Learn From the Social Thought of Benedict XVI," *Communio: International Catholic Review* 35:3 (Fall 2008), esp. p. 442.

midst" (Luke 17:21), and the presence of Christ in our lives—in the "space" we make for him by the conjoining of ascesis and prayer— cannot but transform the worldly order. It does so not only by individual acts of charity, but in many other and unpredictable ways. In the light that shines from the kingdom, self-indulgence, injustice and oppression stand naked and exposed, even if no merely human calculation can tell when God will judge it right to strike them down.

Creative Justice

It is the concept of freedom I have been exploring in this chapter that explains why true justice must be *creative justice*.

Real freedom is nothing to do with a choice between possibilities—at least, not in the beginning. It *makes* possibilities. It is creative, an expression or image of the dynamic freedom of God, who brings everything (and even the *possibility* of everything) into existence out of nothing.[22]

The necessity of choice comes from the Fall. Original (and final) freedom is the ability to do the good. But the good does not yet exist. It must be created. Or it does not yet exist on earth, and bringing it from heaven is necessarily a creative act.

Justice, or acting justly, is one case of doing the good, the right thing. In order to know what that is we cannot simply read it off a page (even if the natural law is in some sense "written on our hearts"). It is not dictated to us. It is not the same as the positive law, the law that men have written down, although the two may overlap.

Insofar as justice is required of us personally, and not simply as a society, we need to rise to a new level, to do something fresh, as though breaking the pattern of the past, or at least the pattern set by sin. Justice goes against the grain of our fallen nature, which is always seeking the advantage of the self. But even if we were unfallen, living in a state of justice, with all our faculties in balance,

22. For the relationship between freedom and creativity see Evdokimov, *Woman and the Salvation of the World*, pp. 48–54. Also Caldecott, *The Radiance of Being*, pp. 212–17.

to find the just thing to do in particular circumstances would often require imagination—imagination to grasp the right thing to do that does not yet exist, and to create social forms and structures that make the good visible on earth.

Justice is to give each his due. This tells us that in order to know the just thing to do we must know the person or people involved. Here again we are in the realm of freedom rather than determinism. A person is never fully revealed. The heart remains mysterious. To understand the person requires an act of faith, of trust. That implies giving and receiving, opening to the other in order to receive what they are prepared to share of themselves. Love, empathy, imagination are all required for truth to be grasped, justice to be done, and a just society to be created, and all of these require freedom—freedom from self, the self that keeps us prisoner.

Asceticism and the living of the Counsels, at least in spirit, is the indispensable foundation of justice—the slaying of self-will. Justice thrives in an atmosphere of prayer. This is perhaps why, in the end, justice melts away, or melts away into mercy. Welling up within the desire for justice, for what the Bible also calls "righteousness," we find the desire to treat all beings as they deserve, and thus to lavish on them nothing less than the love that moves the creator to bestow existence upon them.

Evangelization of Culture

The Christian's only true and specific contribution to the human effort to improve one's condition in society is to bear witness to the religious position as the most completely human stance for tackling the moral, social, and political problems that one meets within social co-existence. We make this contribution above all by re-establishing ourselves as a lived Christian reality, in which the unity of the community is the first miracle pointing to Christ as the catalyst of human values and as a sure beginning of a moral journey, otherwise unthinkable with regard to purity and to the infinite capacity to pick up again. ∼Luigi Giussani[1]

If we look now at the community to which we are introduced by the love of Christ, we see that it is not static or closed, but dynamic and open. The "space" in which we are set free is a rich and boundless land. This is no mere association of individuals, juxtaposed with each other in a juridical structure. We are so made that we can find ourselves only in each other, that is, by "losing ourselves"—or rather by "giving ourselves away" in order to find ourselves.

True community is created not by the abolition of private property, but nevertheless by a process of self-dispossession, whether in some form of explicit service to others, or through formally living a vow. We have seen that the threefold ascesis of the counsels turns us away form an exclusive concern with ourselves, and opens us up to those around us. It is in the encounter with God who alone is able to call forth something new in us (infusing faith, hope, and love) that we are formed as *theological persons*; persons centered on him and on the neighbor who is his "sacrament." This re-centering of the self is a process that leads us deep into the Trinity, into the exchange of love that lies at the root of our being.

---

1. Luigi Giussani, *The Journey to Truth Is an Experience*, transl. John E. Zucchi (McGill-Queen's University Press, 2006).

The Other, who comes to us as Jesus Christ, calls us toward him in particular concrete ways, moment by moment. That is why *Abandonment to Divine Providence* by J.-P. de Caussade can be read as a textbook of true liberation and a remedy against ideological thinking. Ideology is predictable; God is not. "The Spirit blows where he wills. . . ." On a path revealed to us only as we walk it step by step, our Creator recreates us by giving us a task and purpose.

What might this mean, say, to a peasant oppressed by an unjust landlord, or a factory worker forced to slave at a single mechanical task without security or an adequate salary to support his family? It means, first, that personal freedom is attainable even in such situations. Through prayer and response to God, the slave may be freer than his owner. Nor is this a ploy to restrict spiritual freedom to the interior realm, or to postpone any talk of revolution to the end of the world, the *eschaton*. God does not endorse the conditions of an unjust servitude, and we are obliged to strive for justice, even if the initiative must be God's, and any actions taken on behalf of exterior liberation must employ only means that are in harmony with the end being sought.[2]

In section 58 of *Centesimus Annus*, echoed later by Pope Benedict, and of course Pope Francis, John Paul II writes that to obtain global justice "it is not enough to draw on the surplus goods which in fact our world abundantly produces; it requires above all a change of lifestyles, of models of production and consumption, and of the established structures of power which today govern societies." What is this if not a kind of revolution? In section 52, he concludes that the effort to promote development and peace "may mean making important changes in established life-styles, in order to limit the waste of environmental and human resources, thus enabling every individual and all the peoples of the earth to have a sufficient share of those resources."

From all these considerations, it seems increasingly clear that Christian *praxis* in our time should lead in the direction of a new *culture of restraint*—a culture whose very economic mechanisms are

---

2. "Ultimately you can't reach good ends through evil means, because the means represent the seed and the end represents the tree" (Martin Luther King, Jr.).

formed by the Christian understanding of human nature, and shaped by the asceticism of the counsels into a form potentially more receptive of the love of God and thus of the form of the Eucharist. That is where the revolution in truth begins: in a moderate but real voluntary asceticism, refusing to collude entirely any longer with a culture of self-indulgence, escapism, and death.

Evangelization

In his 1975 encyclical *Evangelii Nuntiandi*, Pope Paul VI makes the connection between the Church's social doctrine and evangelization, including "evangelization of culture." Catholic social teaching does not just concern questions of economics and politics, of justice and peace. It concerns the overcoming of the "drama of our time" (n. 20), the split between the Gospel and culture. As Peter Casarella reminds us in his commentary on *Ecclesia in America*, "overcoming this separation is the key to a proper understanding of the correct relationship between Catholic faith and social solidarity."[3]

What is it to "evangelize"? According to Paul VI, "Evangelizing is in fact the grace and vocation proper to the Church, her deepest identity. She exists in order to evangelize, that is to say, in order to preach and teach, to be the channel of the gift of grace, to reconcile sinners with God, and to perpetuate Christ's sacrifice in the Mass, which is the memorial of His death and glorious resurrection" (n.14). It is to do what Christ did, and what he commissioned the disciples to do: to preach the Gospel of the Kingdom, and thus to transform family life, life in society, international life, and conceptions of peace, justice, and development (n.29); to convert the individual and thus the society of which he is a constituent part.

An older Catholicism might have spoken rather of re-establishing the reign of Christ the King. Francis I, in his first address to the people of the media (March 16, 2013), reminded them that "the Church exists in order to communicate precisely this: Truth, Goodness, and

---

3. P. Casarella, "Solidarity as the Fruit of Communion: *Ecclesia in America,* 'Post-Liberation Theology,' and the Earth," in *Communio* 27 (Spring 2000), pp. 98–123. See *Evangelii Nuntiandi*, n. 20. As background to this chapter, read the survey by Glenn W. Olsen in *The Turn to Transcendence*.

Beauty in person." He made it clear in other addresses that rather than evangelizing through the creation of grand structures and plans, he had in mind a call to repentance and conversion at the level of the individual. Have mercy on each other, go to confession, pray, refrain from gossip, do not accumulate wealth . . . live the Gospel.

When Pope John Paul II, from early in his pontificate, first started talking about a "new evangelization," he was building on *Gaudium et Spes* (one of the fundamental documents of the Second Vatican Council) and on *Evangelii Nuntiandi* (Paul VI on evangelization). Aware of the faith that had grown cold in so many of the developed countries, he wanted to emphasize that the Church could not simply accept the way of the world, and especially the disease of Western consumerism. Western nations were once again as desperately in need of the Gospel and of conversion as ever they were before the coming of Christianity. This new evangelization was clearly linked to the idea expressed by Paul VI that faith and culture had become separated from each other, and that this was not merely a fact but a *tragedy*.

It is clear that John Paul II believed that a civilization deprived of its religious roots in faith will inevitably perish. Like the Catholic historian Christopher Dawson, he saw religion as the soul and driving force of a civilization—*every* civilization worthy of the name and capable of survival. Paul VI, if anything, had been even more emphatic. "We are firmly convinced that the basic propositions of atheism are utterly false and irreconcilable with the underlying principles of thought. They strike at the genuine and effective foundation for man's acceptance of a rational order in the universe, and introduce into human life a futile kind of dogmatism which far from solving life's difficulties, only degrades it and saddens it. Any social system based on these principles is doomed to utter destruction."[4]

The object of evangelization, therefore, is never simply persuasion. It is not simply a matter of convincing people to adhere to a certain set of beliefs, or a particular creed. It is not a matter of clever apologetics. It cannot even any longer be thought of simply as a way of initiating people into an existing Catholic culture—starting with

4. *Ecclesiam Suam* (Encyclical on the Church, 1964), n. 100.

136

one's own children, perhaps, but extending to the conversion of those belonging to other civilizations. Naturally catechesis and missionary work remains important, just as apologetics remains important, but today we live in a culture that is increasingly homogenized, becoming the same all over the globe. We speak a great deal about diversity and self-determination, but the real distinctiveness and diversity of cultures is being eroded all the time. Religious traditions, of course, remain; but the erosion of distance between them, and the pressures to conform to modernity, are causing dangerous tensions within and between them, which may be used as an excuse for further homogenization.

In these circumstances evangelization becomes a matter not simply of converting individuals, but of *converting culture itself*. It is a matter of creating in the ashes of a dying fire a new blaze. As we saw, we have to start not just a new society, but a new civilization—a "culture of life." Evangelization will only be effective if it is an evangelization of culture. But are we talking about a new Christian homogenization, a Christian world empire, or are we talking (as I believe) of a genuinely pluralist society, in which different cultures and traditions can live side by side in peace? This is perhaps the most difficult and delicate question facing Catholic social theorists in the present century.

Birth of the Modern

Modern industrial society arose in Britain. How it came about is important to understand, because it helps to explain the religious developments of the period, and the situation we face today. It goes back to the dissolution of the monasteries under Henry VIII, combined with the forced enclosure of common land in the centuries that followed. This helped to lay the foundations for England's industrial and commercial success. For it led to the enrichment of a landed middle class, capable of sustaining huge and sometimes risky commercial enterprises, including trading adventures overseas and factories at home based on new technology.

Modern Britain—in a sense the whole modern world—was founded, in other words, on the deliberate and malicious destruction of a way of life dedicated to contemplation and prayer, the result of Henry's attack on papal authority and the order of marriage, for worldly and pragmatic reasons.

The result was that, after the complex political and religious struggles of the Stuart era and the Civil War, Britain settled down with a political compromise that perfectly suited the development of a prosperous secular empire. The monarch was in most respects subordinate to Parliament, and Parliament was dominated by commercial interests. Britain dominated the seas and her military might was devoted to the establishment and protection of trading interests in the New World and the Far East, including the slave trade. From the Caribbean and the East India Company vast quantities of wealth flowed into the country, creating new possibilities for investment and innovation. Banks, corporations, insurance companies, and the stock exchange were created to support these developments. London became the world's financial capital. The free development of scientific ideas enabled a new breed of entrepreneurs to establish industries based on coal and steam. Cottage industries were replaced by factories, roads were supplemented by canals and eventually railways.

During the reign of Queen Victoria (1837–1901), the British Empire reached its peak. It was geographically the largest *imperium* in history, and economically the richest. This was the "Age of Progress," an age of industry and commerce, and the English felt themselves to be the very crescendo of civilization, if not of evolution itself (natural selection being the discovery of an English gentleman called Charles Darwin).[5] Britain's great rival, France, was left behind for several reasons. For one thing, up until the Revolution, scientific thought and technological innovation was bogged down in a great bureaucracy centralized on the monarchy. The transport system was shaped not by the needs of industry but by military considerations. France remained primarily a rural society, whereas Britain

---

5. The culmination and greatest symbol of the triumph of the materialistic civilization of Britain during the Victorian period was the Great Exhibition of 1851. The Exhibition (actually a triumphant response to the French Industrial Exposition of 1844) was a giant showcase for the arts, trade, technology, and industry, contained within a gigantic glass building known as the Crystal Palace. Altogether it was visited by a third of the British population, and by the royal family three times (Prince Albert being the chief organizer and promoter of the Exhibition).

was increasingly dominated by London and the new cities growing in the coal-rich Midlands. The French Revolution, when it came, diverted the creative energies of the nation into political conflict, whereas by this time Britain's revolutionary era was over.

This is how the whole world, led by Europe and initially by Britain, eventually came to define success in terms of material "progress" and the manufacture of wealth. Technological breakthroughs in the exploitation of natural resources—the building of steam engines and the like—were fostered and encouraged by the new commercial elite, creating a civilization dedicated solely to the ideal of unlimited growth in both production and consumption. The human worker who was still needed to keep the machines running, if he was not an actual slave imported from Africa to the New World (the Empire in its early stages was partly built on slave labor), was a virtual or "wage" slave employed solely to perform a single task, meaningless in itself.

The pure essence of the industrial system was realized in the "scientific management system" of the American inventor and engineer Frederick Winslow Taylor in the 1880s and 90s, and other similar systems developed after that time (for example by Henry Ford), the idea of which was to divide any manufacturing operation into its basic elements and to study these to make them more efficient. This led to the concept of the production line, in which different workers served each separate element in the process. Meanwhile the workers themselves largely fled the countryside and congregated in the growing cities where such work was to be had, creating a new class of urban poor at the mercy of the managerial class that controlled the majority of the wealth.[6] Three reactions followed. The first was that of the Romantic movement, the second the growth of Communism, and the third Catholic social teaching.

In the twentieth century, a second phase of industrial civilization began to take shape, dependent this time on the discovery of elec-

6. The process continued throughout the nineteenth and twentieth centuries, as the Pontifical Council for Culture noted in 1999. "Under various pressures, such as poverty and the under-development of rural areas deprived of indispensable goods and services as well as, in some countries, armed conflicts which force millions of people to leave behind their home and culture, the growing number of

tricity and the invention of the computer. The first stage had led to the swelling of the cities and consequently to an increasingly artificial or manufactured environment. The second went even further by creating a "virtual" world, an omnipresent environment of information and imagery connecting everyone and acting as a medium of instant communication (the "Information Revolution"). The third phase is "transhumanism" or the "Biotech Revolution": the redesigning of nature—even human nature—by tinkering with the genetic code. We have spoken of this in chapter 4. Already it is commonplace to modify human performance with drugs and prosthetics, and it will soon be possible to link the circuits of the human brain directly with mechanical equipment or with the internet. The human organism is increasingly treated as raw material for scientific experiment and technological modification.

The Romantic Reaction

Opposition to these trends has never stood much of a chance, since they follow a cumulative path or "slippery slope." Each development sets the stage for the next. But at the same time, each new development provokes a reaction, not strong enough to reverse things altogether, but indicative of alternative possibilities. Some of these reactions represent the most interesting thought of the era, and plant the seeds of future developments that might flourish years later, when the dominant forces of social evolution have exhausted themselves.

So, for example, the movements known as the Scientific Enlightenment and the Industrial Revolution were opposed by the Romantic movement, associated in England with William Blake, William

---

people on the move is emptying the countryside of people and causing the great cities to expand excessively. In addition to these economic and social pressures, cities have the fascination of the well-being and entertainment they offer, as vividly portrayed by the means of social communication. Through lack of planning, the outskirts or suburbs of every megalopolis are like ghettos. These are often huge agglomerations of people who are socially rootless, politically powerless, economically marginalized and culturally isolated" (*Toward a Pastoral Approach to Culture*, n. 8). As stated earlier, the transition from a largely rural to an urbanized planet took place in the second decade of the twenty-first century.

Wordsworth, George Byron, Samuel Taylor Coleridge, and Edmund Burke. By the late nineteenth century this Romantic stream had become something of a flood, if we take into account the Arts and Crafts movement, Christian Socialism, the Pre-Raphaelites, and the Gothic revival associated with John Ruskin, William Morris, and Augustus Pugin.[7] Before it degenerated (some would say) into mere Aestheticism, these movements helped to reshape the public and domestic face of Britain.

This in turn set the scene for a Catholic Romantic movement sometimes called the Catholic Revival or "Second Spring" (after a famous sermon by John Henry Newman in 1852). Culminating in the first half of the twentieth century, the Revival represents an attempt to recover the balance that had been lost in both Rationalism and in Romanticism. Both these dominant intellectual movements of the time were based on a false conception of meaning that can be traced back to the rejection of Scholastic wisdom by Nominalism and Voluntarism a couple of centuries before the Renaissance.

The intellectual order glorified by Enlightenment thinkers was a mere objectivist and utilitarian rationalism, cut off from the intellectual intuition of essence. The Romantics, on the other hand, tended to value feeling and imagination over reason, glorifying in their turn Beauty over the other transcendentals, Truth and Goodness.[8] Subjective qualities were elevated over the objective—in that respect, the whole conflict can be traced back also to the scientific method of Galileo, with his separation of primary and secondary qualities, only the first of which were amenable to empirical study. But the Catholic Revival sought a new synthesis.

Thinkers and writers such as John Henry Newman, Coventry Patmore, Gerard Manley Hopkins, and later G. K. Chesterton, were interested not in a vague medievalist or pre-Raphaelite nostalgia but in the recovery of a religious and yet rigorously objective per-

---

7. None of these movements was purely nostalgic, of course—the Pre-Raphaelites combined their medievalism with a keen and almost scientific observation of nature, and the Gothic movement was delighted to adapt its preferred style to the modern world by using materials such as brick and iron.

8. John Keats: "Beauty is truth, truth beauty,—that is all / Ye know on earth, and all ye need to know."

spective on the world. They believed that the balance of truth and feeling, of life and intelligence, of imagination and wisdom, could be found only in a "return to religion." And more often than not, this religion turned out to be Catholicism. The Byronic tendency in Romanticism had been to glorify the passions without ordering the soul according to Truth. This was overcome in the Catholic Revival by a re-establishment of the Logos at the center of all things.

The Romantics and the Catholic Revival writers (whether Roman Catholic or Anglican) had very strong views on industrialization and the transformation it had imposed on the way of life of the working man. In a sense, this was at the heart of their rebellion against the spirit of the age—what Blake called the "dark Satanic Mills" in the famous anthem "Jerusalem" he included in the preface to *Milton a Poem* in 1808. The mills were, of course, destined to get a lot darker during the rest of the nineteenth century.[9]

A New Christendom?

In *Christendom Awake*, Aidan Nichols OP situates himself in the tradition of the Catholic Revival and the Christian Romantic reaction to the Enlightenment. He speaks of the evangelization of culture in terms of a renaissance of *doctrine* in catechesis and preaching; a re-enchantment of the *liturgy*; a renewal of Christian *political* thought; a revivification of the *family* through a uniting wherever possible of the domestic and the productive, home and work; the resacralizing of *art and architecture*; and (last but not least) a recovery of the Catholic and spiritual reading of the *Scriptures*. Father Nichols defends the idea of a Christendom State, and perhaps even of a European imperium that would preside over a loose commonwealth of nations (whether those be republics or monarchies). Only a monarch, he argues, can represent the fact that authority (which he distinguishes from "power") descends from above, and thus only a monarch is capable of acting as the symbolic guardian of the natural moral order and the foundational norms of a Christian society.

9. On the theology of work and in particular the critique of utilitarian thinking advanced by the Romantic and Catholic Revival writers see John Hughes, *The End of Work: Theological Critiques of Capitalism* (Oxford: Blackwell, 2007).

An earlier attempt by a major Catholic thinker to conceive of a new Christian social order—Jacques Maritain's *True Humanism*—was conceived in 1934 and published on the eve of the Second World War in 1938. It seems to have been influential in the thinking of the Catholic founders of the European Union: Monnet, Schuman, Adenauer, and de Gasperi. But Maritain's vision of Christendom is very different from that of Nichols. "The unity of such a civilization," he writes, "would no longer be a unity of essence or of a constitution assured from above by the profession of the same faith and the same dogmas" (p. 162). He looks forward not to a *sacrum imperium* of the medieval type, but a pluralist democratic commonwealth organized according to the principle of subsidiarity, granting maximum autonomy to the local and familial level and to individuals in the matter of belief. Unity is to be sought not in a common creed but in the recognition by believers and non-believers alike of a "practical common task."

This social order would, however, be *implicitly Christian* (p. 200). That is to say that while the dignity of the person, the value of economic cooperation, the importance of the family, the responsibilities of citizenship, the common good, and so much else pertaining to the shared social task find their true justification and proper home only in the Christian revelation—as deriving from the Trinity and from the divine image in man—Maritain believes that they will also be acceptable to people who do not share the Christian faith but who want to help bring about a humane society. He saw the wide postwar support for charters of human rights as an example of this process.

Maritain rather optimistically calls for "a change to the primacy of quality over quantity, of work over money, of the human over technical means, of wisdom over science, of the common service of human beings instead of the covetousness of unlimited individual enrichment or a desire in the name of the State for unlimited power" (p. 201). To be fair, he does not see this happening in the real world before some kind of historical transformation (p. 237), perhaps of a catastrophic nature, which would represent "a total reconstruction of our cultural and temporal forms of life, forms which have been built up in an atmosphere of dualism and anthropocentric rationalism" (p. 64). He also has a clear perception of the "radical disorder" of capitalism and consumerism, which at present block any Christianly-inspired transformation of the social order (pp. 107–8, 178–89).

Though I am sympathetic to Maritain's approach, I can't help wondering if the hope of social unity based on the practical tasks pertaining to the common good, rather than on shared philosophical and theological premises (including that of the common good itself), is so unrealistic that it doesn't even work as an ideal. We seem today to be witnessing a kind of intellectual implosion in the culture, due precisely to the lack of a common philosophy or creed. The ideology of rights, divorced from responsibilities and certainly from any Thomistic understanding of the virtues, has grown out of control. Our diversity of aspirations may soon be such that no ordered common life is possible except one imposed by economic necessity and backed by the use of technological force: a prospect that fills many of us with alarm.

Christopher Dawson, writing during the Second World War, was much more positive than Maritain about the prospects of mass conversion to explicit Christian belief as the basis for the next phase of civilization. After analyzing the roots of secularism in Europe's religious divisions, he concluded in *The Judgment of Nations* "that the age of schism is passing and that the time has come when the divine principle of the Church's life will assert its attractive power, drawing all the living elements of Christian life and thought into organic unity" (p. 125). Dawson did not think this would happen quickly or easily, but that the very "strength of the forces that are gathering against the Church and against religion will make for unity by forcing Christians together, as it were, in spite of themselves; or it may be that the Church will react positively to the situation by a fresh outpouring of the apostolic spirit, as Blessed Grignon de Montfort prophesied two centuries ago" (p. 126). He wrote the book, in fact, as a kind of manifesto for a Christian social movement of the time called "The Sword of the Spirit."

Dawson admitted that *The Judgment of Nations* had cost him "greater labor and thought" than any of his other, more scholarly books. The reason was partly spiritual. He was staring in the face a new paganism more terrible "in its cold inhumanity and its scientific exploitation of evil" than either the pre-Christian Romans or

Rome's barbarian conquerors. (Nor did he mean by this merely the immediate threat of German and Italian Fascism!) Nonetheless, he had faith in the ultimate victory of Lord and Giver of Life.

The Spirit of Chivalry

The Crusaders with whom we associate the first Christendom—and who in fact represent one of its greatest failures—made the mistake of confusing an interior and spiritual struggle with an earthly and political one. The most important enemy is within.[10] Nevertheless the name "Sword of the Spirit" suggests a way in which the ideal (if not the historical example) of medieval chivalry remains valid even today. This is brought our particularly by Hans Urs von Balthasar in his book on the German writer Reinhold Schneider, *Tragedy Under Grace*. The West itself, Balthasar goes so far as to say, "was born of the spirit of chivalry" (p. 247), and the spiritual ideal of chivalry is far from being a relic of the past.

> Francis was a knight of Christ, as was Ignatius in turn, while Newman's refinement resists every temptation to take things easy. Knighthood changes its form, depending on whether Christians and the world are willing or unwilling to receive the imprint of its spirit; but it does not change its soul. Were this soul to die, then the salt of the earth would also have perished, and the Church in turn must die. But since she is immortal as long as the world lasts, the glorification of the body of knights is no backward-looking romanticism, no *ancien régime* that turns its face aside from the march of time, no secret front against the birth of tomorrow's humanity, but the only effective equipment with which the Christian can meet the present day.[11]

In this revaluation of Christian chivalry, the "chivalry of the Gospel," I am sure that Balthasar and Schneider are one with some of our great English writers, such as G. K. Chesterton, C. S. Lewis, and

---

10. In authentic Islam, too, the "inner *jihad*" (struggle) takes priority over the outer, and chivalry expresses the meeting of the two, as appropriate behavior on the "righteous path."

11. Hans Urs von Balthasar, *Tragedy Under Grace: Reinhold Schneider and the Experience of the West* (San Francisco: Ignatius Press, 1997), p. 248.

J.R.R. Tolkien. Reading these authors, we are reminded that all is not yet lost; indeed, that there is still a worthy task to achieve with our freedom. The Knight is "sent into the world in order to resist injustice and to preserve justice; but he can do this only serving that which is holy, the hidden Grail and the order that radiates out from this" (p. 255). The body of Knights that the world needs now,

> is the fellowship under obligation to the King of Kings: those who extend the sway of justice, who cannot make compromises with injustice, the consecrated protective lordship, going across all boundaries, extending the guardianship of the valorous over the persecuted, those deprived of their rights, those insulted and distressed, those who take care of creation as it groans, and of the bruised reed, because it is God's will that it not be broken. If the world is torn by divisions, if the peoples are thrown into the confusion of mutual hostility, how is the world to be healed, how are the peoples to be reconciled, if not through such a new body of knights, which is nothing other than the carrying out of the will of Jesus Christ, here and now, in this time?[12]

Are there signs that this hope is about to be fulfilled—that a new Pentecost will soon result in a new chivalry, a new culture of life? We need to approach the question with care. John Paul II was right to say that "man's inner unity" is "threatened by the division and the atomization of his consciousness."[13] This inner unity, which is the condition of our thinking correctly about the world, and perceiving it correctly, can be restored only by *the experience of God's love.* "Our research and our work," he says in the same talk (which was addressed to an academic audience),

> need a guiding idea, a fundamental value, in order to give meaning to and to unite in one direction the efforts of scholars, the reflections of historians, the creativity of artists and the discoveries of scientists, which are all growing at a dizzying rate. Does there exist any other idea, any other value or any other light capable of giving meaning to the manifold commitment of people of science

---

12. Ibid., p. 256.
13. From an address he gave in Poland and reported in *L'Osservatore Romano*, June 16, 1999, p. 8.

and culture, without at the same time limiting their creative freedom? This power is love, which does not impose itself on man from without, but is born deep within, in his heart, as his most personal property.

What the pope said to those in the university in Poland is essentially the same thing that he said to those in economic and political life wherever he went. It underpins the whole of his social teaching. Evangelization is not a program of action, but a mode of being personally present to and for others—of being-for, of living-for. In other words, the evangelization of culture takes place first in *the encounter of one person with another* before it affects governments or organizations.

This seems strange to us only because we are used to thinking in geopolitical terms, in statistics and mass movements. The pope asks us to believe instead that what is most important in the world and in history lies in the smallest and most intimate details: the glance, the invitation, the smile, the encounter with another person, the interior disposition. These are the most important signs and pathways of love in the world.

A secular culture has no conception of the importance of this *encounter*, of friendship, of personal presence (and thus of "sacrament"). Inevitably, in such a society any discussion of evangelization becomes tinged with the attitude that persons are important only as instruments in the fulfillment of a plan, or as subscribers to an ideology. God, in contrast, is concerned with the intimate details of our lives, with the unique character and dignity of each person, who is called to play his or her part in the Trinitarian *communio*, the life of eternal love.

But, indeed, a "mass movement" may well grow from such intimate encounters, as it has done within the Church in the form of the great religious orders, and more recently the "ecclesial movements" such as Focolare and Communion and Liberation. John Paul II, gathering their leaders together for the first time on the feast of Pentecost 1998, wanted the bishops to realize the hope of a new springtime that the movements clearly embody; but at the same time to impress upon the movements themselves that a certain maturity would now be demanded of them: the maturity to work closely and humbly with bishops and parishes, and to avoid the constant temptation to close in upon themselves and become just another cult. For the living spirit of such a movement is always transmitted at the personal level, and is lost when the movement itself becomes too "self-referential" (to use a phrase that Pope Francis, himself a friend of Communion and Liberation, has applied to the Church in general).

John Paul II saw the movements as the key to the revival of faith in the old continent. The spirit of old age and decline, of indifference stultified by bureaucracy, of secret corruption and public compromise, afflicts the parishes, dioceses, episcopal conferences, and even the Curia—but it seemed to him that it did not (yet) affect the movements. In this he was mistaken, judging by the corruption that was later revealed at the very heart of the Legionaries of Christ. Nevertheless, the problems of the movements are usually of another and sometimes opposite kind, to do with excess of enthusiasm and overconfidence. It is easier to keep them in check and channel their youthful energies that to fan the ashes into a blaze without them.

Beyond the Secular

The world of the new evangelization, the world in which modern Catholicism finds itself, is a world of growing religious enthusiasm overall, but many of the more ancient Christian provinces demonstrate a growing hostility towards faith. Christian virtues may survive for a while, and social structures and laws formed under Christian influence, but (one may suspect) not for much longer, so that the persecution of Catholics for perfectly traditional and well-founded beliefs—not just in the Middle East and Africa by Islamist groups and governments, but in Europe and America as well—may become a familiar sight in years to come.

The roots and essence of secularism have been well analyzed by a host of thinkers including Henri de Lubac, Louis Dupré, Zygmunt Bauman, David L. Schindler, and Charles Taylor. We have already spoken of the main causes. The separation of nature and grace led to a view of the world in which God's role in both nature and society seemed peripheral and easy to ignore. The attempt to prevent religious beliefs being used as an excuse for political violence led to the separation of Church and State, and eventually to the privatization of religious belief.[14] With religion privatized, a secular world-view took its place as the generally accepted truth on which society would henceforth be built.

In *Fides et Ratio* (1998), John Paul II describes what he calls the "drama of the separation of faith and reason"—a transition from the "exaggerated rationalism" of the fourteenth century into modern idealism, atheistic humanism, and materialism, positivism and even nihilism. Severed from faith, philosophy lost confidence in its own powers and turned inwards, increasingly obsessed with the question of whether anything could be known at all. Metaphysics gave way to epistemology, and in the end the intellectual elite began to make a virtue out of the fact that nothing can be known for sure.

The rise of science in the Enlightenment period was the product of the Scholastic confidence in reason, combined with a specifically Franciscan attentiveness to nature, together with an almost Platonic interest in the invisible laws or mathematical patterns underlying the phenomena we see around us. But in addition to these influences, it is probably inconceivable without the new nominalist philosophy, which implied that scientific laws are essentially arbitrary, and therefore discoverable only by empirical investigation. The laws and constants which science formulates to "save the appearances" have no permanence and are not regarded as needing any ultimate explanation for their existence (such as a Creator).

Modern man does not need the "hypothesis" of God because he is not interested in explaining the existence of the world as such, but prefers to explain the way the world works in order to exert power over it. Scientific rationality orders the world in terms of the external relations of one thing with another. Atheism is therefore based in

14. Church (grace) and State (nature) had been distinguished by Christ when he said, "Render to Caesar the things that are Caesar's, and to God the things that are God's" (Mark 12:17). However, if the separation had been complete, there would have been no need for the Empire to persecute Christians. Nature has a certain autonomy, but her objectives are limited, and must be ordered to the supernatural. The history of the Middle Ages reflects the long (and losing) struggle to define the correct relation between the two. For a discussion of this point see Christoph Schönborn, *From Death to Life: The Christian Journey* (San Francisco: Ignatius Press, 1995), pp. 99–124.

part on a failure of intellectual insight: an inability to see the need for another level of explanation. John Paul II's encyclical on philosophy was an appeal to the intellectual community to *go on asking questions*, and to ask deeper questions. So, too, Benedict XVI often spoke of the "narrowing of reason" associated with secularism. Meanwhile Charles Taylor's *A Secular Age* shows the positive value in Enlightenment and the new secular modernity—the reasons they "caught on" (other than the advance of technology), and how scientific materialism came to be seen and felt as "the stance of maturity, of courage, of manliness, over against childish fears and sentimentality."[15]

It was not entirely a downward slide. A new humanistic or altruistic concern for the plight of others in distant lands; a rejection of spiritual elitism and an emphasis on the virtues of hard work, domesticity, and fidelity (a legacy of the Reformation); a deep awe at the sheer scale and microscopic detail of the universe revealed by science: these are among the positive factors accompanying a rejection of medieval religion and the emergence of the modern self. Even the impersonality or indifference of the universe revealed by science seemed more plausible than the cosy glow of a world watched over by an anthropomorphic but invisible deity. We need to understand how the new outlook came to be accepted as "common sense," and as patently "more mature," before we can talk about a return to religion.

There is certainly a sense in which we must grow out of both the narrow "imaginary" of medieval faith and the rather sentimental fideism of many modern believers (for whom too often, as Taylor points out, the immense suffering of the world is "painted out" of the picture—which was not the case in earlier ages that had more room for hell). Religion must "grow up," in some sense. But scientific materialism is also immature and unaware of its own limitations, which reveal themselves more and more as time goes by. In particular, it becomes apparent that a rejection of the transcendent source of natural and moral order (in the name of a supposedly "neutral" scientific worldview open to the further investigation of reality) leads to the dissolution of the very idea of truth in an attempt on man's part to

15. Charles Taylor, *A Secular Age* (Harvard University Press, 2007), p. 365.

control that order for himself. This is why diverse religious traditions may find themselves unexpectedly allied against the secular state.

The human heart has an infinite hunger, and cannot be content with this world alone. Furthermore it senses that things are related to each other from the inside, not merely from without. It demands a sense of personal identity and ultimate meaning; it cannot rest in a "liquid modernity" (Bauman) where identity and relationships are entirely fluid. There are limits, and we have nearly reached them. In time we will rediscover prayer as the invisible center and foundation of culture—our opening towards the world of meaning—and from that center will be born a new civilization, imperfect no doubt, but imperfect in other ways than the ones we know. It will be, from one point of view, a Christendom, but distinguished from the old Christendom not least by the fact that it will be shaped by many religious traditions.

The Crisis of the Missions

In the ninth chapter of his great book *Catholicism*, Henri de Lubac writes about the failure of Christian missionaries to communicate the Gospel, partly owing to their refusal to comprehend or appreciate the foreign culture to which they had been sent (Matteo Ricci being a notable exception). The great period of European expansion was marked by a sense of European superiority, as though evolution had reached a peak here, and all other cultures were merely "backward" in comparison. This attitude communicated itself through the missionaries as much as it did through the arrogant representatives of political and commercial interests.[16]

---

16. Though it could be argued that to some this sense of superiority was extremely attractive. It was reinforced by a conviction we have largely lost since the Second Vatican Council, namely that "outside the Church there is no salvation" and pagans are at risk of eternal damnation. The erosion of this sense of dramatic peril during the twentieth century—fostered, critics claim, by theologians such as Rahner and Balthasar—is often said to have caused the crisis of the missions, for unless the missionary is offering salvation from a real danger it is hard to see why he should be there at all, except as a kind of aid worker. If all will inevitably be saved by the grace and mercy of God, conversion to Christianity is unnecessary. Pope John Paul II responded to these concerns in his 1990 encyclical *Redemptoris Missio.*

One important mistake the missionaries made, according to de Lubac, was to identify their faith too closely with their civilization. Now it is true that there was something providential about the particular synthesis of Greek, Roman, and Hebrew culture that produced European Christendom. The Church, de Lubac says,

> is mindful of those providential harmonies which prepared the resources of Greece and Rome for her first expansion, and she well knows that in this conjunction of events something definitive was accomplished, yet she does not share the illusion of some of her children for whom there remains no more to do; since the miracle of the past must continue, she believes in fresh providential harmonies for her further expansion.
>
> She is the Catholic Church: neither Latin nor Greek, but universal. . . . Nothing authentically human, whatever its origin, can be alien to her. . . . To see in Catholicism one religion among others, one system among others, even if it be added that it is the only true religion, the only system that works, is to mistake its very nature, or at least to stop at the threshold. Catholicism is religion itself. It is the form that humanity must put on in order finally to be itself.[17]

Thus the Church is the opposite of a "closed society," according to de Lubac, nor can it be identified with European civilization, or with a particular subculture in the Middle East. And yet, as he goes on to say, these are precisely the ways Catholicism is viewed even by most Christians today, who have concluded that other religious civilizations, perhaps as well as the atheistic civilization based on science, are "impenetrable" by Christianity, which must be content to exist in the ghettoes permitted it by the dominant forces of history and society.

De Lubac's identification of Catholicism with *religion itself* is a far cry from the conventional view—a legacy of nineteenth-century sociology and twentieth-century comparative religion—that there are many religions competing for our attention, faith, and support. Certainly there are many cultures, many traditions, many civilizations; but are there many *religions*? And if we were tempted to agree with de Lubac that there are not, would we not have to concede that

17. H. de Lubac, *Catholicism: Christ and the Common Destiny of Man* (San Francisco: Ignatius Press, 1988), pp. 295–8.

each and every religious tradition would make practically a similar claim to be the truest expression of "religion itself"?

The fact that people of many faiths would each claim "centrality" in this sense is no more surprising than the fact that each of us feels himself to be "I" at the center of the universe. But what if, in one particular case, this claim happened to be true? For example, what if a certain human being—let's say Jesus of Nazareth—both *felt* himself to be at the center of the world, as everyone does, and *actually was* the center of the world? This is in fact the Christian claim. But what does it imply for the pluralism of religious traditions (if we may call them that at least)?

It is not easy, as I have argued elsewhere,[18] simply to assert the truth of Christianity and the utter falsity of every other tradition, since each tradition is a tapestry rich in elements of goodness, beauty, and truth. I believe that wherever Christianity flatly contradicts another faith, it is Christianity that will turn out to be true— or truer—but I also believe that such moments of flat contradiction are fewer and harder to find than at first appears, once the complexity of religious language and the difference of cultural context are taken fully into account.

Nevertheless, given a belief such as de Lubac's, what form of religious pluralism can we accept, and which kind of dialogue can we strive for? Pope Benedict XVI gave us a clue during his 2012 visit to Lebanon. It was a simple remark, seemingly naïve, but no less profound for that. Speaking of Christianity and Islam, he said: "It is not uncommon to see the two religions within the same family. If this is possible within the same family, why should it not be possible at the level of the whole of society?"[19]

---

18. *The Radiance of Being.*

19. He went on: "The particular character of the Middle East consists in the centuries-old mix of diverse elements. Admittedly, they have fought one another, sadly that is also true. A pluralistic society can only exist on the basis of mutual respect, the desire to know the other, and continuous dialogue. Such dialogue is only possible when the parties are conscious of the existence of values which are common to all great cultures because they are rooted in the nature of the human person. This substratum of values expresses man's true humanity." Benedict XVI, Address to Members of the Government of Lebanon in the Presidential Palace, September 15, 2012.

The use of the family as a model of ecumenism is highly significant. Too often we reduce society either to the Market or to the
State. Between the two poles of this dichotomy there is no room for
religion, except as a political or an economic force. But the family is
the fundamental cell of *civil society*, which is both other than Market and State and prior to them—perhaps we should say, more
important than them. It is in civil society that religious pluralism
finds its proper place.

The basis of the family is self-giving love; it is relationality. Members of a family are constitutively related to each other to such a
degree that we commonly say "blood is thicker than water" and
accept the necessity of living together despite the most enormous
divergences of attitude, personality, and belief. Naturally, it is not
possible to ignore the fact that many families are dysfunctional and
broken. Nevertheless, the principle remains in place, and the family
survives, albeit in an eroded and attenuated form. Nor is it a self-
contained unit, as we might say of many other elements of civil society, such as a club or team devoted to a particular sport or hobby.
The family founded on marriage is open not only to outsiders joining it by mutual agreement, as a society may be, but open to the procreation of new members from within. It is supremely, one might
say supernaturally, "hospitable." This again makes it an important
model of ecumenism.

The family suggests a way forward for religious ecumenism
founded on "mutual respect, the desire to know the other, and continuous dialogue." It is, after all, in the family that we normally
learn these things, which we then take and apply in the wider world.
It is the assault on the family and the erosion of such values in civil
society under the economic and political pressures we have noted,
that, more than anything, lies at the root of the tensions we experience in the modern world between religious communities—even
those descended from Abraham—that can no longer recognize each
other as related. The family has been so harassed, atomized, and
isolated that it has lost respect for the person as such. As soon as it
seeks its identity in the political or economic realm, rather than civil
society, it easily becomes the captive of an ideology and a way of life
that excludes and, at worst, persecutes anyone who belongs to a dif-

ferent group. Any oppression, of course, reinforces this false identity and makes dialogue virtually impossible.

> Our human dignity is inseparable from the sacredness of life as the
> gift of the Creator. In God's plan, each person is unique and irre-
> placeable. A person comes into this world in a family, which is the
> first locus of humanization, and above all the first school of peace.
> To build peace, we need to look to the family, supporting it and facil-
> itating its task, and in this way promoting an overall culture of life.[20]

If we were to build our relations with other religious traditions
and communities on the analogy of the family, and work for collaboration and friendship primarily through civil society, rather than
through political negotiation (which reduces even theology to politics), we would also create the optimum conditions for truth to
reveal itself to all, since the truth is ultimately a "person" rather than
an idea, and comes to us through persons, in the radiance and fragrance of those who share our life, those we can love.[21]

---

20. Ibid.

21. In a statement about the principles underlying his work with the Oasis
Foundation, Angelo Scola wrote that we should not have as our goal "the development of a super-religion that is a replacement for historical faiths, but that of an
enriching coexistence between the faithful of the various religions. Such a coexistence leaves wholly untouched the question of whether one of them—for us, faith in
Jesus Christ the living and personal Truth—is in a position to take into itself and
fulfill the truths of the others. On closer inspection, it is precisely this fascinating
question rather than any other which is the keystone for authentic interreligious
dialogue, as also the debate with non-believers, down to the detail of the most
burning anthropological and ethical questions, from the meaning of marriage to
abortion or euthanasia. But if this debate is to be able to develop to its full potential, we need to acknowledge that good which precedes and yet unites—the good of
communication in fact." We must build on the common good simply of "being
together," and the *principle of communication*—"a fundamental 'sharing' (which for
Christians is a reflection of the most radical communication that exists, that
between the persons of the Most Holy Trinity). Communication properly involves
an exchange of different narratives with a view to mutual recognition. Precisely
because of its deep nature, this kind of communication can never be taken for
granted, but is to be considered as the result of a choice, even if sometimes a largely
implicit one." Cardinal Angelo Scola, "The Good which Precedes and Unites,"
Address at the House of Lords, London, June 15, 2012.

The Work of the Spirit

Thus the new imperialism of money gets rid of labor, of all things, which is the way in which man's dignity is expressed, his creativity, which is the image of God's creativity. A speculative economy no longer has need even of labor; it does not know what to do with labor. This leads to the idol of money that is produced by itself. And so there are not obstacles to transforming millions of workers into unemployed persons. ⌁Archbishop Jorge Bergoglio/Pope Francis[1]

We have seen now the real practical "bite" of the notion of purity, or of a life striving against self-indulgence. At the end of this road lies the vision of God. The walking of the road is the building of a Christian civilization. But God did not plant man and woman in the garden of the earth simply to sit around. He created them to *work*. A civilization, a culture, is the fruit of work. Mass unemployment is a sign that something has gone seriously wrong in the way we organize our society.

At the beginning of the Bible, the theme of work is introduced in the following terms: "The Lord God took the man and put him in the garden of Eden to till it and keep it" (Gen. 2:15). After the creation of woman and as a result of the Fall, this work is transformed into "toil" (3:17). The man is told, "In the sweat of your face you shall eat bread till you return to the ground, for out of it you were taken" (3:19). Though exiled, man's vocation is nevertheless reaffirmed: "therefore the Lord God sent him forth from the garden of Eden, to till the ground from which he was taken" (3:23).

From the beginning, man is called to "work"—a work that consists in "tilling and keeping" the land which is his own substance, the soil from which he was made. The work of man is therefore

---

1. Andrea Tornielli, *Francis: Pope of a New World* (San Francisco and London: CTS and Ignatius Press, 2013), p. 127.

both an inner and an outer work, a working on the world around him, and a working on himself.

The purpose of the work is transformative, because you cannot work on something without changing it, but it is also preservative: "to till it *and keep it.*" To modern ears the phrase carries the implication of sustainability, or custodianship. As discussed earlier, the implication hardly needs to be spelled out: God has not created man to consume and destroy the creation that he loves.

In this chapter I want to examine the relationship between inner and outer work in the vocation of man, in order to arrive at a purified conception of the notion of "work" or "labor" itself (as well as of the relation between the notions of work and purity), and thus of the activity that—in the most practical way—generates and shapes a civilization. The question of the relationship between work and prayer will also be raised, for it is by prayer that work is sanctified and offered to God.

The Eighth Day

The Ten Commandments contain a command to keep the seventh day holy. "Remember to keep the Sabbath day holy. You have six days to labor and do all your work" (Exod. 20:9). Note that there is no *commandment* to work here, but simply an assumption that we will—the implication is that work belongs to the very nature and purpose of man, and therefore is not something we can escape. We have no choice in the matter. But work has to be integrated with leisure, with contemplation.

To make the Sabbath holy is to sanctify all the other days too, because it establishes a pattern of seven based upon the first creation narrative in Genesis. By insisting that man should participate (*metoché*) in God's "rest," the Bible is suggesting that each of the other six days must also be a way of participating in the creative acts of God—the acts performed or described on those days.[2]

---

2. The origin of the seven-day week is complicated. It was not derived entirely from the Book of Genesis, but is related to the practice in Babylon of dividing lunar months into quarters made up of seven-day periods, which was also taken up in due course by the Greeks and Romans.

In fact, of course, the "seventh" day of the Christian week is the *first* day of the Jewish week, whose Sabbath takes place on Saturday not Sunday. In the mind of the Church, the day of the Resurrection has been identified with the day of "let there be light" (Day One of Genesis), because in rising from the dead Our Lord has made the world anew. Sunday is a day of "re-creation," in both senses of the word. The rest of the Christian week is to be lived in the light of Sunday, which takes over much of the symbolism of the Jewish *Shabbat* and shifts it one day forward.

What of Christ's abolition of so many Jewish strictures and regulations governing the kinds of activity that can be done on a Sabbath (healing, plucking ears of corn, etc.)? In the Law of Moses it is written that "whoever does any work on the Sabbath day shall be put to death" (Exod. 31:15). Here we must pay attention to the process of death and resurrection in Holy Week to understand what is going on. Christ was crucified and laid in the tomb on Friday, which was the sixth day of the Jewish week, the last day of "work." In that gesture, the whole world in a sense comes to an end.[3] The seventh day, the Jewish day of rest, is transformed by Christianity into Holy Saturday—a day of rest indeed, because God himself lies in the sleep of death. Then with Sunday morning, the first day of a new Jewish week, a new world arises.

The newness of the New Covenant is indicated by the "spiritual" nature of the new Sabbath. The rules of Exodus and Leviticus no longer hold sway, but only the Law of the Son of Man who is "lord even over the Sabbath" (Mark 2:28). This Law is a spiritual law, calling us not to particular external acts but to an interior devotion and special focus on prayer. The essential commandment for Sunday is not a list of "don'ts" but rather one positive "do"—a doing of the liturgy, the joint work of God and man on earth.

In recent years there have been many books rediscovering the profound meaning of the Sabbath.[4] The idea of a special day dedi-

---

3. The "work" of the world, it seems, can only culminate in the killing of the Son of God.

4. I recommend Charlotte Ostermann, *Souls at Rest: An Exploration of the Idea of Sabbath* (Angelico Press, forthcoming).

cated as far as possible to religious duties, contemplation, and leisure is deeply rooted in our traditions, but the sacredness of Sundays has consistently been eroded by secular forces for which efficiency and productivity are paramount. To recover a Sabbath mentality we need to put worldly objectives in second place, and be prepared to consecrate some time to God.

Working with God

So much for Sunday, but what of the other days? How is one to work in the spirit of the Days of Creation? Recall that God states a total of seven times during the Genesis account that the creation, in each of its stages, is "good" (also translated "beautiful"). Thus creation and contemplation, making and appreciation, go hand in hand. The creation itself is a manifestation of the goodness and beauty of being. This same principle must surely govern human work also, even though our task is not nearly as impressive as the creation of the world. Nevertheless, we do help to shape the world that God has constructed, and we adorn it.

Nor is the creative work of God "finished," as though Genesis were describing a series of past events. In fact the acts of God that make and sustain the world continue in every moment, or else the world would cease to be. In that sense it is even more important that our own work be in tune with that of God, for all the time (whether we know it or not) we are necessarily working alongside him, completing—or else perforce spoiling—what he has made.

But how can we do our work in a contemplative spirit, a spirit of thanksgiving and appreciation? Our jobs these days are often so menial, so repetitive, so (we often say) "soul-destroying." Most of the time we work simply for wages, and if we were rich we would not work at all. Our goal in life is to support our family and improve our way of life, to have enough money to buy the entertainment and other consumables we need to fill up our time. In order to achieve that we have to sell things—our labor, our ideas, our constructs . . . ourselves.

In an industrial society, everything revolves around commerce, around buying and selling. The eighteenth chapter of the Book of Revelation, concerning the fall of Babylon, describes it well. Somehow we have been sold a completely false idea about the nature of man and the purposes of human life. A separation seems to have taken place between technology and art, between *techne* and *poesis,* between the workman and the artist.[5] For a human being to *make* things, to transform matter and energy, to "subdue the earth," is in his nature and vocation. The ends of that making, its purposes, are necessarily related to the ends of man as such. The disorder we are speaking of arises when this relationship is disrupted, as it is when a new, naturalistic conception of man and his destiny takes over from the traditional anthropology.

This conception is of the very essence of modernity. If man's end is purely "natural," there is no higher goal to which his work is ordered, and it becomes an arbitrary matter what he chooses to build or do. His own body, reduced to a mere product of evolution, becomes industrial material for the work of other men. Consider this passage from the well-known Catholic critic of industrial technology, Eric Gill:

> Man is a being, an entity. He is not merely an instrument, a tool, a "hand." And the things he makes should properly reflect his nature—not merely his idiosyncrasy, the thing art critics call "self-expression"—his nature as a creature that knows and wills and loves and, above all things, loves. And further, the things men make do not properly exhibit man's nature as a lover unless they are oriented towards the proper object of his love. It is not necessary that there should be any shy-making talk about working for the Glory of God. But it is very necessary, it is entirely necessary that it should be possible to say of men's work that it does in fact give God glory, that the work of man is that *kind* of work. It is not necessary to talk about it; but it is necessary that it be so. It is not

5. With the separation of work from art, both suffer. The workman no longer makes anything whole, anything that can therefore help to make his own soul whole, but by the "division of labor" only serves like a machine to make parts of things to someone else's design. The artist, on the other hand, is reduced from being a prophet to an entertainer. His work has no point but to amuse. See Brian Keeble, *God & Work: Aspects of Art and Tradition* (Bloomington: World Wisdom Books, 2009), also Brian Keeble's *Art: For Whom and For What?* (Ipswich: Golgonooza Press, 1998), and the anthology edited by him entitled *Every Man An Artist: Readings in the Traditional Philosophy of Art* (Bloomington, IN: World Wisdom Books, 2005).

desirable that everybody should always be talking about love; but it is absolutely necessary that, if man's work is to be a proper and normal expression and exhibition and product of his real nature, every work of man should have the nature of a love song.

The most important motives for man's activity in doing or making are neither animal instincts nor caprice. We hold that love is more important and not merely prettier than instinct. Upon such a ground and from such a place we survey the works of men. We see all things as evidence of love. We make what we love—in accordance with our loves we make. A pair of scissors, no less than a cathedral or a symphony, is evidence of what we hold good, and therefore lovely, and owes its being to love.[6]

As though to continue Gill's thought, Gabriel Marcel reminds us that "in the long run all that is not done through Love and for Love must invariably end by being done against Love. The human being who denies his nature as a created being ends up by claiming for himself attributes which are a sort of caricature of those that belong to the Uncreated."[7] Techniques that treat the universe and life itself as raw material for manipulation, without due respect for the order in which they have been given, are in contradiction to the true end of human life, as revealed to us in faith.

This kind of science (Baconian, Cartesian) becomes "inhuman" because it involves an implicit denial of humanity's own *telos*, of "final causes" in general, and of divine Providence—an implicit denial of the Incarnation and the Trinity. It is spiritually incompatible with the kind of humility, the kind of receptivity, the kind of contemplation, which alone enables human beings (riddled though they are with physical and psychological imperfection) to attain a measure of holiness and, therefore, of real humanity.

The Vocational Society

The principles I have been discussing have a bearing on the aim of the political and economic order in general. This is not primarily the

6. Brian Keeble (ed.), *A Holy Tradition of Working: Passages from the Writings of Eric Gill* (Ipswich: Golgonooza Press, 1983), pp. 62–63.

7. Gabriel Marcel, *Men Against Humanity* (London: Harvill Press, 1952), pp. 55–56.

control or protection of society's members as individuals or their contractual relations, but their moral formation, or their formation in virtue, in a way of being that requires the existence of society as such. To create this common good, citizens should be able to support their families not only through work, but through what we might call "good" work—work that nourishes the human spirit, helps to build friendships, and encourages cooperation not just competition.[8] Wealth should be measured not simply in material but in spiritual, psychological, and social terms, since man is not just a material but also a spiritual being, one that lives in and for community.

To anyone who is familiar with the great religious traditions of the world other than Christianity, it will be obvious that the ideas of interior freedom, of human vocation, and of the family as the foundation of society, are practically universal. As such they map out an area where different traditions can potentially collaborate together in the building of a humane society. Against this proposal will be raised the objection that religious cultures have not always found it easy to get along, to put it mildly—and that Islam in particular is one of the major causes of civil and political tension in today's world.

The "Islam" we see in the mirror of terrorism is severely distorted. This distorted ideology often called "Islamism" is a modern and heterodox phenomenon—unfortunately now predominant in many places—the product of a mentality that would have been alien to most Muslims throughout most of history.[9] Certainly it is true that authentic Islam allowed for some use of military force from its origin, in a way that Christianity did not. Even when Christianity became militarized by the conversion of the Empire there always remained a theoretical separation between Church and State, and an ideal of non-violence (turning the other cheek, etc.) that made Christians uncomfortable with military action, at least in

8. See E.F. Schumacher, *Good Work* (London: HarperCollins, 1980); Keeble, *God and Work*; also chapter 7, "The Spirit of Work," below. The "cooperative" aspect of work was traditionally encouraged through the guilds.

9. A link has been suggested between Islamism and the decline of Islam in the face of Western technological and cultural dominance. It occurs to me that the suicide bomber may be motivated (unconsciously) by self-loathing, after in some way taking the guilt of Islam's failure upon himself.

principle. Islam, on the other hand, was founded by an exemplary political leader, and—as in the case of Judaism with its *Halakhah*—a central part of the revelation of Islam was the *Shari'ah* or Law, the social order so determined being regarded as sacred. Furthermore, this sacred order was intended for all mankind, not just for one tribe or group of tribes, giving Islam a universal mission that translated into political expansion.

Nevertheless, if a subject people were at times under pressure to convert to Islam (being subject to various financial penalties if they refused), they were not *compelled* to do so, in accordance with the well-known Qur'anic verse that there must be "no compulsion in religion" (Surah 2:256). In fact the financial penalties just mentioned may be interpreted as payment in lieu of serving in the armed forces or undertaking other responsibilities more appropriate to Muslims—who seem to have remained a minority in many of the conquered territories for the first three or four hundred years in any case.

Islamic militarism, too, was to some extent softened and channeled by moral and spiritual checks and balances—such as the mercy with which a defeated enemy was to be treated, and, in a broader sense, chivalry. The vital element of religion we might call "struggle" in the Way of God (*jihad*) has always meant for Muslims first and foremost the inner struggle to overcome oneself or one's lower nature, before it meant the use of force to defend the Muslim community. In fact, to understand traditional Islam one must take account of three dimensions—not just *Islam* ("submission") and *Iman* ("faith"), but also *Ihsan* (the "beautiful," "perfection," "holiness," or ethics); and not just the exterior forms of these, but the interior transformation they imply (*Tariqah*). Modernist Islamism, by contrast, lives entirely in the exterior world, as though the interior struggle did not exist, judging merit by conformity to certain rigid rules and propositions[10]—just like certain forms of Christian fundamentalism.

---

10. Sachiko Murata and William Chittick, *The Vision of Islam: The Foundations of Muslim Faith and Practice* (London and New York: I.B. Tauris, 1996). See also Seyyed Hossein Nasr, *Traditional Islam in the Modern World* (London: KPI, 1987).

We need to look beyond Islam*ism* in order to find the common ground on which Muslims and Christians (and Jews and others) can work together in building a culture where each religious tradition can find a place.[11] Greater familiarity with the history and culture of Islam is required: the divisions that opened up between different branches of the tradition after the death of the Prophet, the confrontation with Christianity, Buddhism, and Hinduism, European colonialism and the imposition of nationalism, and the demoralizing effect of Western technological "superiority."

Against this background, we can see what has become of the traditional Islamic way of life, "where the individual is related to a greater whole through the extended family, local bonds, guilds, and—on a more inward plane—through Sufi orders."[12] A functioning society of this type flourished in Istanbul up to the beginning of the twentieth century, and elsewhere in the Islamic world until more recently. Of course, the materialistic conception of human development (industrialization, consumption, fragmentation) has changed the way people think in Islamic countries as elsewhere. But authentic Islam is much closer in spirit to authentic Christianity than it is to materialistic individualism.

In the Christian West we tend to think of Islam as standing for quite a different conception of human existence—one of servitude to God. And yet that could also be said to be the concern of Christianity, whose ultimate goal is sonship. For both, freedom and fulfillment is found in submission to God. For Islam, the aim of human existence is to fulfill our calling as "vicegerent" of God, through the knowledge of God and of the "book" he bears within himself, containing all the signs or divine names manifested in creation.[13] Man in that sense reflects the "image" of God. In both religions, I think, man stands before God, and is called to live with

11. None of which is to say that the horrific persecution—amounting in places to extermination—of Christians by Islamist militants (I hesitate to call them Islamic for the reasons already given) should not be condemned and opposed by every means possible, short of adopting the same violence ourselves.

12. Nasr, *Traditional Islam in the Modern World*, p. 117.

13. Ibid., p. 159.

others in a "vocational" society—a society in which our labor can be blessed as a means of education and transformation.

Ananda Coomaraswamy beautifully expresses our common vision of human work. For Plato, he says, "the ideal society is thought of as a kind of co-operative work-shop in which production is to be for use and not for profit, and all human needs, both of the body and the soul, are to be provided for."[14] This leads to a natural kind of perfectionism—for working towards the perfection of the object is identical with working for the perfection of the worker's own soul.

It is a theory of work that is interested in man's needs, not his wants—for wants can be multiplied indefinitely through advertising—and in quality rather than quantity. The implicit critique of modern industry and commerce here is obvious. Of course, Plato had in mind an economy based on distinct vocational occupations determined by birth. The modern version of this ancient idea would modify it by making the determination by choice.

Another key element in the traditional view of a vocational society lies in the conception of what is actually being *produced* by the worker. If we are to serve the authentic human needs of the person, we must have a clear idea of what a person truly is, for this determines what he needs. Man's purpose is to know and serve God, and to recall God at all times, so that anything we produce must be made in such a way that it in some way reminds us of God. It must be beautiful, it must be harmonious, it must be inspiring. It must be not merely decorative (which implies distraction rather than attention), but conducive to contemplation. The English Romantics made this a central principle of their propaganda. According to William Morris, "beauty is once again a natural and necessary accompaniment of all productive labor."[15]

With beauty comes again the possibility of the *enjoyment* of labor, overcoming the "alienation" that Karl Marx found there. In this way, the highest purpose of man can be fulfilled even in the lowest and

14. Ananda K. Coomaraswamy, *What Is Civilization? And Other Essays* (Ipswich: Golgonooza Press, 1989), p. 6.
15. Cited in Hughes, ibid., p. 110.

most menial labor, and the poorest of the poor have access to heaven. Thus for Thomas Carlyle "there is a perennial nobleness, and even sacredness in work," concluding that "a man perfects himself by working," for "even in the meanest sorts of Labor, the whole soul of a man is composed into a kind of real harmony."[16] Again, this is a Platonic insight, and links to his notion of Justice, which means to give everyone his due—and every part of the soul its due—in accordance with the true needs of the body and soul.

The Just Entrepreneur

The vocational society does not depend solely on workers. Not all workers can be craftsmen. Most workers operate within a business enterprise, and this raises the question of the different kinds of enterprise, and the role of the manager or entrepreneur within them. It is here, too, that we find a new use for the concept of "creative justice," for in a vocational society justice must be brought into closer relationship with the creation of wealth.

The word "entrepreneur" originally referred to the manager or the promoter of a theatrical production (it is related to *entreprendre*, "to undertake"). This suggests the possibility of a "theo-dramatic" account of business enterprise. The manager of a business, like the manager of a play, supports the project and makes sure it succeeds. Management is an ethical pursuit, indeed it might as well be a branch of ethics. Almost everything the manager does has a moral dimension.[17] The manager of the play—who for our purposes may also be identified with the director—has a certain freedom; so does the employee or worker. Management is therefore a kind of "liberal art" (a branch of rhetoric, perhaps) that brings about a greater degree of human freedom. The balance between the interests of manager and worker is a balance of freedoms.

The company or organization they both serve also serves them. It

---

16. Cited in Keeble, *God & Work*, p. 49. See also Jean Hani, *Divine Craftsmanship: Preliminaries to a Spirituality of Work* (San Rafael: Sophia Perennis, 2007). For an imaginative reconstruction of a traditional society in which the metaphysical language of the crafts is understood at least by some see Isha Schwaller de Lubicz, *Her-Bak*, Vol. 1: "Chick-Pea," (Baltimore: Penguin Books, 1972).

exists not merely to create capital for a small group of investors or shareholders, but in order to improve their chances of flourishing as human beings. This is the heart of the theo-drama. Both manager and worker are *personae*, persons. They are not just members of a cast, but "I" or "Thou." The organization gives them a role: according to our theo-dramatic model, the manager is not a "player" on the stage *in the same sense* as the worker, but he relates to the one who is, and is "hypostatized" by this relationship.

The organization does exist to generate wealth, and to do so creatively. But wealth is not merely capital. It includes a whole range of resources, many of which are normally ignored or left out of account: time, ideas, personnel, goodwill, imagination, empathy. All such "wealth" is needed by the wider society if not by the firm itself, and by the community of "stakeholders" whose interests are affected. In other words, the creation of wealth is a way of contributing to the common good.

In thinking about wealth, we need to remember that in Catholic doctrine, property and work go together. Our human vocation is to work productively on the "earth and its resources," and we do this in common, in solidarity, collaboratively, looking out for each other's interests. When we appropriate property to ourselves as "private" (my house, my lawn, my car, my land, my tools) it is only as an extension of this principle, in order to be able to work more productively, more creatively, *for others* (since we work best if we are able to focus our attention on some things rather than everything). The "common destination of goods" takes priority.[18]

---

17. See especially the *Compendium of the Social Doctrine of the Church*. "The sense of responsibility that arises from free economic initiative takes not only the form of an *individual virtue* required for individual human growth, but also of a *social virtue* that is necessary for the development of a community in solidarity. Important virtues are involved in this process, such as diligence, industriousness, prudence in undertaking reasonable risks, reliability and fidelity in interpersonal relationships, as well as courage in carrying out decisions which are difficult and painful but necessary, both for the overall working of a business and in meeting possible set-backs" (n. 343).

18. "Goods of production—material or immaterial—such as land, factories, practical, or artistic skills, oblige their possessors to employ them in ways that will benefit the greatest number. Those who hold goods for use and consumption should

The best image of all this is the parable of Matthew 25:14–30, in which three servants are given different "talents" and are expected to make creative use of them while the master is away. The man who buries his talent in the ground and gives it back unchanged is punished, while the man who "invests" it so that it can grow is rewarded. The point is not about investment, but creativity and justice.

"Charity is at the heart of the Church's social doctrine" (*CV*, n. 2). Truth requires charity, and charity truth. In the same way, fairness or justice, like truth, requires love and mercy in order to flourish, and vice versa. This principle can be applied directly to the role of the entrepreneur. The art of management requires mercy and love so that the Spirit of Love may bring life into the organization—life capable of reproducing itself. (*Be fruitful and multiply.*) This is "the way of creative justice," applied to the work of the entrepreneur and manager. It has to be admitted that it is somewhat remote from the model currently taught in business schools.

Alternative Economics

By the nineteenth century, the division of labor, and the separation of property from work, had divided the laborer against his own soul, and alienated society from itself. The Romantics had wanted to present the "Gothic" as an alternative, looking back to a society of spiritually "noble" craftsmen and farmers organized into villages and guilds. But modern society is now so complex, and so gigantic, that it is extremely hard to see how any return to a previous way of life could be managed, except in small islands and oases largely cut off from the mainstream.

The perennial complaint of the Rationalist against the Romantic is that his conception of society is too impractical, too unrealistic, and therefore nothing but an impossible dream. And yet as the mainstream utilitarian culture slides ever closer to the alternatives of global anarchy (financial crisis, climate instability, international terrorism) and the global police state (drones, satellites, CCTV), it

---

use them with moderation, reserving the better part for guests, for the sick and the poor" (*CCC*, n. 2405).

becomes ever harder to support the claim that the *status quo* offers a more practical alternative.[19]

As we have seen, the most recent expressions of Catholic social teaching, such as *Caritas in Veritate*, have done more than gesture in the direction of what has become known as the "alternative" or "new" economics. Catholics are surely obliged, therefore, to take these alternatives seriously. One of the great obstacles is the way these things are presented on paper—the way they are measured. This goes back to the Enlightenment, and specifically the so-called separation of fact and value, which made the notion of *intrinsic value* unintelligible.

In post-Enlightenment societies, an economic value is attached to something from the outside. A commodity is worth whatever someone will pay for it. This means when we calculate the cost of producing something—a calculation that enables us to measure the profit we are going to make—we leave out many of the most important factors, including intrinsic worth, cost to the environment, long-term effects on the community, and the impact on a wider circle of involved stakeholders. If such effects *could* be taken into account, the calculation of profit and loss would appear very different. On a large scale, this would undoubtedly reveal the practical superiority of alternative economics.

There is another important factor that comes into play. A large number of alternative economic experiments have been tried, often with great success. I am thinking for example of cooperatives, the most successful of which until now is Mondragon in Spain, of the Catholic Land Association and Distributist communities such as those at Ditchling and Laxton in England, and the many hundreds of businesses around the world now following the "Economy of Communion" model. These do not depend on special measures such as environmental accounting, but compete with conventional

19. "There is no good reason, economic or otherwise, to wish for the 'recovery' and continuation of the economy we have had. There is no reason, really, to expect it to recover and continue, for it has depended too much on fantasy." From the last page of Wendell Berry's powerful article, "Inverting the Economic Order," in *Communio: International Catholic Review* 36: 3 (Fall 2009), pp. 475–86.

businesses on their own terms. They survive, they grow, they flourish. They show that alternative approaches to business can be successful, even in conventional terms. Cooperatives depend on the fact that the workers are the owners, and therefore deeply committed to the development of the business. Distributist communities are based on bonds between and within families, and the commitment of the community to the support of local farms and small businesses. Chesterton and Belloc's insight was that small, local, and regional businesses thrive when they are working for themselves and their friends and families rather than some distant employer.[20]

As we have seen, the Economy of Communion model developed by Chiara Lubich, rather than making profit available to shareholders, divides it three ways: devoting it either to charitable work in the surrounding community, to the seeding of new enterprise through education, or to the development of the business itself. These businesses seek to promote a culture of giving and social justice, and the inspiration was the life of the early Church described in the Book of Acts, where property was held in common and everyone's needs were taken care of. The poor they serve are people whose needs and potentialities they know personally, so the charitable help supplied to them is never wasted. A similar principle contributes to the great success of the Grameen Bank and other forms of microcredit, where small and effective loans are made to individuals known to the community, as a result of which they are almost always paid back.

The crucial factor that makes these models so successful seems to be the presence of a spiritual impulse—not necessarily a common faith, although the examples cited arise in a Catholic milieu—but at least an orientation towards something beyond the self (what Pope Benedict referred to as the spirit of gratuity). When this spirit drains away or is corrupted, the enterprise becomes like any other, and is likely to fail. Cooperatives that lose the cooperative spirit, communities that fall out among themselves, no longer have a competitive edge and may not even be comfortable places to work.

20. See the Appendix for a more detailed study of the Distributist movement.

A vocational society is one in which human labor itself is a means of sanctification. It is one in which the human person is not dominated by market forces and public opinion but is able, materially and spiritually, to "stand on his own feet." However, the integration of personality that this implies is alien to the world in which most of us have grown up. Joseph Ratzinger once wrote perceptively as follows:

> For Plato, the true location of man's integration is the *nous*, a word that we translate very inadequately as reason or understanding. What is meant is the ability to perceive the true criteria of Being itself, the organ that perceives the divine. It is only through this act, whereby man reaches out beyond himself, that the integration of the individual in himself and with himself, as well as the integration of society, takes place. Men cannot really be united by a common interest but only by the truth; in this way, freedom and justice are brought to realization in their inherent unity.[21]

The call to holiness is universal and undeniable. The call is only heard in the pure heart, in the *nous*, where we glimpse the divine in all things, and find unity in the truth beyond ourselves. This is the core of Catholic teaching—but the same call is heard wherever human beings stand upright under heaven.

> The classes and duties of life are many, but holiness is one—that sanctity which is cultivated by all who are moved by the Spirit of God, and who obey the voice of the Father and worship God the Father in spirit and in truth. These people follow the poor Christ, the humble and cross-bearing Christ in order to be worthy of being sharers in His glory. Every person must walk unhesitatingly according to his own personal gifts and duties in the path of living faith, which arouses hope and works through charity.[22]

---

21. *A Turning Point for Europe?* p. 131.
22. *Lumen Gentium*, 41.

The Way of Beauty

The pitiable state of the modern world, a mere corpse of the Christian world, creates a specially ardent desire for the reinvention of true civilization. If such a desire were to remain unfulfilled and the universal dissolution to take its course, we should still find consolation, because as the world breaks up we see the things of the spirit gather together in places in the world but not of the world. Art and poetry are among them, and metaphysics and wisdom; the charity of the Saints will lead the choir. ⌒Jacques Maritain[1]

Much that might have been said about art has been said about work, and Beauty has been the subject of two other books of mine, so what more remains to add?[2]

One can never run out of things to say about Beauty, especially in a book that is trying to speak of the divine radiance reaching to the ends of the earth. When Balthasar refers to this radiance, he describes it as the work of the Holy Spirit, universalizing Christ's historical, risen reality.[3] Therefore this chapter is not really about art—much less about "gallery" art—but about the Imagination, and about Christ as the Image of God, and the ways in which this Image is embodied in culture and history, beginning (and ending) with the Liturgy.

We will have to conclude that the essence or culmination of all human culture and civilization, and of all evangelization, is prayer —prayer which makes us human, gives life to society, and renders the world translucent to God.

1. Jacques Maritain, *Art and Scholasticism with Other Essays* (London: Sheed & Ward, 1947), p. 83.

2. The literature is of course extensive: I will mention here only Aidan Nichols OP, *Redeeming Beauty: Soundings in Sacral Aesthetics* (Aldershot: Ashgate, 2007). See also the references given in the previous chapter to books by Brian Keeble.

3. Hans Urs von Balthasar, *Theo-Logic*, I: Truth of the World (San Francisco: Ignatius Press, 2000), p. 13.

Diotima's Lesson

In Plato's *Symposium*, the men decide not to get drunk but to discuss Love. The highpoint of the evening is a speech of Socrates, in which he gives an account of his conversation with the wise woman from Mantinea, Diotima. It is undoubtedly a vehicle for Plato to present his own theory. Diotima asserts that what Love desires is not beauty as such, but "reproduction and birth in beauty" (206e). This is our (mortal) substitute for the immortality of the gods, enabling us to come as close as possible to possessing the good forever. At a stroke, she has swept away the visions of sterile love that other speakers have presented. The purpose of human love is to give birth to beauty, and in so doing achieve a kind of immortality.

And "what is fitting for a soul to bear and bring to birth," she says, is "[w]isdom and the rest of virtue, which all poets beget, as well as all the craftsmen who are said to be creative. But by far the greatest and most beautiful part of wisdom deals with the proper ordering of cities and households, and that is called moderation and justice" (209b).

As for the "rites of love" by which this reproduction is to be attained and justice brought about, it is a process of *ascent*.[4] A lover must "become a lover of all beautiful bodies," not just one, and come to value the beauty of the soul and of knowledge even more than that of bodies, until he becomes *beautiful in his virtues*, and tastes the life of the gods:

> one goes always upwards for the sake of this Beauty, starting out
> from beautiful things and using them like rising stairs: from one
> body to two and from two to all beautiful bodies, then from beau-
> tiful bodies to beautiful customs, and from customs to learning

---

4. In *Phaedrus*, Plato puts it that the encounter with earthly beauty causes the soul to sprout wings. Thus Josef Pieper quotes Goethe: "Beauty is not so much a fulfillment as rather a promise." "In other words," Pieper continues, "by absorbing beauty with the right disposition, we experience, not gratification, satisfaction, and enjoyment but the arousal of an expectation; we are oriented towards something 'not yet here.' He who submits properly to the encounter with beauty will be given the sight and taste not of a fulfillment but of a promise—a promise that, in our bodily existence, can never be fulfilled." This passage is from *Divine Madness: Plato's Case Against Secular Humanism* (San Francisco: Ignatius Press, 1995), pp. 47–8.

beautiful things, and from these lessons he arrives at the end at this lesson, which is learning of this very Beauty, so that in the end he comes to know just what it is to be beautiful.[5]

(One is reminded here of the Islamic identification of the virtuous life with *ihsan* or "doing the beautiful.")

Only when he looks at beauty in "the way it can be seen" will he be able to give birth to virtue—and, along with virtue, all the glories of human civilization. This ascent to contemplation is therefore far from being a flight "of the alone to the Alone" (Plotinus), or at least one must say that for Plato it lies at the heart of an active transformation of the world through art and goodness.

The Ladder of Imagination

Diotima's ascent is through a series of levels. We need to understand the levels that exist in our souls. But the traditional picture of the soul does not, I feel, allow enough space for the productions of culture. We can certainly distinguish three main levels: the Body, the Soul, and the Spirit. This rough scheme masks a certain complexity. The highest and main spiritual faculty is the *Nous Poetikos* or "active mind" (*Intellectus Agens*). Below this, the Soul is the home of the faculties of Will, Reason, and Memory. The memory is also the place where sensations from the corporeal world of the Body, among other things, are received and stored.[6]

---

5. From the *Symposium* 211c, in *Plato: Complete Works*, p. 493. Plato demonstrates that Socrates has learned this lesson well, by letting Alcibiades describe in detail an unsuccessful attempt to seduce him.

6. The word "soul" refers to that non-material principle which gives form to the living body from within. No physical entity can do this, be it genetic or otherwise, since anything physical is by definition part of the external world. As to the nature of interiority—the existence of the soul—this cannot be demonstrated empirically for the same reason, but comes to be known in another way. In the experience of *being loved*, we discover that we are not just knowers but can be known by another. We see ourselves in another's eyes. For the "I" to become aware of itself in this way is to reveal its own "interior" (the space between self as knower and self as known), in which the various faculties of the soul are also gradually discovered, but it makes very clear that the source of our being, and a knowledge that enfolds both knower and known, must lie deeper still, in the gift that is the foundation of everything else. In fact this primordial gift is the source of the radiance in which we see everything that exists.

The Thomistic and Aristotelian epistemology speaks of how we come to know the *Forms* of things, their essences (in the Greek tradition *logoi*), by abstraction from the "phantasms" or images of particulars that we receive through the senses. The formal element is then impressed upon the "Passive" Intellect to enable us to know the object.[7] But the "Active Intellect" that performs this abstraction upon them needs to be further divided into two aspects, which we might call the Active Intelligence and the Active Imagination (to borrow a term from Henry Corbin). In this way we can accommodate an insight that comes to us from the Romantics—that the Imagination plays a role in knowing the truth. For the truth of the Forms lies above the human Spirit, and the images we obtain from the senses become the vehicles of the Forms in two distinct ways: through *concepts*, and through *symbols*. Images manipulated and transformed by the Active Imagination may be so fashioned as to reflect or refract the light of the intelligible world in myth or poetry or painting, just as they may be fashioned by the Active Intellect into concepts to be used in discursive argument.

For Plato imagination in the sense of *eikasia* is one of the lowest faculties of the soul, the images it engenders being mere "copies of copies" of the supreme Forms. The imagination in this sense always leads us away from the Forms towards dissipation and unreality. (This is why, comparing them to the direct contemplation of truth, Plato condemns poetry and the arts in general, despite the fact that his own *oeuvre* takes an artistic form.) The Church Fathers and many Christian mystics have also treated the imagination mainly as a danger, as a source of temptation and distraction. Even in Plato,

---

7. This is normally presented as an alternative to the Platonic account. However, it seems to me that St. Thomas leaves the nature of the Active Intellect somewhat mysterious—a kind of mental X-ray that pierces through the matter of the phantasm to reveal the object's nature. To me it seems that this "X-ray" is nothing other than the light of the Forms themselves; that is, aspects or rays of the radiance that is Being, the root and foundation of our own existence. Our situation is therefore not unlike the dwellers in Plato's cave, for whom the light of the Forms is not perceived directly. The fact that our intuition is obscure distinguishes this point of view from that of Ontologism, and leaves Thomistic epistemology virtually intact. But perhaps this account is closer to St. Bonaventure than to Aquinas.

however, there is a sense that the imagination can serve as a ladder in the reverse direction if guided by reason, and also some mention of divinely-inspired images and visions which, unlike the images produced by ourselves, are directly conducive to truth (just as Christian tradition also admits the reality of veridical visions). In *De Anima* Aristotle gave more scope for a theory of the imagination, and Islamic authors extended this further into a full-blown visionary epistemology.

For our purposes we need only be aware that the imagination is ambiguous, depending on whether it is oriented towards the light above, or downwards and away from the radiance of the Forms and of true Beauty. In the latter case, its productions will be depressing and degrading, like those sometimes found in surrealist or expressionist art and even more so in pornography. Fantasy writings such as *Game of Thrones* seem to face away rather than towards the Forms; Tolkien's *Lord of the Rings* offers an obvious contrast, in which the fragrance of the Forms is unmistakable. Other imaginative productions are oriented between these, demonstrating the author's interest in neither that which is below nor that which lies above, but what is too easily taken to be the "real world" around us (I am thinking of thrillers and realistic dramas, which are just as much fantasies but without the magical or futuristic furniture).[8]

The Icon

The purest Christian art form is arguably that of the Icon, which after the iconoclastic crisis of the 8th-9th centuries attained its peak at the hands of Andrej Rublev in the early 15th century and has remained fairly stable ever since—in contrast to the incessant evolution of Western religious art.

The Icon, whether it takes the form of a fresco or a mosaic (as in the early Church) or a panel painting, has a very distinctive pur-

---

8. I developed the thoughts in this section in more detail for a G. K. Chesterton Institute conference on fantasy literature and later as "Landscapes with Angels," a chapter in Justyna Deszcz-Tryhubczak and Marek Oziewicz (eds), *Towards or Back to Human Values? Spiritual and Moral Dimensions of Contemporary Fantasy* (Newcastle: Cambridge Scholars Press, 2006), pp. 84–96.

pose. It is not intended to be a naturalistic, but rather a sacramental representation of a holy person or mystery. To that end it is stylized, and the rules of stylization are the language by which it communicates. The golden background representing heaven or the empyrean, the reversed perspective indicating we are not in optical space, the relative sizes of the figures indicating the focus of our contemplation, the small mouth and large eyes of the saint suggesting silence and receptivity, highlights indicating a light-source above the figure and usually to the left, but at the same time the absence of shadows—these and other techniques, not to mention the colors and the material composition of the paints, are designed to encourage contemplation of the heavenly prototype in the image. The Icon is not a window to heaven, but a ladder that the viewer is supposed to "climb" there. It is an example of a consciously *ontological* style of painting.[9]

Similar rules applied in the East and West right up to the Renaissance. But other forms of sacred art had begun to flourish in the West, evolving from the painted churches of the first millennium—notably statuary and stained-glass windows (large decorated windows only becoming possible once the invention of flying buttresses had diverted much of the weight of the church building from the walls). A growing naturalism was evident already in the International Gothic, where gardens and landscapes become ever more prominent in the background of a sacred image or altarpiece (replacing the symbolic golden background). Fra Angelico (d. 1455) and Rogier van der Weyden (d. 1464) were near contemporaries of Andrej Rublev (d. 1430), but they stood at the beginning of a transformation of art that would accelerate in the centuries following.

An interest in the contemplation of God's wisdom in nature which we associate with the Franciscans may have been the fertile ground into which the seeds of the Renaissance fell (Giotto was a

9. The classic works on this subject are Leonid Ouspensky and Vladimir Lossky, *The Meaning of Icons* (Crestwood, NY: St Vladimir's Seminary Press, 1983) and Paul Evdokimov, *The Art of the Icon: A Theology of Beauty* (Redondo Beach, CA: Oakwood Publications, 1990). Evdokimov emphasizes the horror of a traditional mind presented with modern art, especially its decline (as he sees it) towards abstraction, which he links to pseudo-spirituality and a fascination with the occult (pp. 73–95).

third-order Franciscan), but the revival of pagan learning in the fourteenth and fifteenth centuries, together with the growth of a merchant class and the competition between princelings to patronize the arts, led in both southern and northern Europe to a flourishing trade in naturalistic landscape and portraiture—even sacred art began to acquire a distinctly secular character. With the Baroque it was spiritualized again, but the gold was now heavily mingled with shadows, while the bodies of the saints striving towards heaven were every bit as muscular and dramatic as those of Michelangelo.

Outside the churches naturalism of various kinds remained the thing until the next great transformation, brought about by the Romantic Movement in its later stages. Symbolists who hardly knew what they were searching for prepared the way for Aesthetes, Impressionists, Surrealists, Cubists, Expressionists, and Abstractionists. Conceptual Art has become almost indistinguishable from the entertainment industry. Each new school or movement blazes for a few years before burning itself out. The home of fine art, which had been born on the altar, was now the commercial gallery (or in the case of music, the concert hall) rather than the church—and sacred art underwent a parallel decline (into kitsch and sentimentality) that is hard to reverse.

"To remark that the spiritual curve of culture shows a decline ever since the Renaissance is not to express the wish that the Renaissance be deleted from human history."[10] Not at all: in fact the curve of culture shows great gains and discoveries alongside this "decline" from the Icon (see below). But the price paid for these manifestations of genius was the dissolution of an artistic tradition rooted firmly in contemplation and ontology.

Liturgy

It is said that "the Eucharist makes the Church" (de Lubac *et al.*). Furthermore, the meaning and state of the liturgy is directly related to the state of Christian society, and the building of a Christian civilization depends very largely on the health of Christian worship. Not that every Christian needs to be devout in this sense, although

10. Maritain, *Art and Scholasticism*, p. 82.

that would be desirable; rather the presence of the liturgy serves to open society towards the transcendent—it gives an orientation, just as the glimpse of stars in the sky might do for a traveler in a damp climate.[11]

Increasingly aware during the twentieth century of the growing gulf between faith and culture, and grace and nature, linked to a division within the Church between a passive laity and an active clergy, the Church in the Second Vatican Council sought to "raze the bastions" and reach out to the world. This included an acknowledgement that once again action should be subordinated to contemplation, the visible to the invisible. However, the Council in its *Constitution on the Sacred Liturgy* gave particular prominence to the theme of "active participation" (*participatio actuosa*): "Mother Church earnestly desires that all the faithful should be led to that full, conscious and active participation in liturgical celebrations which is demanded by the very nature of the liturgy" (n. 14). To encourage this participation, the Constitution recommended simplification of the rites (n. 34) on the one hand, and careful attention to the people's responses (acclamations, gestures, etc.) on the other (n. 30).

The Council was reacting against the view that prayer was something the faithful did *on their own* while the Mass was being celebrated by the priest. Nevertheless, the emphasis that the Council laid on the priest's responsibility to ensure this active participation on the part of the faithful in the liturgy *as prayer* did in practice give a great deal of weight to outward and vocal activity, which was observable, as distinct from the more important inner *actio* which this activity was supposed to promote.

The separation of nature and grace had been attacked by the Council, but not at its root. Clericalism was not overcome, but simply adopted another form. Intimations of transcendence—indeed, references to the soul—were minimized. Within the churches, walls were whitewashed and relics dumped in the name of "noble simplic-

---

11. The paragraphs that follow are based on a longer paper of mine in Alcuin Read (ed.), *Looking Again at the Question of the Liturgy with Cardinal Ratzinger: Proceedings of the July 2001 Fontgombault Conference* (Farnborough: St Michael's Abbey Press, 2003).

ity" (n. 34). Unlike the much earlier Cistercian rebellion against artistic extravagances at Cluny, this modern campaign for simplicity was not coupled with the asceticism and devotion that might alone have rendered it spiritually "noble." It fell easy victim to the prevailing culture of comfort and prosperity.[12] These misjudgments were not able to affect the essence of the liturgical act itself or its validity, but they were serious enough to be accounted by many a disaster, and to provoke the schism led by Archbishop Lefebvre.

Again, a great part of the explanation must lie with the cultural moment. All earlier liturgies, Aidan Nichols points out, "formed part of a culture *itself ritual in character.*"[13] The prevailing culture that began to emerge after the Second World War, far from being ritual in character, was one in which ritual, hierarchy, reverence, and custom were regarded with suspicion. Human freedom and creativity depend upon such rules and frameworks, not on liberation from them. A leading anthropologist writing at the end of the 1960s, Mary Douglas, argued that the contempt for ritual forms leads to the privatization of religious experience and thereby to secular humanism.[14] The reformers were blithely unaware of such contemporary reappraisals of liturgy. The very act of undertaking a

12. At the height of the movement in 1967, the American writer Robert W. Jenson wrote an article entitled "God, Space, and Architecture" (*Essays in the Theology of Culture*) in which he rejects the idea in church architecture of a "common focus for all present" and any evocation of an "absolute and changeless Presence," which he terms the "God of religion" rather than the "God of the Gospel." Instead, its forms should be "broken, restless, even nervous.... We should not find a church soothing. The forms of church buildings should be ready to fall, or to take wing. They should have the dynamics of the temporary" (pp. 12–13). They should also be small, since according to Jenson large congregations are obviously a thing of the past. The comparison here is with the theater of audience-participation that was so popular at the time. The fragmentation of ordered narrative is of a piece with postmodernism. These views and others like them were common at the time. Jenson's un-soothing, nervous churches did take shape, but since they were overheated and lined with soft carpets, the aesthetic discomfort they were intended to induce was soon forgotten.

13. *Looking at the Liturgy: A Critical View of Its Contemporary Form* (Ignatius Press, 1996), p. 85 (my italics).

14. See Aidan Nichols OP, *Looking at the Liturgy*, p. 69; and Kieran Flanagan, *Sociology and Liturgy* (London: Macmillan, 1991).

far-reaching reform in these circumstances (however necessary reform may have been) was bound to encourage an activist mentality that would regard itself as the master of the liturgy. Humble receptivity, so essential in matters of worship, was put on hold during the time it would take to make the desired changes. But a virtue once suspended is hard to revive.[15]

The liturgical act is not only a prayer but also a *mystery*, in which something is done to us which we cannot fully understand, and which we must consent to and receive. In the immediate aftermath of the Council, however, the emphasis had swung towards didacticism, the endless preaching and explaining of the action of the liturgy. Furthermore, the liturgy implies a *cosmos*. The reformers' modernistic rebellion against any kind of ordered, harmonious space separating sacred and profane was in fact a rebellion against the symbolism of space, and ultimately against all symbolism in the true sense. Symbols were to be reduced to the status of visual aids, in the service of a purely didactic rather than a sacramental ideal of liturgy. This was a rejection of the sacred cosmology that is intrinsic to the Catholic tradition.[16] With the loss of cosmic symbolism it was as though the vertical dimension of the liturgy had become inaccessible, and everything was concentrated on the horizontal plane, with an emphasis upon the cultivation of warm feelings among the congregation.

Another tendency was mentioned by Cardinal Ratzinger on several occasions, namely the failure to understand the liturgy as a *sacrifice*—not as a separate sacrifice in addition to that of Calvary, or a mere "reconstruction" of the Passion, but as the self-same act performed once and for all, making present the sacrifice of the Cross "in an unbloody manner" throughout the Church, in diverse times and places. Thus the Mass was reduced to one of its aspects: that of a sacred meal, a celebratory feast.

---

15. See James Hitchcock, *Recovery of the Sacred: Reforming the Reformed Liturgy* (Ignatius Press, 1995); Stratford Caldecott (ed.), *Beyond the Prosaic: Reviving the Liturgical Movement* (Edinburgh: T&T Clark, 1998); David Torevell, *Losing the Sacred: Modernity and Liturgical Reform* (Edinburgh: T&T Clark, 2000).

16. See Ratzinger, *The Spirit of the Liturgy* (San Francisco: Ignatius Press, 2000).

The result of all these tendencies was a loss of liturgical beauty. Not that beauty *per se* is sacred: that is the error of the aesthete. The deepest sense of beauty is the splendor of God's glory, perceived by the spiritual senses.[17] With the loss of the transcendent reference of the liturgy understood as a response to the divine glory, beauty was reduced to a purely subjective quality—a matter of personal taste—which was then easily swept aside in the interests of a more seemingly objective content: the moral lesson to be conveyed by the ritual.

Reform of the Reform

The lesson of the liturgical reform of the 1960s and 70s is that the liturgy must ultimately be understood not in isolation, not in purely historical terms, not aesthetically, not sociologically, but *ontologically,* that is to say, in its full metaphysical and meta-anthropological depth. In order to understand the nature of the Divine or Eucharistic Liturgy, in which so many layers of symbolism have been incorporated and overlaid, it is important to locate the deepest and most fundamental structure on which everything else is built. This structure is "nuptial" in nature. That is, the Mass is essentially a wedding between heaven and earth. The liturgy enacts the marriage of the Lamb, combining the wedding banquet of the Last Supper with the redemptive act of the Passion.[18] The "offspring" of this union are Christian souls, indwelt by the Holy Spirit.[19] Jesus Christ, who is the High Priest, the King, and the Sacrifice all rolled into one, is in his own person such a marriage—an intimate union of divine and human nature. Of no previous High Priest could this be said. This is what makes Christianity different from all other religions, as the Letter to the Hebrews makes very clear.

Insofar as he acts in the *persona* and Spirit of Christ, the priest can claim by virtue of his office to be regarded as mediating the presence of the heavenly Bridegroom to his people. The people to whom he

17. Hans Urs von Balthasar, *The Glory of the Lord*, Vol. I, pp. 79–127, 571–583.

18. See the seventh chapter of *Mulieris Dignitatem*, by Pope John Paul II.

19. Seen in this light, the maleness of the priest who mediates Christ in the sacrament becomes highly significant, and it becomes easier to see why it would not be symbolically appropriate to ordain women to the priesthood.

ministers, *if he genuinely loves them* (to the extent of being willing to pour out his life's blood for them), should see in him and follow this same Lord, in whom they find by this means their own true selves. But this love cannot be merely paternalistic in a condescending way. And in fact it is brought out and developed in the priest by the response of the laity themselves, who are able in this mutual relationship to "mother" the priest into the full expression of his vocation, drawing out from him his unique way of *being Christ.*

Authentic social charity cannot be reduced to a dualistic "master-slave" relationship without becoming either sentimental or domineering. During recent centuries it seems the liturgy gradually became separated from any living concern with social justice—or at least, it was hard to see the connection.[20] Naturally, Christians were expected to go out from the liturgy and live virtuous lives, and thus have a transformative effect on society, but they did this by crossing from sacred space into secular space, rather than by discovering a deeper relationship between the two. This could be described as a profanization of charity; a secularization of solidarity. That is why the post-conciliar reaction was to emphasize the horizontal dimension of the liturgy (social concern) over the vertical (the act of worship), or even to confuse the two. Whole religious orders went into steep decline as the communitarian aspect of their mission took precedence over the liturgical, the love of neighbor over the love of God. The problem of liberation theology was therefore a product not of the 1960s, but of the dualism of an earlier era.

Social solidarity is more securely grounded on right worship than on common feelings: the love of neighbor is founded on the love of God. This is in fact one of the clear implications, not only of the Ten Commandments themselves (the first three of which are devoted to the worship of God), but of the new Christian anthropology. The human person is by its very nature other-centered. We love God, and this opens us to the life of the other in our neighbor; we love our neighbor, and this opens us to the love of God. We do not simply go out to do good to another in the world, inspired by our worship of God in the church. Rather, the love of God sends us out to

20. See Michael J. Baxter, "Reintroducing Virgil Michel," *Communio* (Fall 1997).

do good, because it reveals who we are and who is our neighbor. We are not (only) imitating the love of God that we see demonstrated in the liturgy, but *living the liturgy out in the world*.[21] The liturgy is not (merely) separate in a horizontal sense from what goes on outside, but separate in the sense of being "interior," or revealing the inner meaning and purpose of what lies outside. Sacred space, sacred time, and sacred art are distinctive, not (just) as belonging to a parallel world, but as defining the center of *this* world: the world in which we live and work.

The Eucharistic liturgy reveals us to ourselves, because it reveals "the mystery of the Father and his love" (*Gaudium et Spes*, n. 22). The Father's love is not a *thing*, not an object to be known and researched, but an act, a deed, an event, which may be known only through participation. In the Son, in the reception of his Gift which is the Holy Spirit and Redemption, we are broken open and poured out for the world, mingling our lives with his in the communion of the Church, and our "most high calling" is brought to light. In this way I hope it is clear that the call of Pope Francis to a renewed concern for the poor, for refugees, and for the victims of violence is not in contradiction to, but on the contrary is an extension of, the "reform of the reform" initiated by John Paul II and Benedict XVI.

In Search of Beauty

Culture is the offspring of our search for beauty, as Diotima taught Socrates. Jacques Maritain gives this a Christian interpretation in *Art and Scholasticism*. "It is indeed the ardent desire, the earnest prayer of the mind, taken in its pure state, to beget a living creature in its own likeness."[22] But "you see that to establish fully the dignity and nobility of art, we have found it necessary to go back as far as the mystery of the Trinity."[23] For everything the artist does is in the image of God, not least this begetting in beauty—for the Son is the Father's "work of art."

---

21. The point is developed in *Hymn of Freedom* and *Heart in Pilgrimage*, both by Michael L. Gaudoin-Parker.

22. *Art and Scholasticism*, p. 96.

23. Ibid., p. 97.

If we revisit those schools and movements of secular art that seemed so profane when contrasted with the purity of the Icon we may find much that will surprise us. In many landscape paintings we find glimpses of paradise, and in the paintings of Monet—ostensibly intended to capture a fleeting moment—a search for the eternal heaven located in a world of light. In the quiet still-lives and domestic scenes painted by Vermeer we find the banal, domestic universe enfolded in a loving, contemplative gaze. In the deceptively naïve paintings of Paul Klee we find attempts to imitate the way nature works in reality, and a revelation of the humor of the Creator. Even the conceptual art of the late twentieth century—though it seems trivial, like fireworks for the mind—can change the way we look at the world, at least for a moment or two.

A similar story unfolds in music, which evolves from chant to polyphony and thence (*via* Romanticism) to elaborate concert pieces abstracted from any overt religious significance. A high point of spiritual serenity is achieved with Palestrina, Taverner, Bach, Handel, Mozart, de Victoria, but the rampaging emotionalism set loose by Beethoven leads eventually to the breaking of previously sacrosanct laws of composition by Schoenberg and John Cage, and the merging of classical music with popular commercial music through cross-fertilization, film scores, and the rest. Yet here too the same history can be viewed as one of tremendous achievements, and a religious sensibility breaks through (Saint-Saens, Tavener).

In architecture, the elegance of Art Deco marked a last aesthetic gasp before the high hopes of Bauhaus functionalism led to the sad spectacles of Modernism and Brutalism in the mid- to late-twentieth century. Yet the human phenomenon that is Manhattan stands almost as a vindication of the skyscraper (although nothing can justify the tower blocks of a thousand other cities), and Antoni Gaudi stands against Le Corbusier as the representative of Catholic genius in whom new architectural visions are still capable of revealing themselves.

Literature followed the same cultural trajectory, the same "curve," in which we can find both an upward and a downward path. From the great genius of Shakespeare and Cervantes we can trace through the European "turn to the subject" a flowering of great plays and novels in which the human psyche and social mores are laid bare—preparing the way, strangely, for Freud and Jung, and (in a different way) Karl Marx. There can be no argument against Jane Austen, Elizabeth Gaskell, Charles Dickens, or the great Russians, yet in James Joyce and J.P. Donleavy, in D.H. Lawrence and Hemingway, we find indulgence mixed with genius in equal measure. Poetry, so much closer to metaphysics in its attempts at verbal precision, blossoms in Patmore and Hopkins and Eliot but coherence is lost until, here and there, a process of recovery can begin. The cycle continues, and it is driven by the search for *beauty* even if the word is held in abhorrence by many of the masters of our time, and is hidden under words such as "function," "efficiency," "integrity," or even "originality."[24]

The Rediscovery of Prayer

For Maritain, "[w]hat makes the condition of modern art tragic is that it must be converted to find God again. And from the first conversion to the last, from baptism to the habit of virtue, there is a long way to go."[25] Yet he did not rule out such a conversion, nor did he despise all modern art.

Balthasar, famously, condemned the modern era more sweepingly as follows:

> We no longer dare to believe in beauty and we make of it a mere appearance in order the more easily to dispose of it. Our situation today shows that beauty demands for itself at least as much cour-

24. A "cosmic pessimist" would see overall decline mitigated in part by brilliant developments within each field. It is as though each historical cycle needed to exhaust its cultural possibilities, these being impossible to achieve without the release of inhibitions and the abolition of taboos that had preserved standards during the previous phase. In such a way, for example, rock music may be seen as a positive development, in which technical genius (Hendrix) and spiritual influences (U2) may be expressed, despite the fact that the genre as a whole contributes to the agitation of the modern world and the decline of tradition. In fact the picture is yet more complex, since old traditions rarely die out completely but remain and even flourish to some extent alongside the new. See Robert Bolton, *The Order of the Ages: Word History in the Light of Universal Cosmogony* (Ghent, NY: Sophia Perennis, 2001), especially Ch. 10, "The Submergence of Distinctions."

25. *Art and Scholasticism*, p. 92.

age and decision as do truth and goodness, and she will not allow herself to be separated and banned from her two sisters without taking them along with herself in an act of mysterious vengeance. We can be sure that whoever sneers at her name as if she were the ornament of a bourgeois past—whether he admits it or not—can no longer pray and soon will no longer be able to love.[26]

Yet we do believe in beauty, as I have suggested, even if we are confused about what it is and where to find it. The search goes on, whether in the gutter or among the stars. Nor are we deprived of all freedom and grace. What we lack, for sure, is a science of ascent, which takes place through *ascesis*. Perhaps this science has been preserved more effectively by the Orthodox Church than in the West,[27] and any effective renewal of our civilization will have to await the reunion of the two traditions.

In the meantime we need to pay attention once more to the Sermon on the Mount and the Beatitudes, which imply a very different path to freedom than the one dominating society at present. As we saw already, freedom in the modern sense—the power to choose between A and B—is a debased freedom, and this explains why we feel so trapped within the downward curve of our culture. True freedom, attained through a measure of self-mastery, gives the power to choose, or create, an entire situation, including the choices to be made within it.[28] God's freedom is not to choose between pre-existing possibilities, but creates the very possibilities themselves. By analogy, our own full human freedom is a creative freedom, a creativity that in some degree changes the world. It can be achieved only by integrating the will with the other human faculties, including intellect and imagination.

The liturgy and, more generally, prayer, is the school of this higher freedom and creativity. It is this turning towards the Transcendent in faith and worship that orients our ascent within ourselves, and gives

26. *Glory of the Lord*, Vol. I, p. 18.

27. See, e.g., Dumitru Staniloae, *Orthodox Spirituality: A Practical Guide for the Faithful and a Definitive Guide for the Scholar* (South Canaan, PA: St Tikhon's Seminary Press, 2002)—and, of course, the classic compilation of the Orthodox Fathers, *The Philokalia*, four volumes of which have so far appeared from the publisher Faber.

28. Robert Bolton, *Keys of Gnosis* (Hillsdale, NY: Sophia Perennis, 2004), p. 76.

a direction to our search for beauty. The liturgy is a crucible in which our transformation is accomplished. It is more than art, then, that is "born on the altar"—the whole of civilization depends on this act of sacrifice, though we have done our best to render it invisible. The widespread destruction of the unborn and the collapse of the family is a clear indicator. How can we ignore the annual killing of 40–50 million children worldwide, or the appalling poverty in which so many grow up?[29] It becomes ever more obvious that without a place for the sacred, society becomes a death trap for the "unwanted."

All through the Old Testament, the prophets speak of the fact that one day the power and spirit of God will be poured out upon the whole People of God. What happens at Pentecost is more than a reminder of God's spiritual presence in the world; it is a new beginning, akin to a birth, or the conception of a new life. The fullness of God's life, possessed by Jesus, is shared with all, infusing new faculties and possibilities into the human condition.

Christ is not merely a model for us to imitate, an exemplar. As God-Made-Man, he is God's gift of grace to us, the gift of God's own self, making it possible to live in the way he shows to us. Jesus Christ, as Balthasar puts it, "empowers us inwardly to do the Father's will together with him."[30] Surpassing even the "first gift" of existence, the gift of grace offers us eternal life—enables us to share, even now, in the life of the Trinity, which is perfect love, perfect freedom.

29. Statistics from the World Health Organization.
30. See his essay in Schurmann et al., *Principles of Christian Morality* (San Francisco: Ignatius Press, 1986).

Conclusion

At the end of this book we come back to the implications of the title. A Christian theology of *gift* helps us to rediscover a relational perspective that is both ancient and universal.

The model of *homo economicus* that we inherit from the Enlightenment was based on man understood as an individual rather than as a "person" in the relational sense. It turns man into a solitary and conflictual actor in the market, an isolated and docile subject of the state, pursuing his own survival, pleasure, and power.

The alternative offered by the Church's teaching recognizes man as originally "in-relation," an "*I-in-relation*," whose needs and therefore self-interest involve social goods founded on gift, and specifically on self-gift and self-reception—which manifest as trust, generosity, altruism, friendship, cooperation, and charity. Man is a relational creature, whose being is received rather than self-made, and whose only fulfillment comes through loving his neighbor as himself.

If modernity in its negative aspect is associated with a tendency to favor an active and aggressive attitude over a receptive and contemplative one, then the theology of gift has implications in all the areas where we perceive the fruits of that tendency, and not just in economics. This includes environment and conservation, sexuality and bioethics. It helps us respond to the challenges of secularism and inter-religious dialogue, and the contemporary crisis in education. It does all this by restoring our vision of nature (including our own human nature) as a gift to be appreciated, cultivated, and respected.

The theology of gift signifies openness to being, to the whole of reality. This openness lies at the heart of religious experience. Variously interpreted, it is expressed in the many cultural traditions we attempt to transmit to future generations. If we are indeed creatures of gift, who find ourselves only by striving to love, then our political and economic structures, our ethics and philosophy, have a single goal: *solidarity through communion*, the common good of humanity in harmony with nature.

The Beatitudes teach us how to be happy, how to find a happiness that the world cannot give. These teachings are not just words but deeds. In becoming man—assuming our flesh, our human state—God lives these words, these teachings. The Word becomes flesh. No man has ever been less of a hypocrite than Jesus of Nazareth. And because no man is alone, but is always constitutively related to God and to neighbor, the Word has also become *human society*. We cannot ignore the Church, or separate Catholic social teaching from the rest of theology.

The creation of ideal cities has a long history, going back at least to Plato. From the very beginning, it was clear that the outward city would mirror the interior city, and that disorder in the one would breed disorder in the other. Justice is the key to order. But it requires imagination to create a just society, and to build a culture of life in which the beauty of God's love shines through, in which every mother is supported, every child protected, every sick person helped, every stranger welcomed. This is creative justice.

Man is a microcosm, and a fallen, broken one at that. Our ideal city is a dream, a fantasy, until we see it arriving like an impossible resurrection. Plato and the others were right: the soul is the key. The ugly struggle for power, the lies and hypocrisy that are so common in the realm of Caesar, can only be defeated by an "inner struggle" like that of the hesychasts in the desert—though even monks rarely attain the social harmony of the earliest disciples (Acts 2:44–47).

Nothing is possible without prayer, but with God all things are indeed possible. A Christian society may seem a long way off, but that is a mistake: it exists already, in and among those who show mercy and kindness to those around them.

Appendix

E S S A Y S

Francis of Assisi

The original version of this article appeared in Resurgence 104 *(May/ June 1984), pp. 9–12. I include it here partly because Francis was the saint I associate with my conversion, and also because he demonstrates one way of trying to live according to the Gospel—a way that may be extreme, but can still be a source of inspiration to us.*[1]

In 1980, Blessed John Paul II declared Francis of Assisi the patron saint of ecology. Francis was the "raving lunatic" (Voltaire) whose linen drawers caught fire one night as he was sitting by the hearth, and who was so reluctant to harm "Brother Fire" that the blaze had to be extinguished against his will. When he washed his hands, he used to choose a place where the water would not have to be trampled underfoot. He would move worms, too, off the road in case anyone should tread on them, and put honey and the best wine out for the bees in the depths of winter. He instructed the friars not to cut down the whole tree when they went for firewood, so it could have hope of sprouting again.

So far, so good—crazy, but with a touch of nobility. But then we read that this same Francis scourged himself and rolled naked in snow or brambles to cure himself of lust, and fasted so much that his body finally gave out under the strain. He once addressed the devils who were keeping him awake in the following terms: "Devils! I command you on behalf of God almighty, use all the power given you by the Lord Jesus Christ to make my body suffer. I am ready to endure everything, for I have no greater enemy than my body; in this way you will avenge me on this adversary and enemy."

---

1. The sources for this article include Marion A. Habig (ed.), *St Francis of Assisi: Omnibus of Sources* (Chicago: Franciscan Herald Press, 1973); Arnaldo Fortini, *Francis of Assisi* (New York: Crossroad, 1981); André Vauchez, *Francis of Assisi: The Life and Afterlife of a Medieval Saint* (Yale University Press, 2012).

Does this not confirm an accusation often leveled against Christianity: that at its heart flourishes a sinister dualism, a masochistic hatred of everything that binds us to the earth? Even a saint who loved animals as Francis did, it seems, could not resist this sickness of Christianity, and was forced by his conditioning into despising his own flesh—the flesh that he nevertheless shared with the animals he loved. Francis, to this way of thinking, was a man divided, a living symbol of the ultimate failure of Christianity to acknowledge the unity and goodness of all creation. What follows is a rather different interpretation.

Mortification

In each of us there are two selves: the real and the illusory, the true and the false. One of these has to prevail at any given moment. The struggle is as old as Eden. The victor is that person whose self "has become the self of all beings," and who, "having renounced the fruit of action, attains perfect peace" (*Bhagavad Gita*).

Outside Christianity, the true self is known only by not-knowing. It is what manifests when the false self disappears, just as the light shines when a cloud blows away. What we *know*—or what we think we know—is that "idol" which is the false self; the true cannot be known, although its presence gleams through the lives and personalities of those we acknowledge as "wise" the world over. It was the coming of Christ that fully revealed the true self, the New Adam; those who open themselves to his grace find that he has fought and won the struggle for us.

To be "saved" we must renounce the "fruit of action," the mysterious fruit that was forbidden to Adam and Eve, and instead let God act through us, or become incarnate in us. Our artificial self, the Old Adam, must die, so that "I live, and yet no longer I but Christ lives in me" (Gal. 2:20). As St. Francis comments in his *Admonitions*: "A man eats of the tree that brings knowledge of good when he claims that his good will comes from himself alone and prides himself on the good that God says and does in him. And so . . . the fruit becomes for him the fruit that brings knowledge of evil."

Now obviously Francis had no horror of physical substance as such, or of human flesh. Indeed, his path to sainthood could be said to have begun when he faced and overcame his disgust at leprosy, forcing himself to kiss a leper in friendship. By so doing, he confronted biology at its most terrible, and was able to find God in the midst of it. "What had previously nauseated me," he said, "became a source of spiritual and physical consolation." This act of doing something his false self shrank away from was one of his first "mortifications," the practice of which he kept up all his life.

Another typical example was during a time of freezing wind: Francis became aware that he was afraid of the cold blowing through his thin habit, so he rushed to the top of the nearest hill and stripped naked, standing there until he had overcome his fear.

Francis' whole method involved discovering whatever the false self desired, and doing the exact opposite. It was this false self that that was his "adversary and enemy"—the self that is accreted together by thieving things that do not belong to it. His hatred was directed not at the cells or sinews or sensations of his body, but at the false will that misused them, and the sense of being separate from God. No wonder that those devils left Francis to sleep in peace, after being told to attack his body. They *could not* obey: they were being told to attack their own Master, Francis' false self.

As for the apparent contradiction involved in all mortification— trying to destroy our will by exerting it, or acting in order to renounce action—this dissolves when looked at more closely. Francis was not aiming to *save himself* by penance, only to signify his willingness to be saved. Like all "religious actions," this was a ritual performance, a kind of gesture made in acknowledgment of the invisible world, an invitation to God.

Truth comes when it chooses, but it would not be fitting for it to arrive without having been asked, so first of all it inspires us to ask. In something of the same spirit, a Zen monk who believes in instantaneous *satori* will sit for hours at a time in *zazen*, refusing to fall asleep or fidget. The Sufis have a saying: "The truth is not found by seeking; but only those who seek will find it."

Lady Poverty

Francis grew up in relative comfort. His father was one of the rising merchant class of Assisi, and named his son after France, the country where he did most of his trade. The boy learned the popular songs of the French troubadours, and as he got older could afford to lead the wild youth of Assisi in the latest fashions, spending his father's money on the pleasures of the body. Along with many of his friends, he fought against Perugia in a vicious local war, and was imprisoned for a time. After that, he set his sights on leaving the merchant class behind. He wanted to become a knight, a nobleman, to serve some fair lady by might and daring. He did not get very far. Riding off towards Apulia dressed as richly as could be, a generous impulse made him give most of his finery to a destitute knight he met on the road. And before long he was turned back by a dream to Assisi.

After a long period of self-questioning, it is said that a crucifix spoke to him in a ruined chapel. It told him to repair the church. Taking this rather literally, Francis rushed off and sold some of his father's precious fabrics without permission, bringing the money back to the local priest to help him repair the building. When his father, raging mad, came looking for him, Francis was hiding in a hole in the ground. He stayed there a solid month, afraid to come out. On going home, he was beaten severely and locked up in disgrace. It was his mother who finally let him out—his mother who had wanted to name him John, after John the Baptist, the Herald of the Great King.

Then came the dramatic gesture by which he ended his old life once and for all. In front of the whole town, which by this time had been thoroughly scandalized, and in front of the Bishop, to whom his father had appealed for justice in the matter of the stolen money, Francis tore off his clothes, renouncing everything he had from his human father. From that day on, Peter Bernadone would curse his son whenever he saw him pass by. A servant of the Bishop gave Francis a cast-off tunic, and he marched off into the woods, determined to repair old churches with his bare hands. He was singing as he went.

Francis had not given up his chivalrous romanticism,[2] nor his

2. See Mark of Whitstable, *Gospel Chivalry: Franciscan Romanticism* (Leominster: Gracewing, 2006).

desire to serve a great lady. He had merely transformed them. Some time before, he had started to think of Poverty as a person. He called her "the most beautiful woman in the world." In his eyes, she was the Bride of Christ. In his new life he wanted only to be found completely faithful to her. He would consistently refuse to touch money or property, and took the Gospel so literally that he would not even store up food for tomorrow. With those who followed him, he elevated begging for alms into a sacred ritual, a symbol of total dependence on the God of charity. It is in the context of this love for Lady Poverty that his enthusiasm for every kind of mortification can be understood.

Undoubtedly, he derived joy from his penances. There was nothing gloomy about them. As G.K. Chesterton wrote, "He devoured fasting as a man devours food." Of course, in his enthusiasm he tended to overdo it. He would often fall ill, and only then start to be gentler on himself. And yet once Brother Stephen was rebuked for cooking the friars too good a meal; and when on the next day he served only crusts of bread, he was met with Francis' wry remark, "Dear son, discretion is a noble virtue, nor shouldst thou always fulfill all that thy superior biddest thee, especially when he is troubled by any passion."

To his companions—the embryonic Franciscan order—Francis showed more discretion than he did to himself. He threw away their hair shirts and the painful metal hoops that some of them had started to wear. If he noticed any of them going around with long, hungry faces he would advise them to eat a proper meal, and to pray for their joy to be restored. Awareness of the presence of God always drives out depression. They should be happy, not "gloomy and depressed like hypocrites." He told them once: "If, in the matter of eating and drinking we are obliged to deny ourselves those superfluous things which are harmful to the body and the soul [note that it was not his intention to damage the body], we must forego even more so excessive mortifications, for God desires loving kindness and not sacrifice."

Perhaps the greatest temptation Francis had to face came from his very devotion to Lady Poverty. In 1210 he obtained the first papal approval for his way of life, and permission to preach without being a priest. His followers became an Order within the Church (although the Rule was not finalized until 1223). This is where the subtle Serpent raised his head. Francis had fallen into the feeling that this was "his" Order. After all, he had started it, and was at the center of it. It revolved around him. Only after a long struggle could he renounce all desire to lead except by example, give up the exercise of power completely, and hand the movement over to the Holy Spirit, the "true Minister General of the Order," and to the Church. It was at that time that he had several prophetic visions, and knew that the days of strict poverty were coming to an end. He knew he could not impose his Lady on those who came after.

As he lay dying, his words showed that he was at last at peace with himself. "I have done what was mine to do: may Christ teach you what you are to do."

The Franciscan Movement

Meister Eckhart (admittedly a Dominican, not a Franciscan) calls detachment the "greatest and best virtue," by which we can "by grace become what God is by nature." Detachment starts with the realization that any desire to know *who I am* is just another ploy of the false self, the Old Adam. Any self that I am capable of knowing—of turning into an object of my own consciousness—cannot possibly be me. That self, the true me, can be known only by and in God. Therefore our role is not to *know* but to *be* ourselves. We must be content to say with Francis, "What a man is before God, that he is and nothing more."

Detachment in this sense is the inner dimension of Franciscanism. Whatever compromises have taken place under the pressure of history and society, and with the end of begging from door to door, the relationship with Lady Poverty will remain secure for those who are not attached to any image of themselves. This is the path of humility. Anyone who is fully detached in this way is pure in heart, poor in spirit, meek—a "peacemaker," too, because he or she no longer participates in the game of self and other, friend and enemy, so necessary for those who think they have something to defend.

By detaching him from all things, including himself, Lady Poverty freed Francis to look for the good in everything and everyone

198

he met. Without a "self" to worry about, he could not be concerned about possible personal advantages and disadvantages, and consequently he was able to respond to things as they really were. Through "Brother Sun" he saw the Light of Life; through "Sister Water" he saw the baptism of rebirth; in a lamb on its way to market he saw the Lamb of God; through wood the Tree of the Cross. The Book of Nature reflected the Book of Scripture, and in both he read only a single Word, the divine Logos.

The ability to make a lasting peace depends on the ability to see and address the good on both sides. Against the advice of the townsfolk of Gubbio, Francis went to speak to a wolf (some say a local bandit) that was preying on them and their flocks. He told it that if it would stop doing this the people would no longer hunt it, and that because he recognized its need to eat he would persuade the townsfolk to lay out food on a regular basis. The wolf shook hands on the bargain, and for the rest of its natural life came and went freely in the town without incident. Eventually the people buried it affectionately under their church.

In Trevi, where Francis was trying to preach, a noisy ass got loose in the square and nobody could catch it. Francis said to it, "Brother Ass, please be quiet and allow me to preach to the people." When it did so, immediately standing perfectly silent, everyone was amazed, and "fearing that the people might take too much notice of this astonishing miracle," Francis "began saying funny things to make them laugh."

In both cases, what made a miracle possible was the fact that the saint cut through the ordinary way of looking at the world, and instead of treating the animal like a dumb beast addressed it as it existed in the presence of God. He was dealing, not with some fragment of the world outside himself, but with a particular aspect of the wholeness reflected in his own heart. He spoke as though the animal could understand him, because he was really speaking to God, through one of the innumerable types or forms of beauty and goodness that subsist in the Maker of All.

All things are equally intelligent in God: flocks of birds and crowds of people listened to Francis' sermons with the same attentiveness, responding not to the words as much as to the intention of spirit which animated them. Of course, it did not always come off. People tend to be entrenched in their habits and unprepared to give them up long enough to pay attention to a funny little man speaking in the town square. And there is at least one story of Francis turning aside to preach to a flock of birds, who flew off when they saw him approaching. "Then he came back and began to accuse himself most bitterly, saying: 'What effrontery you have, you impudent son of Peter Bernadone'—and this because he had expected irrational creatures to obey him as if he, and not God, were their Creator." For a moment, he had become attached to the image of himself that others saw and projected onto him—that of "the saint who speaks to animals." But birds are hard to fool. Only God can hold their attention; never the false self, the thief of Eden.

A Christian Society

Francis rapidly became the most universally popular of Christian saints, canonized only two years after his death. He is the patron saint of Italy as well as of ecology. There are three main Franciscan Orders in the Church: one for men, one for women, and one for men and women remaining "in the world." The women's branch was founded by one of Francis' most devoted disciples, Clare of Assisi who in 1212 ran away from her aristocratic family to join his band of brothers. The family reacted violently, but Francis protected her, welcomed her into the religious life, and established a community for her and her sisters at San Damiano. She was always the most faithful of his followers when it came to the rule of poverty, refusing to let the pope mitigate it in any way. ("Holy Father, release me from my sins, but not from the vow to follow our Lord Jesus Christ.")

According to one biographer (Fortini), the idea of a Third or "Secular" Order began to germinate on the very occasion I described in which Francis quieted the birds. Villagers who had listened to his sermon came and asked how they could participate, how they might dedicate themselves en masse to his movement. But it was not until 1221 that a way was found for this to happen—when the merchant Lucchesio and his wife asked to join Francis, without being forced to separate from each other. As soon as the Third Order had been established with its own Rule, it spread rapidly throughout Italy and beyond. And it transformed medieval society by helping to bring feudalism to an end. The Rule forbade the bearing of arms or the swearing of oaths of fealty, on which the almost perpetual warfare between feuding city states all over Italy depended. That very year (1221), tertiaries in Faenza refused to take up arms for the Emperor, and the pope upheld their right not to go to war if they had chosen peace. Whole villages and towns all over Italy now claimed the same right.

St. Francis also wanted to solve a much greater conflict. In 1219 he voyaged to the Nile (the front line in the Fifth Crusade) to persuade the warring sides to cease fighting. Unsuccessful in his preaching to the Christians, he took advantage of a truce to walk across to the opposite camp and ask for an audience with Sultan Malik Al-Kamil, the nephew of Saladin, the conqueror of Jerusalem.

The sultan may have recognized in Francis a spirit like that of the Muslim mystics and holy men called Sufis, with whom he was himself associated. At any rate, he seems to have greeted him warmly, and listened politely to his exhortations to convert to Christianity. His advisers declined the challenge Francis threw down to walk with him into the fire to see whose God would save them. Francis was given gifts and sent on his way. But later the sultan gave most of Jerusalem back to the Christians and, later still, it was the Franciscans who were entrusted with care of the Holy Places.

Biographer André Vauchez thinks Francis was as much influenced by his conversations with the Muslims as they were by him, or more so. His last written words on the subject, in the Rule of 1221, suggest he had moved away from a simple desire to provoke martyrdom, and so perhaps win converts through his death (if that had originally been his intent). He asked his friars to act with discretion and humility, not seeking doctrinal confrontations that would lead to violence—in other words, not attacking Mohammed or deliberately seeking martyrdom, but "being subject to every human creature" and serving them, whether Muslim or not.

This is, in a sense, a very "modern" approach, closer to that of Mother Teresa than one might have expected of a medieval saint. Francis seems also to have been impressed by the regular call to prayer in the Muslim camp, as well as by the courtesy with which he was treated and perhaps the great respect given to the name of God by devout Muslims. He stands, then, as a reminder that evangelization begins with service and humble charity towards every human being. We are all in search of the beautiful face of God. Only that beauty, dimly reflected in our own lives, will have the power to draw people closer to Christ.

Despite the enormous impact the Franciscan movement continued to have at every level of society, from peasants to kings (Louis IX), poets (Dante), scientists (Grosseteste), and artists (Giotto), the betrayal of Francis' ideal of poverty came swiftly, with the Rule progressively softened and the head of the Order, Brother Elias, conspiring with the pope to build a vast basilica in Francis' honor. But such things are only to be expected. The inspiration to live a Gospel life (and it has to be admitted that Francis' reading of the Gospels was rather selective) is hard to sustain. The energy derived from doing so flows into other cultural channels. Civilization itself depends on such energy, periodically renewed, and the Italian Renaissance can be said to have had in large part a Franciscan inspiration.

Other betrayals followed—some of them far-reaching indeed. The "Spiritual Franciscans" reacted to what they saw as the growing laxity in the Order by reviving the ideal of strict poverty, and many were influenced by the writings of Joachim of Fiore (d. 1202) to see Francis as the herald of a Third Age of the Spirit (after the ages of the Father and the Son). In this new era of peace and freedom, the Church herself would no longer be necessary, for God would rule directly in men's hearts. Though the Spirituals were suppressed, their influence and that of Joachim can be seen in the Reformation, in the philosophies of Marx and Hegel, and even in the New Age movement of the twentieth century. The Age of Science, too (foreseen by Friar Bacon, who died in 1294) owed much to the new attention the Franciscans were paying to the natural world, while the philosophical ideas of Duns Scotus and William of Ockham (both Franciscans) contributed to the breakdown of medieval realism, with a growing emphasis on the individual and the supremacy of will over intellect.

If there is any truth to this summary, the impact of St. Francis on modern society has been immense, if confusingly complex. We never know how our actions will affect the future—how they will be interpreted, and what will come of them. All we can do is live in the moment we have been given, faithful to the Spirit. Nothing else is our concern. What we see in the case of Francis—the enormous spiritual and cultural energy released into the world by someone who tried to live by the Gospel—should also teach us that the status quo is more vulnerable than we ever believed, more fragile than its palaces and boardrooms would have us think.

In truth the whole of this fragile world and its history has already been taken over from within and reshaped by a force and a life infinitely more powerful even than Francis, or all the saints combined. Francis' master, Jesus Christ, has absorbed that world, and imprinted on that history the pattern of his own life, death, and resurrection. In that great story, still unfolding, Francis has done what was his to do; may Christ teach us our part.

Gay Unions and Marriage

In many parts of the world, matters of sexual preference and expression are increasingly regarded as on a par with any other right to choose. The social and political pressure to abolish the distinct privileges of the traditional married couple, or to extend them to same-sex couples, has become intense. Many nations and states have by now not only made provision for the legal recognition of same-sex unions, but (more seriously from a Catholic point of view) have redefined marriage in order to be able to apply the term also to gay unions. This essay should be read in conjunction with 'The Mystery of Gender', above.

Marriage is a reproductive covenant for the procreation and education of children. If that Catholic teaching is true and valid, it requires lifelong celibacy of all those who are *not* called to marriage, including all those who happen never to find a suitable mate for whatever reason.[1] (Of course, this assumes the falsity of the post-Freudian dogma that genital activity is an essential part of human health and happiness.)

Conceiving from Within

It may be objected that the new technologies available to assist reproduction might open an era in which gay marriage itself could become a kind of "reproductive covenant," at least for those gay couples that want to have children. But it makes a crucial difference if the child is not conceived from within the act itself.

We should consider this in terms of the impact of the problem on the bias of researchers, evidence of the effects on children of being brought up by gay parents is often unreliable. In any case, to the extent gay marriage is a new phenomenon, proper sociological

---

1. It might seem that my description of marriage disqualifies naturally infertile couples, as indeed it would if that condition were known for certain beforehand. Impotence was traditionally regarded as an impediment to marriage, for example. If a couple had married with good intentions but only later discovered their inability to have children, the Church would judge the marriage in the light of the intention, no doubt—though I suspect this might be accepted as grounds for an annulment.

studies of its results will not be available for several generations. But we already know that a child's sense of its own identity is largely formed in relation to the parents, both by example and through education. Some have spoken of an "ontological wound" reported by children of divorced parents.[2] A similar wound may be suffered by those orphaned when they were very young, or brought up by two mothers or two fathers.

The added dangers in the latter case include the fact that not only is the child deprived of something concrete (a mother or a father),[3] but another and untried model of child-rearing and of living intimately together has been imposed upon it. It may be difficult for the child subsequently to admit any problems or difficulty with this experience, not for "political" reasons but because to do so would offend and hurt those who love and care for it. Just as the child of divorce may be forced to take sides, or find its identity divided between the parents, so the child of a same-sex union may find itself playing the role of "mirror" in which the two parents seek to contemplate themselves. The child is not (in its origin) a living communion of the two with the Holy Spirit in one flesh, but has been co-opted to play that role—a burden that may prove to be too great to bear.

But the deepest reasons why gay "marriage" is impossible are to do with the nature of marriage itself. At the level of feelings there may indeed be a profound bond between two people of the same sex. But a friendship, however deep and intense, is not the same as a marriage.[4] Feelings obviously have a place in marriage, but as an institution and as a sacrament it does not depend upon them.

2. Andrew Root, *The Children of Divorce: The Loss of Family as the Loss of Being* (Ada, MI: Baker Academic, 2010).

3. This is more significant than it may appear, since man and woman are both made in the image of God, but as father and mother reveal different and complementary aspects of the divine image to the child. A child deprived of either or both is at a disadvantage in terms of developing his knowledge of God at a formative age—which is not to say that the deficit cannot in some ways be compensated for.

4. One view is that homosexuality represents a confusion of the intimacy of friendship with the erotic desire to merge physically with another—which can only be done in reality by conceiving a child, since any other form of merging would involve the destruction of the other person.

Marriage brings into existence a new reality: a unity composed of two people and potentially their child(ren)—a whole greater than the sum of its parts. This ontological union, once freely entered upon in full consciousness by two baptized Christians (who by virtue of their baptism are each members of Christ's "mystical" body), is so strong that it is indissoluble except by physical death.[5]

There seem to be several essential conditions to bring about this ontological union. One is the intention of the couple to create just such a union, which they express in the words of the marriage vow. Another is the fact that each member of the couple is a baptized Christian (not necessarily a Catholic). A third is that the couple consists of a man and a woman. Finally the marriage must be consummated—or these three conditions ratified—by sexual intercourse, since in no other way can it be open to offspring.[6] How are these conditions inter-related?

Marriage and the Trinity

The "giving of the word" in a marriage vow, which is in essence the conscious *giving of the self*, each to each, is the decisive intentional act that establishes the basis for a marriage. It is this intention that seals the analogy between the human and the divine. In God, too, a Word is given. Marriage is an image both of the Trinity as a communion of equal persons, and of the Church as the union between God and man. This resemblance or analogy that exists

---

5. It can, of course, be annulled; but this merely constitutes recognition by the Church that the marriage never really existed, owing to the incomplete intention of one or other partner or the failure to consummate. It is worth noting that such an indissoluble union could not conceivably be brought about simply by an agreement between two consenting adults; that is, by legal contract alone. A mere contract, as distinct from the stronger form of personal union sometimes signified by the word "covenant," can always be dissolved. In fact it is highly unlikely that most of those currently campaigning for same-sex "marriage" want such unions to be *indissoluble* in that sense. But without indissolubility at least in principle, there is no "marriage" in the full sense understood by Catholics. The Orthodox tradition also regards marriage as indissoluble in principle, and divorce as a sin, though it allows more scope for the recognition of failure in marriage and the possibility of remarriage in some cases, even if second marriages are a concession.

6. Except in the exceptional case of the Blessed Virgin Mary and her spouse Joseph, where the single offspring was conceived miraculously.

between marriage, the hypostatic union in Christ, and the divine Trinity in heaven "connects" the married couple with God in a particular way, making them a living icon of the Trinity.

However, the image is only complete if the couple is already baptized. Baptism means that Christ dwells within a person, through the Holy Spirit. This is a more intense form of presence than the universal presence of the Creator within the creature. Before being baptized, God is within me, and I may pray to him there; but after baptism I am also within God. Baptism initiates me (even before I fully realize it) into the mystery of the Incarnation, into the "within" of God, so that the life of God as man is being lived through me; my life is that of the Son. The within of God is the Trinity.

Thus for the married couple who are baptized, marital union becomes part of this living out of the Incarnation, and specifically the union of Christ with his Church (the extension of the Incarnation into communion with others). There may even be an implication that the Church recognizes that without being joined to Christ by baptism, a human being is probably incapable of the fullest kind of self-gift—or, at least, that it should not be expected of him. (Nevertheless, the teaching on marriage is offered to mankind in general, at least as an ideal.)

In sexual intercourse the couple forms a biological unit. The whole is greater than its parts: literally so in the case of a union that results in the conception of new life. The biological incompleteness of each sex on its own, such that it can only fulfill this aspect of its nature by merging with the other, specifically excludes marriage between two persons of the same sex. In the act of procreation, and in no other act, two individuals *function as a single principle*, because it takes an act performed by both of them to give rise to a new human life. Their union is more than a felt or imagined union of two consciousnesses or of two sets of feelings into an ecstasy of sensation; it is an objective union of two embodied persons in a unity that transcends the couple.[7]

---

7. I have touched on this already. For more, see Anthony Fisher in the context of a related debate, "HIV and Condoms within Marriage: *Communio*, 36:2 (Summer 2009), especially pp. 341–7. Bishop Fisher argues that homosexual intercourse is "not a reproductive type of act" capable of making them "an organic unit."

The Battle for Marriage

At the time of writing, the battle for and against same-sex "marriage" is still raging, with millions in France demonstrating against the proposed changes in law that would permit same-sex couples to define their union as "marriage." Part of the concern here is not the question of gay sexuality as such. It is clear enough that according to Catholic teaching homosexual inclinations are intrinsically disordered, but nevertheless not culpable unless encouraged and indulged. Instead, as Plato shows in the *Symposium*, 211c, they can and should be sublimated and transformed in the search for a beauty that transcends the physical and sensual.[8] The more urgent problem is that such a change in the law would lead to changes in the definition of marriage for heterosexual couples—perhaps even eliminating the concepts of consummation, or of adultery, since these cannot easily be defined in a homosexual context. In fact, of course, with the admission of no-fault divorce and other changes in marriage law in the past century, the civil concept of marriage and the Catholic concept of sacrament have already long since parted ways.

The compromise most likely to emerge involves a complete separation of civil from sacramental marriage, opening the former to gay couples (and eventually perhaps other groups who may demand to be included), but reserving a term such as "matrimony" for the sacramental marriage, to signify the inclusion of components that Catholics would regard as essential, such as indissolubility, exclusivity, sexual difference, and openness to conception. But the effect of such a compromise on society at large might neverthe-

---

8. In *Love and Responsibility* (Boston: Pauline, 2013), though he does not speak of homosexuality as such, Karol Wojtyla writes that "the sexual drive in man is a fact that should be acknowledged and affirmed by him as a source of natural energy" (p. 269). He speaks of "supra-material energies" (p. 272), transformed by the attainment of the human vocation to love, and the mastery of these energies to create an authentic interior freedom. Our desires are in fact infinite, because they were made for God. It is not surprising they go on the rampage when God is removed from view. We must integrate the sensual desire for the body within an appreciation and love of the whole person, since sensual desire tends precisely to focus on the physical dimension to the exclusion of all else. Ultimately we must fix our desires on their proper object, which is the beauty of God, and in that way lead each other to heaven.

less be catastrophic. Anglican theologian John Milbank has even suggested that the movement to open marriage to gay couples has nothing to do with LGBT rights or the widespread demand for equality before the law. Rather, it represents a step in the drive by the State and the Market to take control over human reproduction for political and economic reasons—a step towards technocracy:

> We are not talking about natural justice, but about the desire of biopolitical tyranny to destroy marriage and the family as the most basic and crucial mediating social institution.
>
> It is for this reason that practices of surrogate motherhood and sperm-donation (as distinct from the artificial assistance of a personal sexual union) should be rejected. For the biopolitical rupture which they invite is revealed by the irresolvable impasse to which they give rise. Increasingly, children resulting from anonymous artificial insemination are rightly demanding to know who their natural parents are, for they know that, in part, we indeed *are* our biology. But this request is in principle intolerable for donors who gave their sperm or wombs on the understanding that this was an anonymous donation for public benefit.
>
> The price for this severance is surely the commodification of birth by the market, the quasi-eugenic control of reproduction by the state, and the corruption of the parent-child relation to one of a narcissistic self-projection.
>
> Once the above practices have been rejected, then it follows that a gay relationship cannot qualify as a marriage in terms of its orientation to having children, because the link between an interpersonal and a natural act is entirely crucial to the definition and character of marriage.[9]

It does seem that the war against "bio-political tyranny" in the case of marriage was lost some time ago, with the acceptance of divorce and contraception, and that the legal acceptance or promulgation of same-sex unions is simply an inevitable consequence that has somehow caught Catholics and other "conservative" groups by surprise.

9. John Milbank, "The Impossibility of Gay Marriage and the Threat of Biopolitical Control," *ABC Religion and Ethics*, April 23, 2013 (www.abc.net.au).

Beyond Catholic Neoconservatism

When it first appeared, several Catholic Neoconservative writers in America saw Pope John Paul II's Centesimus Annus—*published to mark the end of a century from* Rerum Novarum—*as a clear endorsement of the dominant American free-market or liberal approach to economics. In 1994 the present author was (along with representatives of a number of journals from* Communio *to the* New Oxford Review*) one of the signatories of a manifesto called "Towards a Civilization of Love" which criticized this Neoconservative interpretation of the encyclical, calling attention to the fact that the pope had gone so far as to question the "models of production and consumption" in present-day economic theory, and even "the established structures of power which today govern societies" (n. 58). In no way, it seemed to our group, was the document a simple rubber stamp for American-style capitalism. The following brief essay looks back on this debate from the early days of the pontificate of Pope Francis.*

While the Church's magisterium is careful not to offer us any model economic system, it encourages members of the Church, especially the lay faithful who are most fully engaged in economic society, to develop such models by applying the principles of Catholic social teaching to their own concrete historical and personal circumstances, drawing on their experience and expertise. This is where more work is urgently needed, not least to prevent Catholics from being swept away by the ideologies which dominate in this field, and which may lead us to fail to recognize the cultural and moral logic of the economic system itself.

The argument between the Neocons and "Paleocons" has never been formally resolved.[1] Neocons draw comfort from the fact that that John Paul II did endorse the market economy. Nevertheless, he

---

1. It still bubbles under the surface, even though a neoconservative writer such as Michael Novak is capable of writing in language borrowed from the *Communio* school, as in the first part of this quotation: "For Catholics, all social energy flows

also writes about the "limits of the market" and the need for economic and political freedom to be circumscribed by a "strong juridical framework" (nn. 34, 40, 42, 39). A market in which goods are exchanged is only "free" within certain limits. Those limits reflect the moral-anthropological assumptions of the lawmakers. But such constraints, whether ethical or cultural, are not imposed from "outside" the market. *The market itself is a juridical framework, standing on certain moral and anthropological assumptions.* It is a kind of game, though a serious one, and every game is constituted by the rules that define what it means to play—in this case what counts as property, fair exchange, and so on. As the British writer John Gray puts it:

> The forms of property, and of contractual liberty, which go to make up the market are themselves legal artifacts, human constructs that human design may amend or reform. The idea, common among latter-day liberals, of the market as a spontaneous order may be illuminating in so far as it generates insight into the ways in which unplanned market exchanges may coordinate human activities better than any plan; but it is profoundly misleading if it suggests that the institutional framework of the market process is given to us as a natural fact, or can be deduced from any simple theory. There will, in fact, be considerable variation, across countries and over time, in the forms of property, the varieties and limits of contractual liberty and the kinds of competition which the institutions of the market encompass. The view of the market that is to be rejected, accordingly, is that (common in the United States) which theorizes its institutions as flowing from some underlying structure of rights.[2]

For Gray (who is not a Catholic), both market institutions and human rights are social or cultural artifacts, justifiable mainly in terms of the human well-being they promote. This is surely not far

from the inner life of the Trinity. Everything is gift. We signal our gratitude by developing our own talents to the full, by becoming free, responsible, initiative-showing, creative agents of a better world. . . ."—in Finn (ed.), *The Moral Dynamics of Economic Life*, p. 34. Signaling our gratitude to God by becoming an entrepreneur is not, however, quite what Pope Benedict meant by integrating the "spirit of gratuity" into the market.

2. J. Gray, *Beyond the New Right: Markets, Government and the Common Environment* (London and New York: Routledge, 1993), p. 83.

from the pope's view. An economy does not exist at all except as a set of patterns and customs of behavior: i.e., as the material aspect of a moral-cultural system. Economic activity—like political activity—is a subset of cultural activity. It has a moral structure, as well as requiring certain standards of human behavior in order to function harmoniously. This structure will either be compatible with Christianity or not. If it is not, Christians may be obliged to push for a more radical change in the economic system than, say, a few restrictions on pornography, arms sales, or the accumulation of wealth at the expense of the poor.

The Cult of Consumerism

In *Centesimus Annus* John Paul II managed to speak of economic freedom and creativity without ever endorsing the modern cult of economic growth—the commitment to a continual increase in GNP or GDP.[3] It is implied that we should be aiming at stability and long-term sustainability (within a context of global solidarity), rather than the mere multiplication of financial transactions within an economy. When the "creation of wealth" is defined solely in terms of increasing production and consumption, society will be driven inevitably towards consumerist attitudes that are condemned by the encyclical in the strongest terms (nn. 36, 41).

A leading Catholic neoconservative, Michael Novak, building upon and adapting the insights of Max Weber and others, often speaks of "three fundamental orders of liberty"—political, economic, and cultural—that need to be carefully distinguished. Socialism, he writes, is "a moral, economic and political system all in one. But capitalism is the name only of an economic system which, for its full and free development, requires a democratic polity and a humanistic and pluralist culture."[4] The combination of democracy,

3. There is, fortunately, growing pressure to incorporate in the calculation natural as well as other forms of capital. Britain, for example, is committed since the 2012 Rio Conference to produce "Green accounts" by 2020. Recognition of the depreciation of natural assets leads to a much more realistic estimate of growth. How to measure environmental costs or offset them remains problematic.

4. M. Novak, *The Catholic Ethic and the Spirit of Capitalism* (New York: The Free Press, 1993), p. 147. Novak's "three orders of liberty" bears a striking resemblance to Rudolf Steiner's "threefold structuring of the social organism," a theory

capitalism, *and* religious freedom is the only viable "third way" between capitalism and socialism,[5] while the confusion of the three systems—moral-cultural, economic, and political—Novak argues, will inevitably lead (and did lead under state socialism) to both injustice and stagnation.

The economic system *per se*, therefore, according to Novak, is morally neutral, and certainly religiously neutral. Of course, "important ethical assumptions are built into the free economy."[6] These "moral skills" or praiseworthy habits include initiative, enterprise, and public spiritedness.[7] (He might have added trustworthiness, among others.) The economic system presupposes such virtues, but they have little to do with its inherent structure or design: they simply enable it to function correctly, as a machine needs oil or fuel.

It has to be said at this point that the *non*-neutrality of the economic system is not always clear either in *Centesimus Annus* or in the later encyclical of Pope Benedict, *Caritas in Veritate*. In the later document, for example, Benedict says in one paragraph (part of n.36) that the economy is an instrument that can be used badly or well, depending on the motivations of those at the helm. That sounds a bit like Novak. But to pull those words out of context would be a mistake. In the very next paragraph he adds that "the economic sphere is neither ethically neutral, nor inherently inhuman and opposed to society. It is part and parcel of human activity and precisely because it is human, it must be structured and governed in an ethical manner"—that is, *structured* as well as governed,

---

the Anthroposophists developed after 1917 and which led to the creation of a "League for Social Threefolding" in Germany between the wars. Here also the fundamental idea was that the correct functioning of society depended on the autonomy of the economic, political, and spiritual (or cultural) spheres of society, correlated with the three principles so dear to the French Revolutionaries: Equality, Fraternity, and Liberty. Later commentators, such as Charles Waterman in England, stressed the inseparable interweaving of the three elements based on the unity of human nature underlying all economic, political, and cultural activity. But the idea of a "free market" appears to require the separation of the economic sphere from the others.

5. Ibid., p. 147.
6. Ibid., p. 113.
7. Ibid., pp. 232–5.

so that fraternity can find its place "within normal economic activity," and not just as an add-on or beneficent gesture.

From Bourgeois to Imbecile

I remain convinced that Novak and his colleagues cannot be right, for every culture has at its heart a conception of what it means to be human, and this shapes our activity in every field. He himself assumes this, as we can see in his classic work *The Spirit of Democratic Capitalism*, where he writes that the Founding Fathers of the United States "chose as their model citizen, for whom the system was designed, neither the saint nor the preacher, neither the hero of war nor the aristocrat, neither the poet nor the philosopher, neither the king nor the peasant, but the free man of property and commerce."[8] Of course, not all economic and political systems are consciously "designed," but each does suit one set of human types more than another, and thus exerts a subtle pressure on others to conform to it—in this case the *bourgeois* type, which sooner or later degenerates into the *consumer*, or even into what Georges Bernanos called the *"imbecile,"* the post-Christian who lives on the surface of his own being, and eventually prefers killing to thinking.[9]

Neoconservatives, I imagine, also find it hard to criticize consumerism, since on what else can economic growth and "wealth creation" depend? But consumerism implies the construction of a false self, based on enjoyment and desire.

> The construction of the self as a consumer implies the removal of ends which are held to be objectively more desirable than others. The individual consumer is to choose his or her own ends; desire itself is therefore the only proper end, the only thing which is

---

8. M. Novak, *The Spirit of Democratic Capitalism* (New York: Simon & Schuster, 1982), p. 343.

9. See Hans Urs von Balthasar, *Bernanos: An Ecclesial Existence* (San Francisco: Ignatius Press, 1996), pp. 358–68. The term "imbecile, which he calls "a new form of poverty," is discussed by David L. Schindler in "The Meaning of the Human in a Technological Age: *Homo Faber, Homo Sapiens, Homo Amans*," in *Communio* 26:1 (Spring, 1999), pp. 82–4. The imbecile may be an expert, but he is only half-cultured and shallow; for him knowledge is power. His logic can be shattered only by the childlike spirit of the Beatitudes (pp. 84–97).

inherently good. We are told to buy to keep the economy moving; what we buy makes no difference. The goal is not the promotion of the good, but only the making of profit. Dissociated from ends, consumption becomes a sheer arbitrary movement of the will. Where there are no true ends to move the will, the movement of the will is determined by power, that power which is most pervasive and most able to dominate the channels of persuasion.... The experience of coercion in a free market is not primarily a matter of too few choices, therefore, but the fact that what one chooses doesn't matter. There are, as Bruce Springsteen sings, "57 Channels and Nothin' On."[10]

There are two main conceptions of morality: one is based on what it is good to *be*, and the other on what it is good to *do*. The first path leads to natural law and virtue ethics, the other to the glorification of the human will (voluntarism and pelagianism). The separation of the "three liberties" flows from the latter conception, because they define three main fields of human choice and action— what we *do*—whereas in each of these fields we are striving to *be* only one thing, namely (in religious terms) "holy." Moral restraint will always come too late and exert an inadequate influence, if in both the political and the economic realms the value of the *act of choice* (exercised by voting or paying) has been elevated above the value of what may or may not be available for the choosing. (The result of this is that I am thought to be freer the more varieties of baked beans or sugary drinks are sitting on the supermarket shelves, and the more money I have in my pocket to pay for them.)

Transformation through Love

The main flaw in Neoconservatism seems to me this. Christianity is concerned with *inner transformation*, and therefore it affects all

10. William T. Cavanaugh, "Coercion in Augustine and Disney," *New Blackfriars*, June 1999, pp. 283–90. And, we might add, the world of consumerism comes increasingly to resemble a giant hotel, from which, as the Eagles sing in *Hotel California*, "you can check out, but you can never *leave*." For an analysis of consumerism see Zygmunt Bauman, *Consuming Life* (Cambridge: Polity Press, 2007). For Bauman, a consumer society is one in which consumers themselves are turned into commodities. One might also say it is one in which the interior life is drowned and dissolved in a sea of distraction.

human activities—including political and economic ones—from within.[11] It cannot simply accept an existing structure and add to this a Christian nuance or intention. The structure must be refashioned in accordance with the truth about human beings and their destiny. Christianity reveals that our nature fulfills itself only in self-giving love. If this is true, it affects the goals and methods of economics, and we must be able to envisage a "sane economy" that is just as concerned with quality as it is with quantity.[12]

Thus economic values in the market should be determined not simply by what happens to be desired, but what leads to our true end. In fact, every economy is not only a "cultural economy," but also an "ethical economy," the expression of an *ethos*.[13] And ethos is ultimately a matter of *telos*. Morality is rooted in anthropology, in what we are as human beings: our goal and calling. Detached from this anthropology, both Market and State easily become expressions of the "culture of death."

At the time of writing Pope Francis is only at the beginning of his papacy, but each of his major statements to date, including both interviews and documents such as *Evangelii Gaudium* (2013), have had a bearing on social questions quite at odds with the views of the neoconservatives. What we hope for now is a genuinely creative new direction.

11. David L. Schindler, "The Anthropological Vision of *Caritas in Veritate* in Light of Economic and Cultural Life in the United States," in *Communio* 57:4 (Winter 2010), p. 564.

12. D. Stephen Long blames a great deal on Weber's introduction of the Enlightenment's "fact-value" distinction into economics, coupled with the translation of liberty into mere formal ability to choose. For many "dominant" social thinkers (among whom he includes Novak), the "free market is based on fact," and "theology provides values that help it operate freely," where the ultimate "value" is simply freedom itself. D.S. Long, *Divine Economy: Theology and the Market* (London and New York: Routledge, 2000), p. 19.

13. In his Letter to the British Prime Minister on the eve of the G8 summit, June 17, 2013, Pope Francis put this very clearly: "the present global crisis shows that ethics is not something external to the economy, but is an integral and unavoidable element of economic thought and action."

The Joy of the Gospel

Before this book went to press, Pope Francis published his first major "solo" document, laying out a vision for his pontificate: the Apostolic Exhortation Evangelii Gaudium *(EG). In this remarkable document, evangelization, spirituality, and Catholic social doctrine are fully integrated.*

EG begins with a call to joy through a renewed encounter with the risen Lord. It includes a reiteration of John Paul's appeal for help in transforming the papacy itself in *Ut Unum Sint* (n. 96)—a "conversion of the papacy" and of the "central structures of the universal Church," all of which "need to hear the call to pastoral conversion" (*EG*, n. 32). He clarifies many of the remarks he made in interviews soon after his election, which had been widely misinterpreted. Sections 34 to 39 are particularly helpful, where he speaks of the "hierarchy of truths" (citing St. Thomas Aquinas and Vatican II) and the priority of the virtue of mercy.

The pope also points out that theology, doctrine, and pastoral practice (and the way they are expressed) continue to develop. "For those who long for a monolithic body of doctrine guarded by all and leaving no room for nuance, this might appear as undesirable and leading to confusion. But in fact such variety serves to bring out and develop different facets of the inexhaustible riches of the Gospel" (nn. 40–41).

In this summary of some of the main points of the Exhortation, without claiming to mention every element of importance, I will touch on those with the most direct bearing on the themes of the present book.

Social Teaching

A number of paragraphs are devoted to economic, social, and political issues. This is not a social encyclical (see n. 184) and therefore the treatment must be somewhat cursory, but the basic outlines are clear. Francis condemns the "throw-away culture," a culture of exclusion, and the idea that wealth will "trickle down" to the poor from the rich (it sometimes does, but hardly enough), the idolatry of money, the obsession with consumption, the accumulation of debt, and the spread of corruption, calling for a financial reform based on a firm grasp of ethics (nn. 53–59). "We can no longer trust in the unseen forces and the invisible hand of the market. Growth in justice requires more than economic growth, while presupposing such growth: it requires decisions, programs, mechanisms, and processes specifically geared to a better distribution of income, the creation of sources of employment and an integral promotion of the poor which goes beyond a simple welfare mentality" (n. 204).

He points out that inequality and unbridled consumerism corrode the social fabric and lead to violence (nn. 59–60). The hope for peace lies in the human heart unified by the Holy Spirit: "If hearts are shattered in thousands of pieces, it is not easy to create authentic peace in society" (n. 229).[1]

He speaks of the way ideas and ideologies mask and distort reality (n. 231–33). Connected with this is the importance of the local and the small (n. 235)—Francis elevates the polyhedron over the sphere, because the sphere implies an erosion of differences, each point on the surface being equidistant from the center, whereas the polyhedron preserves the distinctiveness of many social, cultural, and economic elements, represented by the different facets into which the surface is divided (n. 236).

In another section he speaks of our role in the defense of unborn human life (n. 213–214)—"a human being is always sacred and inviolable, in any situation and at every stage of development"—and as custodians of nature (n. 215). With regard to the latter, he writes, "Thanks to our bodies, God has joined us so closely to the world around us that we can feel the desertification of the soil almost as a physical ailment, and the extinction of a species as a painful disfig-

---

1. In a subsequent document, which I will not summarize here (*Message for the World Day of Peace 2014*), Pope Francis develops the notion of "fraternity" as a foundation for peace.

urement. Let us not leave in our wake a swath of destruction and death which will affect our own lives and those of future generations."

Evangelization of Culture

Evangelii Gaudium is about "a new phase of evangelization," and the above themes are situated within this context. In a similar way Francis mentions the integration of faith and reason, faith and science (nn. 242–43, and see also nn. 132–34). If reason arrives at a conclusion it cannot refute, faith cannot contradict it. Nevertheless scientists often exceed their competence in making statements that cannot be proved. Ecumenical dialogue between Christians is also "an indispensable path to evangelization" (n. 246) through an "exchange of gifts" sown by the Holy Spirit. "If we really believe in the abundantly free working of the Holy Spirit, we can learn so much from one another!" (n. 246).

Francis also reaffirms the Church's teaching on other religions, discussing each of them in turn (nn. 247–53), with an emphasis on Judaism and Islam. "Non-Christians, by God's gracious initiative, when they are faithful to their own consciences, can live 'justified by the grace of God,' and thus be 'associated to the paschal mystery of Jesus Christ.'" Some commentators have seen this as going further than the teaching of the Second Vatican Council in *Nostra Aetate* or later clarifications such as *Dominus Iesus*, but he is saying only that God's grace can work outside the Church, and can justify those whose rejection of Christianity is non-culpable. This "associates them with the paschal mystery"; meaning that no one is saved except through the sacrifice of Christ (making them members of the Church even if they are unaware of the fact).

What is interesting, and does perhaps go slightly further than previous teaching, is what he says next—that "due to the sacramental dimension of sanctifying grace, God's working in them tends to produce signs and rites, sacred expressions which in turn bring others to a communitarian experience of journeying towards God. While these lack the meaning and efficacy of the sacraments instituted by Christ, they can be channels which the Holy Spirit raises up in order to liberate non-Christians from atheistic immanentism or from purely individual religious experiences" (n. 254). This suggests that the actual forms projected by these other religions—their rites and practices—have a sacred and perhaps a saving quality, in the sense that they lead whole communities in the direction of God. Francis is careful to distinguish these rites from sacraments, but he calls them "channels" for the Holy Spirit.

This enables us to find a place for other religions in the economy of salvation, rather than simply dismissing them as an elaborate form of "invincible ignorance." They may even be seen as a helpful provocation to Christians. "The same Spirit everywhere brings forth various forms of practical wisdom which help people to bear suffering and to live in greater peace and harmony. As Christians, we can also benefit from these treasures built up over many centuries, which can help us better to live our own beliefs." Here the pope speaks again of social dialogue, including the fundamental right to religious freedom, which includes the right to manifest those beliefs in public life, not just privately.

The pope speaks of the dangers of what has come to be known as fundamentalism (n. 250), and the need for mutual respect and genuine reciprocity. "We Christians should embrace with affection and respect Muslim immigrants to our countries in the same way that we hope and ask to be received and respected in countries of Islamic tradition. I ask and I humbly entreat those countries to grant Christians freedom to worship and to practice their faith, in light of the freedom which followers of Islam enjoy in Western countries! Faced with disconcerting episodes of violent fundamentalism, our respect for true followers of Islam should lead us to avoid hateful generalizations, for authentic Islam and the proper reading of the Koran are opposed to every form of violence" (n. 253).

The pope's statements on social dialogue as an essential element of evangelization even incorporate people of no particular belief. "As believers, we also feel close to those who do not consider themselves part of any religious tradition, yet sincerely seek the truth, goodness and beauty which we believe have their highest expression and source in God. We consider them as precious allies in the commitment to defending human dignity, in building peaceful coexistence between peoples and in protecting creation" (n. 257).

The Way of Beauty

The central section of the Exhortation, Chapter 3, contains rich instructions on the methods and spirit of Christian evangelization—the "proclamation of the Gospel"—and the role of the Holy Spirit therein. He begins with an ecclesiology, describing the Church as a People of God animated by the Spirit and incorporating diverse cultural expressions. The presence of the Spirit gives the People "an instinct of faith—*sensus fidei*—which helps them to discern what is truly of God . . . a certain connaturality with divine realities, and a wisdom which enables them to grasp those realities intuitively, even when they lack the wherewithal to give them precise expression" (n. 119). The missionary activity of the People finds expression not only in the "preaching" of the Gospel to those we meet, but in popular piety, and in both cases is driven by the presence of the Holy Spirit (n. 122), who distributes the many diverse charisms in the Church (n. 132).

A substantial section is devoted to the art of the homily. Here the pope reminds us that the Church is more than a People; she is a Mother (n. 139, cf. nn. 103–104), who "preaches in the same way that a mother speaks to her child, knowing that the child trusts that what she is teaching is for his or her benefit, for children know that they are loved." The "mother tongue" of the Church is a kind of music that she sings to us—the music of the Gospel (n. 141). The Spirit sets hearts afire, evoking our desire for "the Father who awaits us in glory" (n. 144).

From preaching, the pope goes on to discuss the way we can understand the Word of God more deeply—through study, by living the faith, and *lectio divina*. This leads into a discussion of catechesis (n. 163ff), including mystagogy (n. 166)—which has been neglected in recent years—and the "way of beauty." Lest we should think that this refers simply to the use of prettier artworks in our churches, he adds: "This has nothing to do with fostering an aesthetic relativism which would downplay the inseparable bond between truth, goodness and beauty, but rather a renewed esteem for beauty as a means of touching the human heart and enabling the truth and goodness of the Risen Christ to radiate within it" (n. 167).

The essence of evangelization lies in our relationship with the other, the neighbor. He is the "sacred ground" before whom we remove our sandals (n. 169), listening with utmost patience in order to accompany him spiritually. "In other words, the organic unity of the virtues always and necessarily exists *in habitu*, even though forms of conditioning can hinder the operations of those virtuous habits. Hence the need for 'a pedagogy which will introduce people step by step to the full appropriation of the mystery'" (n. 171).

The Four Pillars

Because evangelization concerns the building up of a supernatural society, the pope then returns to the social dimension of the Gospel; specifically, "the inclusion of the poor in society, and second, peace and social dialogue" (n. 185). This means "working to eliminate the structural causes of poverty and to promote the integral development of the poor, as well as small daily acts of solidarity in meeting the real needs which we encounter" (n. 188). The pope believes that "openness to the transcendent can bring about a new political and economic mindset which would help to break down the wall of separation between the economy and the common good of society" (n. 205).

> Economy, as the very word indicates, should be the art of achieving a fitting management of our common home, which is the world as a whole. Each meaningful economic decision made in one part of the world has repercussions everywhere else; consequently, no government can act without regard for shared responsibility. Indeed, it is becoming increasingly difficult to find local solutions for enormous global problems which overwhelm local politics with difficulties to resolve. If we really want to achieve a healthy world economy, what is needed at this juncture of history is a more efficient way of interacting which, with due regard for the sovereignty of each nation, ensures the economic well-being of all countries, not just of a few. (n. 206)

Francis describes four pillars on which the Church's social doctrine rests. "Progress in building a people in peace, justice and fraternity depends on four principles related to constant tensions present in every social reality" (n. 221).

(1) The first is that *"time is greater than space."* This means we can work slowly but surely, without being obsessed with immediate results" (n. 223). "Giving priority to time means being concerned about initiating processes rather than possessing spaces" (n. 223).

(2) The second is that *"unity prevails over conflict."* The peacemaker is often the one who faces the conflict head on, and finds unity on a higher plane (n. 228). "The message of peace is not about a negotiated settlement but rather the conviction that the unity brought by the Spirit can harmonize every diversity. It overcomes every conflict by creating a new and promising synthesis. Diversity is a beautiful thing when it can constantly enter into a process of reconciliation and seal a sort of cultural covenant resulting in a 'reconciled diversity'" (n. 230).

(3) *"Realities are more important than ideas"*—a principle based on the central mystery of our faith: the incarnation of the Word. In our weakness and foolishness, we mask reality with "angelic forms of purity, dictatorships of relativism, empty rhetoric, objectives more ideal than real, brands of ahistorical fundamentalism, ethical systems bereft of kindness, intellectual discourse bereft of wisdom" (n. 231). "Ideas disconnected from realities give rise to ineffectual forms of idealism and nominalism, capable at most of classifying and defining, but certainly not calling to action. What calls us to action are realities illuminated by reason. Formal nominalism has to give way to harmonious objectivity. Otherwise, the truth is manipulated, cosmetics take the place of real care for our bodies" (n. 232).

(4) *"The whole is greater than the part."* Here the pope is speaking about the "tension between globalization and localization" (n. 234). Both are needed, but the local must not be reduced to a "museum of local folklore." "The whole is greater than the part, but it is also greater than the sum of its parts.... We need to sink our roots deeper into the fertile soil and history of our native place, which is a gift of God. We can work on a small scale, in our own neighborhood, but with a larger perspective" (n. 235). It is here that the pope affirms the polyhedron over the sphere as an image of unified diversity.

The Holy Spirit in the New Evangelization

Jesus wants us to "proclaim the good news not only with words, but above all by a life transfigured by God's presence" (n. 259). That means we must be transfigured by the Holy Spirit, and that is the theme of the final chapter of the Exhortation.

"What is needed is the ability to cultivate an interior space which can give a Christian meaning to commitment and activity" (n. 262). An "interior space"—precisely the action of the Holy Spirit, who opens in us the "secret room" where we can pray to the Father, and from which we can go out to renew the face of the earth. Evangelization depends upon having a "contemplative spirit" (n. 264), an openness to God at the center of each soul.

This is the same as to say that it depends on friendship with Jesus, on living with him, and knowing him. Pope Francis is concerned with giving the Church a new understanding of the reasons for evangelization. Why do we proclaim the Gospel? The reason is actually very simple. "We have a treasure of life and love which cannot deceive, and a message which cannot mislead or disappoint. It penetrates to the depths of our hearts, sustaining and ennobling us. It is a truth which is never out of date because it reaches that part of us which nothing else can reach. Our infinite sadness can only be cured by an infinite love" (n. 265).

This truth is a Presence that does not disappoint—in whom and with whom we devote ourselves entirely to the praise of the Father. But in that life of praise we are not seeking to escape the "maelstrom of human misfortune" (n. 270). That would be nothing but a "slow suicide" (n. 272). Instead, we throw ourselves into the life of Christ. "We have to regard ourselves as sealed, even branded, by this mission of bringing light, blessing, enlivening, raising up, healing and freeing" (n. 273). As a result, "our lives become wonderfully complicated and we experience intensely what it is to be a people, to be part of a people" (n. 270). For every human being is "the object of God's infinite tenderness, and he himself is present in their lives" (n. 274).

The Resurrection is an "irresistible force." "Each day in our world beauty is born anew, it rises transformed through the storms of history" (n. 276). "No single act of love for God will be lost, no generous effort is meaningless, no painful endurance is wasted. . . . It may be that the Lord uses our sacrifices to shower blessings in another part of the world which we will never visit. The Holy Spirit works as he wills, when he wills and where he wills; we entrust ourselves without pretending to see striking results. We know only that our commitment is necessary. Let us learn to rest in the tenderness of the arms of the Father amid our creative and generous commitment" (n. 279).

The New Evangelization is inspired by the Holy Spirit, and the Holy Spirit comes into our lives through the prayer of the Blessed Virgin Mary at the heart of the Church. She is the gift of Jesus to each one of us. "At the foot of the cross, at the supreme hour of the new creation, Christ led us to Mary. He brought us to her because he did not want us to journey without a mother, and our people read in this maternal image all the mysteries of the Gospel. The Lord did not want to leave the Church without this icon of womanhood" (n. 285).

"Contemplating Mary, we realize that she who praised God for 'bringing down the mighty from their thrones' and 'sending the rich away empty' (Luke 1:52–53) is also the one who brings a homely warmth to our pursuit of justice. She is also the one who carefully keeps 'all these things, pondering them in her heart' (Luke 2:19)" (n. 288). It is in Mary—the heart, icon, and mother of the Church—that action and contemplation are united into a single dynamic force, and evangelization, the road to God's kingdom, comes into being.

The Example of Distributism

I have for some time been sympathetic to and interested in one particular attempt to apply Catholic social teaching in the modern world, and that is Distributism—a social philosophy developed by the English writer and convert G.K. Chesterton and his cradle-Catholic friend Hilaire Belloc. The following lecture has been given on various occasions, and it seems appropriate to publish it here.

Gilbert Chesterton was born in 1874, and as a young man became a well-known man of letters and denizen of Fleet Street. In 1916 he became the editor of his brother Cecil's weekly, the *New Witness*. This was renamed *G.K.'s Weekly* in 1925 and kept going (partly on the proceeds of his Father Brown stories) until his death in 1936.

The *Weekly* became the vehicle for promotion of Chesterton's social philosophy. But his literary interests remained wide: he was a poet, a playwright, a novelist, a controversialist… and many of his greatest works were studies of such figures as Browning, Blake, Tolstoy, Shaw, Chaucer, and Dickens. But it is not possible, with Chesterton, to isolate one part of his character and interests from any other, and his literary writings often betray a consuming concern for social justice and an interest in political and social matters. The range of his interests and the depth of his vision made him totally unsuited to be a specialist. He belonged to one of the last generations of English schoolboys who received a good all-round education, and he grew up to be a *universalist*, in the sense of "catholic"—at first only with a lower case, then with an "Anglo-" attached to the word by a hyphen, and finally (in 1922, when he was 48) with a capital letter; being named by Pope Pius XI a Knight Commander of St Gregory.

One of the twentieth century's most persuasive exponents of Catholic Christianity, Chesterton is regarded by some as the main successor in this respect to John Henry Newman. The Tractarians and the Oxford Movement of the nineteenth century had restored a healthy intellectual respect for religious dogma and revived a patristic spirituality in the Church of England. At the same time another movement was gathering force in England, and this is associated less with the name of Cardinal Newman than that of Cardinal Manning. It was a Christian response to the excesses of capitalism and the rise of socialism, to the injustices and ugliness of the industrial economy. Pope Leo XIII's encyclical *Rerum Novarum* in 1891 (perhaps influenced by Manning and certainly effectively promoted by him) was a kind of watershed for this movement, and it marked the beginning of a stream of authoritative social teaching emanating from Rome but widely respected beyond the visible boundaries of the Church. Chesterton managed to combine the inheritance of both movements—to reconcile Newman and Manning.

Distributism and the Historical Imagination

Through writing for a political paper called *The Speaker,* Chesterton had become acquainted with Hilaire Belloc. This is the man credited by Gilbert's biographer Maisie Ward for teaching him "a certain realism about politics—which meant a certain cynicism about politicians," for introducing him to the Christian alternative to socialism, and for showing him how to set English history back into the history of Catholic Christendom.[1] Their meeting in the year 1900 almost did not take place, Belloc having been warned by an anti-Semitic friend that Chesterton's style revealed him to be too "Jewish" to be worthy of attention.[2] Ironically, for most of his life Gilbert's own writing would be flawed by a tendency to indulge in literary stereotypes that led to him also being labelled "anti-Semitic," though he had Jewish friends and as a Zionist supported a Jewish state. (By the mid-1930s in fact, in the face of the Fascism that he despised, he had declared himself ready to "die defending the last Jew in Europe.") When he did write about the Jews, his real target was often the financial tycoons of his day.

1. Maisie Ward, *Gilbert Keith Chesterton* (London: Sheed & Ward, 1949), pp. 115–16.
2. Ibid., p. 113.

Chesterton carried a sword stick. But rather than slashing at men or their institutions with cold steel, he preferred to slash at the *ideas* which supported the foundations of a corrupt civilization. He was not a mere anarchist. The same man who yearned to carry a real sword (and upon getting married went out to buy a revolver so that he could defend his wife from brigands) also built himself a house around a tree-trunk in Beaconsfield. In his writing he would set up pillars capable of supporting a new kind of social architecture. The inspiration for this more constructive strategy came in part from his imaginative vision of English history. By "imaginative" I do not mean purely fanciful, although Chesterton was candid in his Introduction to *A Short History of England* (1917) that he was no historian, and offered "no swagger of sham scholarship" but only the insights of an amateur into the large patterns and meaning of events.[3]

Chesterton believed that England before the Reformation, however imperfectly Christianized, had at least been a working model of a "Distributist" state. That is to say, before the advent of modern capitalism, which tended to concentrate ownership and therefore power into the hands of the industrialists (just as socialism tends to concentrate it in the hands of the "State"), property had been spread more evenly through the whole of society, or at least through a landowning peasantry in the countryside (and through the guilds in the towns) sufficiently numerous to form a backbone for England. He traced the process by which social justice grew up under Christendom: how the slave turned gradually into a serf, and the serf into a peasant proprietor. "No laws had been passed against slavery; no dogmas even condemned it by definition; no war had been waged

---

3. Imagination may be defined as that faculty of the soul which employs the memory to mediate between the intellect and the senses, between ideas and observation. History is therefore an art as much as it is a science, indeed much more so, since it is certainly not an experimental science. *A Short History of England* (New York: John Lane Co., 1917) is a commentary more than a textbook, precisely because it assumes that the historian has already done his job—and that the reader is already familiar with the facts. It demonstrates a phenomenal grasp of its topic, but because it is written in the mode of commentary, with imagination and interpretation very much to the fore.

against it, no new race or ruling class had repudiated it; but it was gone."[4] It was gone, but in such a way that it could (and did) return, almost before its absence had been noticed. For "[t]he new peasant was still legally a slave."[5] The fabric of this (in some ways) admirable social system was therefore fragile. The rights of the peasants being founded on custom rather than on law, they could not stand against the forces of self-interest once these were aroused. The turning point Chesterton places some time before Henry VIII, in the reign of Richard II in the late 14th century. The leader of the Peasants' Revolt, Wat Tyler, was treacherously stabbed by the Lord Mayor of London in front of the young King. To prevent further bloodshed, Richard himself promised to accept the peasants' demands; but he was forced to betray his trust by Parliament. A new governing class was rising; the King's word had been broken; the ordinary people had been betrayed—and the overthrow of the King was the natural result. The Crown could now be kicked around like a football during the Wars of the Roses, and those who seized it thenceforth were lesser men seizing a lesser thing.

At this point Chesterton really lets his imagination take flight. He writes of what *might have been*.

> If Richard II had really sprung into the saddle of Wat Tyler, or rather if his parliament had not unhorsed him when he got there, if he had confirmed the fact of the new peasant freedom by some form of royal authority, as it was already common to confirm the fact of the Trade Unions by the form of a Royal Charter, our country would probably have had as happy a history as it is possible to human nature. The Renascence, when it came, would have come as popular education and not the culture of a club of aesthetics. The New Learning might have been as democratic as the old learning in the old days of mediaeval Paris and Oxford. The exquisite artistry of the school of Cellini might have been but the highest grade of the craft of a guild. The Shakespearean drama might have been acted by workmen on wooden stages set up in the street like Punch and Judy, the finer fulfillment of the miracle play

4. *A Short History of England*, p. 66.
5. Ibid., p. 89.

as it was acted by a guild. The players need not have been "the king's servants," but their own masters.[6]

In similar vein, he writes in *The Common Man* ("If Don John had Married"):

> There was a moment when all Christendom might have clustered together and crystallized anew, under the chemistry of the new culture; and yet have remained a Christendom that was entirely Christian. There was a moment when Humanism had the road straight before it; but, what is even more important, the road also straight behind it. It might have been a real progress, not losing anything of what was good in the past. . . . There was a moment when religion could have digested Plato as it had once digested Aristotle. . . . And England would have gone the way of Shakespeare rather than the way of Milton. . . . Perhaps there are things that are too great to happen, and too big to pass through the narrow doors of birth. For this world is too small for the soul of man; and, since the end of Eden, the very sky is not large enough for lovers.

Chesterton was accused of romanticizing the Catholic features of Merrie England. I think his accusers did not quite appreciate the depth of realism that lay disguised under Gilbert's sympathetic but deliberately simplified account—simplified in the way a sketchbook artist captures aspects of a scene he knows is complex. (It is worth noting that Eamon Duffy's tremendous scholarly achievement in *The Stripping of the Altars* has gone some way towards vindicating his vision of the Reformation as an act of brutality visited on the people by their rulers.) He is, however, "romantic" in one indisputable sense; being firmly in the tradition of rebellion against oligarchy, plutocracy, and industrialism, alongside notorious Romantics like Blake and Wordsworth, Dickens, Ruskin, and William Morris. With William Cobbett and Max Weber, he saw the origins of the modern economy in the appropriation and exploitation of monastic property and the suppression of the guilds after the Reformation, together with the enclosure of common land. Hilaire Belloc identified the Statute of Frauds under Charles II as one of many measures

6. Ibid, p. 100.

that enabled the village landlord to aggrandize himself at the expense of traditional tenure and hereditary freehold. The industrial revolution in turn was made possible by the existence of this new class of wealthy, often absentee landowners with an abundance of cheap labor for hire. The destruction of the monasteries is particularly poignant as a symbol of what was taking place. It is as though our modern world was actually built on and presupposed the *destruction of contemplation*—or at least the destruction of that (largely Benedictine) ideal, the synthesis of contemplation and action that lay at the heart of Christendom. The erosion of the concept of sacred time and the cultural importance of Sundays and Holy Days was all part of the same process, which continues even now.

The Distributists

According to Chesterton, something like medieval Distributism has to be possible under modern conditions if England is to survive (or revive) as a civilization. As he wrote in his main book on the subject, *The Outline of Sanity* (1926), a family needed to own the means of production, its land or tools, "in order to defend itself and to be free." In fact neither wealth nor equality but *freedom* was the whole point of Distributism—freedom not for some abstract many-headed entity dubbed "the working class" or "the proletariat," but for individual men and their families, bound together across the generations in a complex of communities and mutual responsibilities. Without the freedom to exercise responsibility the development of Christian personality, let alone a Christian culture, is impossible. The opposite of a Distributist state was what Belloc called, in a book of the same name, *The Servile State* (1912); meaning by this a state in which the majority of men are servile, for they labor to the advantage of others for mere money, at a job that can no longer be regarded as any kind of "vocation."

The Fordist factory and production line is, of course, the clearest example of this. Not to own the means of production but to live at the service of the few who do is, Belloc and Chesterton argued, to be effectively a slave; and a society in which this is the norm is precisely servile. Of course, in compensation for losing control of our lives in this way, we modern slaves may have considerable "wealth," in the sense of purchasing power and access to material goods. As Chesterton remarked somewhere: "Comforts that were rare among our forefathers are ... multiplied in factories and handed out wholesale; and indeed, nobody nowadays, so long as he is content to go without air, space, quiet, decency and good manners, need be without anything whatever that he wants; or at least a reasonably cheap imitation of it."

G.K.'s Weekly gave birth to the Distributist League (the "League for the Restoration of Liberty by the Distribution of Property") in 1926. This was an attempt by the leading intellectual lights of the group to organize those who felt some sympathy for their ideas into an effective force for the transformation of society. The initial response was great, and Chesterton (naturally elected as President) must have felt that he was sitting on a real social movement. Subscriptions to the newspaper doubled to over 8,000 in a couple of months. Branches opened in many towns and cities. The first Distributist communities had already sprung up: for example under Eric Gill and Hilary Pepler at Ditchling (1916), and at Laxton in the north of England; others were to follow, and some have even survived to our own day.

The Distributists were full of ideas.[7] They proposed to "re-establish the peasant, the craftsman and the small (and secure) retail tradesman." Although in favor of what is now called "subsidiarity" and so against government interference wherever possible, they were not above appealing to the government for help in getting Distributism started by framing legislation to shelter the small and differential taxation to handicap the large. If such measures might seem to work against freedom, it could be argued that they were

---

7. Apart from the books already mentioned, the most important "textbook" of Distributism may be found in Hilaire Belloc's 1936 *Essay on the Restoration of Property*. The history of the Distributist League has been explored in detail by J. Michael Thorn in *The Chesterton Review* (August 1997), and numerous other articles in that journal. See also Tobias J. Lanz, *Beyond Capitalism and Socialism: A New Statement of an Old Ideal* (Norfolk, VA: IHS Press, 2008); Race Mathews, *Jobs of Our Own: Building a Stakeholder Society, Alternatives to the Market and the State* (Irving, TX: Distributist Review Press, 2009); John Médaille, *Equity and Equilibrium: The Political Economy of Distributism* (Irving, TX: Distributist Review Press, forthcoming).

intended only to hamper the freedom of the few who wished to destroy the independence of the many. The point was not, as the name "Distributism" may have misleadingly suggested, to share out land or property more equitably between citizens, but to create the conditions under which the dispossession of the poor could less easily take place.

The Distributists wished to encourage local democracy, education in handicrafts and farming, and a less centralized market system for distributing produce—supported by the mutual agreement of consumers to buy mainly from approved smaller shops. As a transitional stage in the direction of owning the tools of one's trade and the land necessary to support one's family, some of the Distributists recommended the widespread ownership of shares in big industrial or agricultural enterprises, even though the control exercised by a shareholder over a privatized business can only be (as Belloc pointed out) "distant, indirect and largely impersonal."

But while Distributists shared several general principles, there continued to be sharp controversy and discussion within the League concerning the *application* of these principles. In fact, many commentators have seen in this tendency to become a talking shop, and in the very real (sometimes even violent) disagreements that broke out between individuals and branches of the League the main reasons for its failure and disappearance.

The failure of the Birmingham Land Scheme is quite a good example. This was a practical proposal put forward in 1928 by the Birmingham branch (enthusiastically supported by Liverpool) to acquire pieces of land on which to settle some of the unemployed in family plots. It was thoroughly researched, and many volunteers stepped forward. But not only did other branches (including London) oppose it, saying that the League should stick to its main function of making propaganda, but the government of the day was able to squash the scheme easily, simply by decreeing that volunteers would lose all unemployment benefit, and by refusing to offer any form of support until the first crops and returns became available. The League itself did not come up with any proposal (so far as I am aware) for supporting the volunteers through the voluntary contributions of members. By 1930 the League had given up on parliamentary democracy altogether. After all, had not Chesterton himself said in *G.K.'s Weekly* in 1925 that "[w]hat we desire is not a paltry party programme, but a Renaissance"? But this made it increasingly likely, especially after Chesterton's death in 1936 and the conversion of *G.K.'s Weekly* into the *Weekly Review*, that the League and the movement would fall into the hands of curmudgeonly "little Englanders" and even out-and-out Fascists, like its sometime Editor, Gilbert's highly dubious and in fact rather distant relative (though with confusingly similar initials), A.K. Chesterton.

Most commentators agree that the movement suffered from a "Luddite" tendency, closely linked to the ruralist mentality, which led to a perennial tension over what to do about modern technology. Chesterton had pointed out that only a fool could claim that it is impossible to turn back the hands of a clock—but this was mainly a joke. (As he also famously said, Christianity has not been tried and found wanting, it has been found difficult and left untried—and that must apply to a large extent also to Christendom.) He didn't really want a "return to the Middle Ages" so much as the birth of a new, more humane civilization. He thought that machinery should be limited, not abolished. But others in the movement, notably the brilliant Dominican Vincent McNabb (of whom it was said somewhere that "[h]atred of machinery combined with a love of poverty sundered him from his typewriter"), represented another extreme—a kind of principled extremism that was prepared to question even the necessity of a dentist's drill, and insisted on a return to the land: a kind of "Amish Catholicism." Eric Gill, first at Ditchling and after 1924 at Capel-y-ffin and then High Wycombe, managed to put this ideal into some kind of effect, thanks mainly to his own charisma and skill. But other experimental "cells of good living" were less successful—and even Ditchling had its darker side.

Chesterton himself was a moralist and a contemplative, not an activist in any practical sense (in fact his *im*practicality is legendary). Maisie Ward points out, too, that from the 1920s on he was increasingly aware of an impending apocalypse, a catastrophic break-up of the social order. If this did not succeed in entirely destroying his good spirits, perhaps it did reinforce his impracticality with the sense that nothing much could be done until the world should be converted. At any rate, it was partly the tendency of the Distributists to spend too much time and energy disagreeing among themselves, combined with their unwillingness to make the kind of compromises that would have enabled them to engage in British politics, that led to their inability to make common cause with other Christian-inspired social movements of the time, notably the Christian Democrats of the Catholic Social Guild, founded in 1909.

Continuing Influence

Two important facts should be remembered. Firstly, the fundamental *idea* of Distributism was no merely eccentric English wackiness but mainstream Catholic social teaching. Leo XIII himself had written that "law should favor ownership and its policy should be to induce as many people as possible to become owners," so that property and land will be "more equitably divided." Secondly, Distributism was not as great a failure, or as impractical, as might appear on the surface. For one thing, it was not a completely isolated phenomenon but overlapped with many other movements and groups, both Catholic and Anglican, that had a considerable and long-term effect on society—including the Christian and Guild Socialists, and the "Christendom Group" that was launched in 1922 with a book to which Chesterton contributed a lively Epilogue in the year before he became a Roman Catholic. That group went on to regular Summer Schools and started a quarterly journal of its own in 1931, before it was swallowed up in the great social changes of the 1940s and 50s. Many of its members had a wide influence in the Church of England: Maurice B. Reckitt (the first Treasurer of the Distributist League), V. A. Demant, Arthur J. Penty, and T. S. Eliot among them. The attempt of this group to revive an interest in the "natural law" as applied to economic life has been dismissed by those who understand economics (for example Ronald Preston and Denys Munby) as naive and medievalist, as no doubt in many ways it was. Nevertheless, it was taken seriously by no less a figure than Archbishop William Temple, whose Malvern Conference of 1941 and resulting book *Christianity and Social Order* undoubtedly contributed to the creation of the Welfare State.

Maisie Ward was one of the first to begin to assess the wider and longer-term influence of Distributism, in her biography of Chesterton, but even at that early date (1944) she had to give up the enormous task of tracing the spread of these ideas around the world. This influence was by no means only among reactionary political groups depressed by modernity, nor in the continuation of the "arts and crafts" movement to which Eric Gill and David Jones had given such an impetus. Obviously, it helped that Chesterton and Belloc were read and admired by multitudes who had no involvement with the Distributists. Gilbert's famous public debate with his friend, the Fabian socialist George Bernard Shaw, which was broadcast by the BBC in 1927 and continues to be restaged as a theatrical event, demonstrates the kind of popularity he had as a lecturer and debater. He was a media superstar of his day, and by no means only known among his fellow Christians—for he was prepared and able to defend Christian dogmas and the principles of Christian civilization most entertainingly against all comers and under any circumstances. (This despite the fact that he often did not remember where *or whether* he was supposed to be speaking, and in consequence several times had to make up his lecture on the spot.)

Maisie Ward points out that the direct influence of Distributism seemed to be greater in the colonies of the British Empire than in the heartland. She calls this a "magnificent revenge" for the harsh words Gilbert had sometimes penned about them. An effective Distributist paper was started in Ceylon and had an influence in India—perhaps even on Gandhi. In that other onetime colony, the United States, numerous publications and initiatives of the Catholic Rural Life and Country Life movements, and especially the group known as the Southern Agrarians, also testify to the influence of the Distributist ideal in the United States.[8] The Catholic Worker movement of Dorothy Day and Peter Maurin, which was founded in New York but spread worldwide under the influence of the Catholic encyclicals and personalist philosophers such as Maritain, Berdyaev, and Mounier, can also be attributed in part to Chesterton. In Aus-

---

8. See Peter A. Huff, *Allen Tate and the Catholic Revival: Trace of the Fugitive Gods* (Mahwah, NJ: Paulist Press, 1996).

The Example of Distributism

tralia the Bishops of the entire Province adopted the main Distributist ideal as the aim of Catholic Social Action in a statement of 1940. Some of the most impressive developments in applied Distributism took place in Nova Scotia, where the Antigonish Movement fostered St Francis Xavier University flourished from the 1920s until the 1950s, creating co-operative stores and savings banks, houses and workshops across the country. It was led by two Catholic priests who found in the British co-operative and credit union movement (started among cotton-weavers in Rochdale in 1844) the missing practical ingredient to make Distributism really work against poverty. Eventually, however, even this movement petered out as a growing bureaucracy came between the organization and its own membership.

Jobs of Our Own, the study of Distributism and the co-operative movement by Race Matthews of Monash University in Australia, argues that although the Antigonish Movement ran out of steam, it influenced the development by another Catholic priest (Fr Jose-Maria Arizmendiaretta) of a much more successful co-operative in the Basque region of Spain from the 1940s, namely Mondragon, which he calls a form of "Evolved Distributism." Mondragon survived in a competitive modern economic environment, becoming (under the name Mondragon Co-operative Corporation or M.C.C.) one of the largest business groups in Spain, with annual sales of billions of US dollars and a workforce of tens of thousands. As Pope Leo XIII wrote in 1891 in his "charter" for Distributism, "Men always work harder and more readily when they work on that which is their own."[9]

Mondragon is a particularly spectacular example of what I find the most interesting stream of Distributist influence: the one which flowed through the co-operative and various ruralist and regionalist

9. Mathews focuses on Antigonish and Mondragon as two major attempts to put the ideas of Distributism into practice. His central thesis is that Distributism only works when people have *jobs* (that is, work) of their *own*. In the early 20th century, Antigonish was a movement of *consumer* co-operatives in Nova Scotia which flourished for a time, but ultimately failed. Although Mathews finds much to praise in their work (and plenty of consumer co-ops flourish today), he uses Antigonish to illustrate how the basic *agency dilemma* will weaken any co-operative that

movements into what has become known as the "New Economics," represented in part by Catholic writers such as Leopold Kohr (*The Breakdown of Nations*) and convert E. F. Schumacher (*Small is Beautiful, Good Work,* etc.). In England alone we now have the Intermediate Technology Development Group, the Schumacher Society, magazines like *Resurgence* and *The Ecologist,* the New Economics Foundation and "The Other Economic Summit," plus a whole range of Green-oriented communities, networks, and organizations that share many of the ideals (and sometimes the failings) of the early Distributists. While some of these writers and activists are utopian dreamers, many—such as Paul Ekins and Richard Douthwaite—have considerable economic expertise.[10]

Some more examples from the literature will suffice to show the continuity of the New Economics with the Distributism of the 1920s. The Agrarian writer Wendell Berry writes in *Resurgence* that the "central figure of agrarian thought has invariably been the small owner or smallholder who maintains a significant measure of economic self-determination on a small acreage. The scale and independence of such holdings imply two things that agrarians see as desirable: intimate care in the use of the land, and political democracy resting upon the indispensable foundation of economic democracy."[11] Other writers in the same issue of *Resurgence* describe the brave new world of "genetic patents" in terms vividly reminiscent of the Distributist critique of industrial monopolies, of imperialism, and of the earlier enclosure movement by which huge swathes of common land were appropriated for private estates. In

---

operates only on the consumer level. You may have a food co-op, but if you hire outside managers to run it, there's nothing particularly co-operative about *their* incentives. They may as well be working at the mall. In contrast, Mondragon is a *worker* co-operative. This co-operative (really a co-operative of co-operatives) is said to be the seventh largest corporation in Spain. Mathews examines the intricate mechanisms by which a worker in a Mondragon factory has a real voice in how his shop is run, a real stake in the success of the whole enterprise, and a real safety net for keeping at *work*, not getting welfare payments.

10. On all of this please see Joseph Pearce, *Small is Still Beautiful: Economics as if Families Mattered* (Wilmington: ISI Books, 2006).

11. May/June 1998.

her book *Cities and the Wealth of Nations* (1984), Jane Jacobs argues for Community Land Trusts, worker-owned and managed businesses, non-profit banks and regional currencies, controlled locally. Herman E. Daly of the World Bank and John B. Cobb, Jr, in *For the Common Good* (1989) argue for maximizing the distribution of privately owned property, and hold up Mondragon as proof that alternative models of industrial organization are perfectly feasible. They want to re-tune the economy to the ecosystem, and re-establish agricultural communities based around the family farm. Unfortunately, like many in the Green movement and *unlike* E. F. Schumacher (who was a great admirer of the encyclical *Humanae Vitae*), some of the methods they advocate are inconsistent with their stated aims. Chesterton would have been the first to point out that the rebuilding of economics around human relationships and small communities like the family cannot proceed by means of an attack on the freedom of the family, in the form of coercive population control policies. It is unfortunate that the new economic ideas are no less likely than the old to be found in association with a dubious ethics and distorted anthropology.

Nevertheless, in the light of all this, one can definitely say that Distributism did not die. The new Distributists are all around us. For a while Distributism—the modern agrarian and anti-industrial movement—became detached from Christianity, and certainly from Catholicism. But as Wendell Berry writes, the "agrarian mind is, at bottom, a religious mind." A new wave of Distributist activity is gathering momentum in the face the contemporary economic crisis—for example in Italy, on the Adriatic coast, the Italian Chesterton Society has founded credit unions, schools, farms, and cooperatives. We can see also signs of a new and vigorous interest in Distributism (admittedly more theoretical in nature) among thinkers associated with Radical Orthodoxy, the most lively cross-denominational theological movement in Britain. John Milbank goes to the heart of Distributism and brings out its continuing relevance when he writes, for example:

> Today very few people, even middle-class "well-off" people, possess any real property as opposed to a mass of temporary commod-

ities that they have been more or less constrained [or seduced] into buying. For all the neoliberal talk of freedom, it is not an accident that so few are allowed the kind of property that permits one to leave a creative mark in the world. This is above all true of land—but we are made to pay most dearly of all and on almost a life-time lease for the very space in which it is possible to sleep, make love, be born, die, prepare food, engage in play or the arts. We should instead seek a way to provide people as widely as possible with real property, commencing with landed property itself.[12]

Implications for Catholic Social Teaching

What made it possible to think in terms of a rediscovery by the Church of her radical tradition is above all the fall of Communism at the end of the 1980s. The effect of this was to make possible a more serious critical engagement with consumerist capitalism. Take for example the 1997 report of the Pontifical Council for Justice and Peace, *Towards a Better Distribution of Land: The Challenge of Agrarian Reform*. This is a document which summarizes Catholic teaching on land reform and sustainable development, applying it to the very severe injustices we see in the developing countries. It is perhaps the most explicitly "Distributist" of Church documents to date.

It begins: "The development model of industrialized societies is capable of producing huge quantities of wealth, but also has serious shortcomings when it comes to the equitable redistribution of its fruits and promotion of growth in less developed areas." It criticizes in particular the concentration of land into a few large holdings, often administered by absentee land barons using hired help. It promotes policies based on "family owned and farmed enterprises," encouraging the authorities to "ensure the adoption of laws to uphold and protect the effective distribution of private property," particularly "one's own equipment in artisan enterprises and farms of family size, of shares in middle-size and large firms," and tax policies that "ensure continuity of ownership of material goods within the context of the family" (nn. 37–8). It talks, too, of the need for "administrative decentralization" to empower local communities. In other words, in this document *the Church herself has revived the*

12. Milbank, *The Future of Love*, p. 255.

fundamental idea of Distributism and exhorts us to apply it urgently in the third world, for the sake of justice to human beings and for the sake of the global environment. For in Africa, Latin America, and parts of Asia there still remains what Chesterton would have called a "peasantry" and the basis for a rural economy of extended families, of the kind that was destroyed in England by the Reformation, the enclosure movement, and the industrial revolution.

There is hope, too, for the radicalization of the Church among the dynamic young lay movements and secular institutes that are now flourishing in Europe and America, as the life of our parishes and religious orders (with few exceptions) continues to decline. I am thinking of movements like Focolare and Communion and Liberation, whose members take Catholic teaching and the lead of the pope extremely seriously, and who enter public and economic life with an energy and creativity that generates new models of co-operative enterprise and communitarian social action. It may be that we will find that among the aging and declining populations of the developed world, where conventional welfare and pension arrangements are likely to collapse due to lack of funding from governments and contributions from the young, and where large numbers of people are increasingly unable to find work even as wage slaves (thanks to a combination of automation and the expansion of the workforce), that conditions are ripe for the recovery of the principle of mutual support and associations of common interest, such as the medieval guilds.

It is, I am suggesting, possible that we will increasingly see New Economic thinking being absorbed and co-opted—perhaps even surpassed—by Christian thinkers and lay ecclesial movements. But it important to understand that something deeper is going on here than a paradigm-shift in social theory that Catholics are catching onto a bit late in the day. When we consider the range of perils that now threaten the basis of our civilization—ecological disasters, the assault on childhood innocence, the instability of the world financial markets, the likelihood of major acts of nuclear or biological terrorism, the unstoppable trade in drugs, the emotional and moral chaos that will follow in the wake of genetic engineering—enormously varied, of course, but all largely brought on by the exponential development and indiscriminate application of technology, we are forced to a conclusion we should have reached long ago. It is a paradoxical conclusion, as Chesterton would have noted: namely that the world is in this very *material* crisis for non-material, indeed for *spiritual*, reasons.

As I have argued in this book, then, the solution, if there is to be one before the final breakdown of our civilization, must come at a spiritual level; at the level of ideas, attitudes and above all, prayer. What we need is not merely a new political ideology, nor even a process of moral rearmament, brought about in reactive flight from the threat of anarchy, but a full-scale spiritual renewal. What we need is a "Marian revolution" that would enthrone the Mother and Child (and everything they represent) at the center of the values, institutions, and assumptions of society. A new culture must begin to be born even before the death of the old, a culture based not on activism, but on the contemplative receptivity that Mary exemplifies.

Chesterton understood this. All his social activism flowed from a deeper and more fundamental receptivity, a gratitude and thankfulness that was bound up with his continual amazement at the very act of existence. "Thanks," he said in *A Short History of England*, "are the fundamental form of thought." And in *The Common Man*:[13] "Human beings are happy so long as they retain the receptive power and the power of reaction in surprise and gratitude to something outside. So long as they have this they have as the greatest minds have always declared, a something that is present in childhood and which can still preserve and invigorate manhood"—can still, we might add, renew Christian civilization. The Marian "culture of life" that is beginning to be born will also (I realize more clearly now) be a "Josephine" culture, for Joseph is the most Marian of saints, the one who lives closest to Mary. I propose him as the patron of Distributists: of workers, craftsmen, and dreamers.

Summary and Conclusion

Distributism is the view that private property should be widely distributed through society, rather than concentrated in a few hands,

---

13. *The Common Man* (New York: Sheed & Ward, 1950), p. 252.

in order to enable more or even most people to be able to take responsibility for their own families by means of productive and dignified labor.

It is not supposed by Distributists that property should be stolen from the rich and given to the poor, but rather that legislation should make it easier for the small landowner, tradesman, shopkeeper, or craftsman to survive, and harder for the would-be "tycoon" to accumulate so much wealth and power that he can force the former to become a mere employee or wage-slave entirely dependent upon him.

This of course assumes that there is a will and a desire among most men to work productively and creatively as work that is truly worthwhile and dignified. But this desire is all but eliminated in a society where men have become addicted to earning money and spending it purely as consumers, for the sake of individual enjoyment. So the real enemy of Distributism is individualism and consumerism—a spirit and a way of life opposed to the Gospel.

Correspondingly, Distributism is not a mere economic policy or a political platform, but a spirit and a way of life. It is based on the fact that, in the long run, men are happiest not through the possession of great wealth and leisure at the expense of others, but through the possession of *freedom*, in the sense of self-responsibility and self-determination, especially the freedom to create and support a family. A man should be allowed to stand on his own two feet, not dangle from another man's belt.

Distributism is "personalist" rather than "individualist," which is to say that it views people as relational and therefore cooperative by nature. The good of the individual is not separable from the common good. We fulfill ourselves by serving others. The Church proposes the best form of social organization, in very general terms, as *subsidiarity in solidarity*, based upon the integrity and initiative of families as the foundation of a healthy civil society.

In Christianity we always stand at the very beginning of things, which is partly why the image of the Holy Family is so important to us. By the unique power of Christianity, which is the power of the Resurrection of Christ, hope need never die. In our day I think we stand not at the very end of the world but near the end of a cycle of history, perhaps in the death-throws of a civilization that will be looked back upon by later generations as a kind of sunken Atlantis. Over the last century the principles of Catholic social teaching have been set out for us in the clearest of terms, and with *Caritas in Veritate* a bridge opened both to the deepest metaphysics and to the New Economics.

Benedict's successor, Pope Francis, is leading us over that bridge into a new world. His teaching is founded, like everything in Christianity, on a Cross: on the integration of a horizontal with a vertical principle, of the principle of solidarity (horizontal) with the principle of subsidiarity (vertical). He assumes, too, the integration of justice and mercy in charity (the interior "form" of all the virtues); and of Spirit with Letter, of means with ends, and of heaven with earth. This cruciform teaching will always shatter the worldly wisdom of men, and provide a framework for those who want to try the experiment of Christianity in their own lives and time—even if their act of faith strikes others as foolish as that of Noah and the teaching as useless as an Ark on dry land.

Slow Evangelization

Léonie and Stratford Caldecott[1]

Popes John Paul II announced a "Decade of Evangelization" in the 1990s, and Benedict XVI continued to rally Catholics in the West around the call to a "New Evangelization" and the hope of a "new springtime of the faith." What have we learned during all this time— and from bringing up, in the midst of it, our own children?

Cultural Catholicism, which depends on the handing-on of the faith from mother to child, generation after generation, has become a luxury the Church can no longer count upon. It is simply not going to happen the way it used to, in a world where the electronic media inserts itself between parents and children within the home itself. Before the faith has time to set down its roots in the soul, a new culture has already colonized that soul, with alternative values, aspirations, and heroes. We don't believe the Church has taken this enough into account. Up until now, Catholics have too often relied on maintaining a sense of community and tradition, without conveying a sense of *why* people forcibly uprooted within their own homes by technological and social change should want to belong to either. This general problem is made worse by the scandals of recent times, with the accelerated loss of confidence in bishops and priests.

The Church's call to spread the Gospel in lands that were formally—and may still be nominally—Christian is a natural response to this situation. But the conditions in which Christians are called to evangelize must be taken into account. We have to face the mayhem stored up for our society through the abortion holocaust, the experimentation on embryos, the acts of mass destruction, the degradation of the environment, the undermining of families, the pollution

---

1. A shorter version of this paper first appeared in *Second Spring* 16 (Fall 2012).

of the imagination, and a cultivation of desires to excess. Our education system is a shambles, our health services overstrained, our cultural heritage vandalized and vulgarized. New plagues, new wars, lie just around the corner. Genetic weapons that target particular ethnic groups, children born without parents or as the result of laboratory experimentation, cruelty on a scale never before imagined or perpetrated: all of this is part of the legacy of the twentieth century—even if we must not lose sight of the good that is also a part and an expression of the modern world.

Nor is it the case that Christians are united against the threat of secularism. Instead, they are divided into factions. Anyone who approves of *Humanae Vitae* tends to be labeled "right-wing," and someone who questions it is placed on the "left." Or it may be one's stance on abortion rather than contraception that is the criterion. But if the focus is switched to economics or liturgy, quite different groups of people may suddenly find themselves in the same camp. In liturgy, the ideal of the "Right" is a revival of Tridentine Catholicism, while the "Left" favors freedom of expression and liturgical experimentation. On the other hand, one may find a right-winger in liturgical matters sitting next to an opponent of *Humanae Vitae*. In economics the "Right" believes that markets must be as free as possible, and the Left that they should be controlled by the State. Left-wingers on sexuality or liturgy may find themselves in either camp when it comes to economics.

There is a psychological analysis that may help us identify what is going on when people use these terms. The Right is associated with order or rigidity and a kind of macho masculinity, the Left with movement, fluidity, and feminism. Thus for the Right the rules of morality, or liturgical correctitude, or economic growth, are relatively simple and it is generally accepted that they should apply to everyone. The Left, on the other hand, is all about pluralism and variation, about pragmatic adjustment and a lack of absolutes. That doesn't mean, of course, that the Left does not have an ideology of its own, far from it. It is just that left-wing ideologies tend to be more pragmatic and relativistic. They affirm (often in absolutist terms) the lack of absolutes.

Roots of Modernity

In the "Culture Wars," abortion, family, liturgy, and the economy tend to be the hot-button issues. But a more philosophical analysis reveals that much of this surface conflict signifies nothing, because *both sides* in these conflicts share certain assumptions that will prevent them from ever managing to do anything to change the world for the better. These are assumptions that transform every dispute, every argument, into a struggle for power instead of truth. Religion is reduced to politics. Unless we correct these profound errors, evangelization will always fail, because we will have already conceded too much to the *Zeitgeist*.

The nominalists of the fourteenth century argued that universal Forms do not exist except perhaps as abstractions in the mind, and that all that really exists is a collection of particular, individual things. Their influence led to a growing emphasis on the individual and his will. Eventually, the working-out of this philosophy in all its implications led to a world without objective values and qualities, in which reality is essentially material and can be divided and subdivided down to the subatomic level, where it dissolves into a kind of unimaginable "foam" of energy (or something very like Aristotle's *materia prima*).

With no hierarchy of ordered Forms to draw upon (since the existence of such Forms was now questionable), God's rule over the universe became "free" in the sense of arbitrary, or whimsical. There being no such thing as "right" and "wrong" except what God happened to decide arbitrarily to command or forbid, the new image of God was that of an absolute dictator. Similarly, if the only Forms are those we invent, the social and political order of human society has to be created by the imposition of will—if not by God, then by a divinely appointed king, and if not by him, then by individual choices made at the ballot box—or by those capable of manipulating those choices, by means subtle or crude. Along with this there took place a narrowing of human reason. Previously we had looked for at least four types of explanation of things, each of which was necessary in a different way to make something happen. The four causes of things were termed in the Aristotelian tradition as formal, final, efficient and material. But with the rise of empirical science formal and final causes dropped out of the picture.

In hindsight we can see that this philosophical shift prepared the ground for the Reformation, which emphasized individual conscience and pared away the fabric of mediation—the traditions, sacraments, and sacramentals—by which the self had been embedded in a social cosmos. But without those ties, without that embeddedness, nature was drained of grace, and our connection to the transcendent God became less a matter of imagination or intellect or feeling than of sheer willpower. All that was needed was for us to stop willing it, and it would effectively cease to be, which is what happened in the later stages of the Enlightenment.

In the context of economics, free-market conservatives prioritize an understanding of freedom based on the assumption that all moral obligations stem from individual acts of will. In a contract, each party voluntarily binds itself to do or give something in exchange for something else. The contract becomes the basic paradigm for all human relationship. Opposed to this is the traditional understanding that obligations (i.e. duties and rights as the two aspects of responsibility) are often *prior* to acts of will, because they flow from the relationships constitutive of our identity as creatures in society, creatures who are called to love.

Obligations (such as the duty to pay one's workers a just family wage, or to allow them time for worship, or indeed the obligation to respect the lives of others), are rooted in our constitutive relation to God, not in a decision to grant them in return for some advantage to myself. As Pope Benedict says in *Caritas in Veritate* (2009), "if the only basis of human rights is to be found in the deliberations of an assembly of citizens, those rights can be changed at any time" (n. 43). Rather, they are based on the needs of each person to fulfill himself according to his nature—that is, what is "due" to us as persons—and those needs impose a duty on others to permit that fulfillment.

The mistake of liberalism is to assume that my freedom from constraint is the same as my capacity for self-realization. In other words, if (some of) the external restraints on my behavior are removed, I will be to that extent freer to express and perfect myself. But the

Catholic understanding of freedom presents it as freedom to do something, not just freedom *from* something. Freedom is necessary to self-realization, because it is necessary to love; but it is love that fulfills us, not freedom. In the words of the encyclical, "we must reappropriate the true meaning of freedom, which is not an intoxication with total autonomy, but a response to the call of being, beginning with our own personal being" (n. 70). How do we do this?

The Interior Dimension

"The more Christianity acts in a triumphalist and absolutist manner in the world of today and tomorrow, the more it is felt to be a ghost."[2] By this Balthasar does not mean that Christ will not, in the end, triumph, nor that there are no absolutes in Christian teaching. He is drawing attention to the *way Christians act*, and the way they assert and defend the truth. But notice the paradox. The more solid and assertive Christianity becomes, the more insubstantial and ghostly it appears. And a ghost is just an echo, a vestige, a ghastly prolongation of something long dead.

The very efforts we make to assert the truths we believe are what turn us into ghosts.

What is the answer? How do we start to "feel real" to our contemporaries? By acting differently. The opposite of a "triumphalist and absolutist manner" is not "defeatist and relativist" but perhaps something more like "humble and tentative." Humble because we are not inflated by what we believe, and tentative because we do not know how best to express it—only if the "the Spirit gives us words" will we know how to communicate at all, and the Spirit speaks only through the humble.

The triumphalist thinks he knows the answer to everything—and if he doesn't, then he knows where to look it up (in the *Catechism* or the *Summa*). Christian doctrine seems to him like a watertight, logical structure, with everything neatly in place. Yet if you really look at this structure, if you read cutting-edge theologians like Balthasar (or Rahner or Lonergan or Barth, if that is your preference) you find that the whole thing balances on a knife-edge of mystery. The

2. Hans Urs von Balthasar, *Theo-Drama*, V, p. 491.

teaching of the Church does not dispel the mysteries: it depends upon them.

The overconfident Catholic thinks that the existence of God explains the universe, and smirks at the scientist who suggests it just popped out of nowhere. Yet in fact our doctrine denies that God was *compelled* to create anything. The world therefore rests on the "groundless ground" of divine freedom. In other words, we cannot explain it after all. A similar mystery confronts us in the origin of evil and therefore suffering. The devil was an angel of light. He was not deceived or confused when he rejected God: he just did it. But *why* he did is a mystery.

The Bible begins and ends in profound ambiguity. The foundational narrative concerning Eden and the Fall cannot be interpreted literally, and its real meaning is inexhaustible. The Book of Revelation is even stranger. These books appear to posit a beginning state and an end state of the world not subject to death and entropy, but this is something we lack the experience to imagine and the physics to account for.

Even Jesus remains elusive. "My teaching is not mine, but his who sent me" (John 7:16). This leads Balthasar to ask, so does he have a teaching, or not? Jesus is called "the image of the Invisible" (Col. 1:15), but is this not a contradiction in terms? He has saved us from sin, and yet "All things have continued as they were from the beginning of creation" (2 Pet. 3:3). Sin and death continue, even in the Church and sometimes even more intensely there than outside. Our fellow Christians, too, have become more mysterious than ever. "It is no longer I that live, but Christ who lives in me" (Gal. 2:20).

St. Paul states categorically, "If any one imagines that he knows something, he does not yet know as he ought to know" (1 Cor. 8:2). God does not become less mysterious the more we read theology; he becomes more so. That is the way of faith; the reason it has to be an infused supernatural gift and not a rational conclusion from an argument. In faith we grasp by not grasping; by "letting go" and allowing ourselves to be changed.

Not that faith contradicts reason. Faith *stimulates* reason, precisely because we have to work out how to express what we believe, and what has happened to us, in a way that does not contradict it. It comes close to contradiction in paradox, but here is that knife-edge again: it never quite contradicts. And the closer the two become, the sharper our intelligence has to be. Thus for Balthasar, "As clarity increases, the mystery grows" (*T-D*, V, p. 496). Mary, for instance, is both illuminated and thrown into shadows by the angel's announcement that she will give birth to God's child—that the Spirit will "overshadow" her. The meaning of the paradoxes and all the strangeness of Christianity is only to be found in "the Trinitarian character of truth itself" in which there is no closed, absolute system, but only a continual going beyond oneself in freedom.

What does this imply for evangelization? It means that we must turn things around. We are told to evangelize our own culture, our own society, which has become indifferent to God. But there is a first frontier of the New Evangelization to be crossed, and it is to evangelize ourselves—or to allow ourselves to be evangelized, to be changed by the Gospel. That doesn't mean simply that we must become better Christians, although that would obviously help in all sorts of ways. It means that we have to become a new creation, a new people. The first disciples were transformed by the Holy Spirit. We must be too. Christianity itself must be changed into a force for change, not just for maintaining the *status quo*, or keeping the show on the road.

The key to evangelization, and the reason it is failing, is that it cannot work without spiritual transformation. In other words mysticism, spirituality, whatever you want to call it—even *gnosis* perhaps (not in the heretical but in the Christian sense)—is not an add-on, not an indulgence for those who are so inclined, while the rest of us get on with the serious business of intellectual argument and social action. It is at the very heart of any intellectual or practical engagement with and expression of the faith, and without it we remain on the outside of the problem. Even artistic and aesthetic evangelization—the "way of beauty"—though it reaches parts other forms of evangelization cannot, is doomed to fail and become self-indulgent or tasteless without it.

The Slow Revival

Ever since Carlo Petrini's protest against a McDonald's in the Piazza di Spagna in 1986, there has been a "Slow Movement" of people and organizations committed to the idea that the curse of modernity is an obsession with speed, efficiency, and economic growth. You can read on Wikipedia about Slow Fashion, Slow Cities, Slow Money, Slow Parenting, and even a World Institute of Slowness. The Slow Movement believes that quality of life and thus real wealth comes from slowness, care, and contemplation, rather than non-stop activity and frenetic speed. Perhaps the same idea—for all the reasons we have just given—should be applied to evangelization. Too much has been expected too quickly: we need Slow Evangelization.

In recent years the focus in evangelization has been on methods aimed at bringing about rapid results. The aim has been to grab the attention and in that moment direct it towards an aspect of Christianity that will be immediately appealing and attractive. Christian apologists, for example, concentrate on knocking down false arguments and smoothing the intellectual road to faith. That is important work, though here in England we live in an anti-intellectual culture where few people are prepared to listen to such arguments. Another growingly important approach revolves around what the Church has to say on social and economic questions ("Catholic social teaching"). Those who are made aware of the Church's wisdom in this field are more likely to take her seriously in others. The use of art and imagination to lead people towards the truth has already been mentioned.

All of these methods are important. But Slow Evangelization is about putting down roots. Naturally we need to grab the attention, and we need to persuade. There will always be moments of conversion, and sudden realignment. But we also need to create *islands of faith*, or *oases of truly Christian culture*, starting with our children and friends. That is a slower process, because it follows the rhythms of natural growth and the development of personality. You cannot have authentic Christian evangelization without seeing, among and between those who speak and those who are addressed in the name of Christ, the birth of a new order of human living. The evangelization of the culture starts with the way we relate to others. A culture is created or reborn and reshaped when friends work together creatively, share their freedom with one another, refusing to be bound merely by memory and prejudice, and instead taking responsibility for their lives.

In Section 83 of *Evangelium Vitae*, Blessed John Paul II writes of the attitude of mind that is needed for the building of a culture of life:

> we need first of all to *foster* in ourselves and in others, *a contemplative outlook*. Such an outlook arises from faith in the God of life, who has created every individual as a "wonder" (Ps. 139:14). It is the outlook of those who see life in its deeper meaning, who grasp its gratuitousness, its beauty and its invitation to freedom and responsibility. It is the outlook of those who do not presume to take possession of reality but instead accept it as a gift, discovering in all things the reflection of the Creator and seeing in every person his living image (Gen. 1:27; Ps. 8:5). This outlook does not give in to discouragement when confronted by those who are sick, suffering, outcast, or at death's door. Instead, in all these situations it feels challenged to find meaning, and precisely in these circumstances it is open to perceiving in the face of every person a call to encounter, dialogue, and solidarity.[3]

This is the "outlook" of Slow Evangelization. It is evangelization for the long haul. And it requires creativity. To be open to each other is also to be open to the future; it is the opposite of being closed within the narrow circle of oneself. We are kept open to each other by love and prayer. In that attitude of openness and prayer, of hospitality and kindness, the faith we represent may grow and develop in a new way, not imitating the patterns of the past, but finding new forms that answer the needs of our age.

Call to Glory

These are challenging times for Roman Catholics across the world, and in our country Catholicism manifests itself as a kingdom rather

---

3. He also wrote: "The drama of contemporary culture is the lack of interiority, the absence of contemplation. Without interiority culture has no content; it is like a body that has not yet found its soul. What can humanity do without interiority? Unfortunately, we know the answer very well. When the contemplative spirit is missing, life is not protected and all that is human is denigrated. Without interiority, modern man puts his own integrity at risk" (Pope John Paul II, Madrid, May 3, 2003).

dis-united than united. What we want to offer here is a small plea, the sort of manifesto that a mother scatters in the ears of her children, piecemeal, spread across the stress and strain of daily life, like autumn leaves that swirl in the wind, and are gone—except that the impression of their gorgeous shapes and colors sticks in the memory, and creates an atmosphere that cannot be entirely swept away. Glory, however fleeting, cannot be erased. It stays with us, an *anamnesis* on which the soul can feed even in the darkest hours.

Glory is what this life is all about. You will find Catholics who tell you that it is about suffering, purgation, purification. They are not wrong. The problem is that everyone except the most heroic souls (and these are few and far between) has to admit, eventually, that they cannot hack the tough stuff. And so a gulf opens up in the Church, between a so-called "progressive" or "liberal" wing, and a so-called "conservative" or "orthodox." Ironically each berates the other for their pusillanimous response to the Gospel. Yet if we were only to bring into focus a vision of God's glory—the ultimate "realism"—we could drop our swords and turn them into ploughshares. This has to happen: without it we are lost.

There is no glory on this earth without a participation in that mystery which is at the heart of what it means to be human. That mystery is a spousal one. It reaches its highest point in the synthesis of natural and supernatural in the mystery of the Eucharist, which is where the Incarnation touches us and nourishes us individually. But this possibility of union with God is rooted, as Blessed John Paul II and Pope Benedict have tirelessly reminded us, in an aboriginal fact of our being: the fact that we are created for each other, male and female. This relationality is a reflection of something in the nature of God himself. The Trinitarian dynamic at the heart of the Godhead is reflected in the I/thou of human experience, represented by the man saying to the woman "this at last is flesh of my flesh," and the woman saying to the man, "I have conceived with the help of the Lord."

All of human experience is a waltz with the divine, a communication between one heart and another heart, with the result that a third heart comes into focus. The third heart is the heart of God. Only because of, and *within*, that Third Heart can a human child, a human soul (or even a wholesome ecclesial reality) come into being. This should not surprise us. God is, after all, Creator.

If we want to be where God is, where Love resides, we must be prepared to participate in his mysterious creativity. We must be prepared to become people for whom "progeniture" is possible. Not just on the biological level, but first and foremost on the spiritual level. Every man and every woman is called to become a father or mother. Even celibate men and women must embrace this, or their work, their apostolate, their mission, will be without issue. Spiritual fecundity is the only thing that makes the Church grow and thrive.

How many times does scripture use images about growth and fecundity, whether of the land or the human body? The seed sown on fertile soil, not on rock or among the thorns. The flourishing vineyard that yields good wine, not sour grapes. The father giving his son bread and eggs, not stones and scorpions. The mother in anguish for delivery who forgets all her pain when she sees her child, that startling envoy of the Absolute. The images have been made to seem hackneyed through over-use, or even misuse. But enter into them anew, as images of the life of just one human soul: your own...

The growth of the soul, the new life that is sown in the soil, may be slow in appearing. It may take more time than we sometimes feel we have. The baby grows for nine months in darkness. But the slowness is part of the process, and we shouldn't wish for it any other way.

Bibliography

Papal encyclicals and other documents of the magisterium are freely available online at www.vatican.va and in print from the Catholic Truth Society (London).

Anderson, Gary A. *Charity: The Place of the Poor in the Biblical Tradition.* New Haven: Yale University Press, 2013.

Augustine of Hippo. *On the Sermon on the Mount.* Accessed June 10, 2013. limovia.net.

Balthasar, Hans Urs von. *Bernanos: An Ecclesial Existence.* San Francisco: Ignatius Press, 1996.

———. *Explorations in Theology,* Vol. I: The Word Made Flesh. San Francisco: Ignatius Press, 1989.

———. *Explorations in Theology,* Vol. II: Spouse of the Word. San Francisco: Ignatius Press, 1991.

———. *New Elucidations.* San Francisco: Ignatius Press, 1986.

———. *The Christian State of Life.* San Francisco: Ignatius Press, 1983.

———. *Theo-Drama: Theological Dramatic Theory,* Vol. IV: The Action. San Francisco: Ignatius Press, 1994.

———. *Theo-Logic,* I: Truth of the World. San Francisco: Ignatius Press, 2000.

———. *The Office of Peter and the Structure of the Church.* San Francisco: Ignatius Press, 1986.

———. *Tragedy Under Grace: Reinhold Schneider and the Experience of the West.* San Francisco: Ignatius Press, 1997.

Balthasar, Hans Urs von, and Joseph Cardinal Ratzinger. *Mary: The Church at the Source.* San Francisco: Ignatius Press, 2005.

Barber, Benjamin. *If Mayors Ruled the World: Why They Should, and Why They Already Do.* Yale University Press, 2013.

Barker, Margaret. *The Great High Priest: The Temple Roots of Christian Theology.* London: T&T Clark International, 2003.

Bauman, Zygmunt. *Consuming Life.* Cambridge: Polity Press, 2007.

Belloc, Hilaire. *An Essay on the Restoration of Property.* Norfolk, VA: IHS Press, 2002.

Bergoglio, Jorge Mario, and Abraham Skorka. *On Heaven and Earth:*

Bibliography

Pope Francis on Faith, Family, and the Church in the Twenty-First Century. New York: Image, 2013.

Bernanos, Georges. *Tradition of Freedom.* London: Denis Dobson, 1950.

Bolton, Robert. *Keys of Gnosis.* Hillsdale, NY: Sophia Perennis, 2004.

———. *The Order of the Ages: Word History in the Light of Universal Cosmogony.* Ghent, NY: Sophia Perennis, 2001.

Borella, Jean. *The Secret of the Christian Way.* New York: SUNY Press, 2001.

———. *The Sense of the Supernatural.* Edinburgh: T&T Clark, 1998.

Caldecott, Stratford. *Beauty for Truth's Sake.* Grand Rapids: Brazos Press, 2009.

———. *Beauty in the Word.* New York: Angelico Press, 2012.

——— . (ed.). *Beyond the Prosaic: Reviving the Liturgical Movement.* Edinburgh: T&T Clark, 1998.

———. *Catholic Social Teaching: A Way In*, 3rd edn. London: CTS, 2007.

———. *Fruits of the Spirit.* London: CTS, 2010.

——— . *Seven Sacraments: Entering the Mysteries of God.* New York: Crossroad, 2006.

——— . *The Radiance of Being: Dimensions of Cosmic Christianity.* New York: Angelico Press, 2012.

Charles, Rodger SJ. *Christian Social Witness and Teaching.* Leominster: Gracewing, 1998.

Chesterton, G.K. *Collected Works*, Vol. IV. San Francisco, CA: Ignatius Press, 1987.

———. *A Short History of England.* New York: John Lane Co., 1917.

———. *Orthodoxy.* New York: Dodd, Mead & Co., 1908.

———. *The Common Man.* New York: Sheed & Ward, 1950.

———. *The Outline of Sanity.* New York: Dodd, Mead & Co., 1927.

Clément, Olivier. *The Roots of Christian Mysticism.* New York: New City, 1993.

Coomaraswamy, Ananda K. *What Is Civilization? And Other Essays.* Ipswich: Golgonooza Press, 1989.

Dante, *The Divine Comedy*, trans. Allen Mandelbaum. New York: Knopf, 1995.

D'Arcy, Eric. *Conscience and Its Right to Freedom.* London: Sheed & Ward, 1961.

Dawson, Christopher. *Religion and the Modern State.* London: Sheed & Ward, 1935.

———. *The Judgement of Nations.* London: Sheed & Ward, 1943.

Deszcz-Tryhubczak, Justyna, and Marek Oziewicz (eds). *Towards or Back* to Human Values? *Spiritual and Moral Dimensions of Contemporary Fantasy*. Newcastle: Cambridge Scholars Press, 2006.

Dupré, Louis. *Passage to Modernity: An Essay in the Hermeneutics of Nature and Culture*. Yale University Press, 1993.

Dupuy, Jean-Pierre. *The Mark of the Sacred*. Stanford University Press, 2013.

Ellul, Jacques. *The Technological Bluff*. Grand Rapids: Eerdmans, 1990.

Elvins, Mark Turnham. *The Call to Hospitality: The Origins of the Hospitaller Vocation*. Leominster: Gracewing, 2013.

Evdokimov, Paul. *The Art of the Icon: A Theology of Beauty*. Redondo Beach, CA: Oakwood Publications, 1990.

_____. *Woman and the Salvation of the World: A Christian Anthropology on the Charisms of Women*. Crestwood, NY: SVS Press, 1997.

Finn, Daniel K. (ed.). *The Moral Dynamics of Economic Life: An Extension and Critique of Caritas in Veritate*. Oxford University Press, 2013.

Flanagan, Kieran. *Sociology and Liturgy*. London: Macmillan, 1991.

Fortini, Arnaldo. *Francis of Assisi*. New York: Crossroad, 1981.

Francis and Clare of Assisi. *Francis and Clare: The Complete Works*, Classics of Western Spirituality. Mahwah, NJ: Paulist, 1986.

Francis de Sales. *Introduction to the Devout Life*. London: Burns & Oates, 1956.

Gaudoin-Parker, Michael L. *Heart in Pilgrimage: Meditating Christian Spirituality in the Light of the Eucharistic Prayer*. New York: Alba House, 1994.

_____. *Hymn of Freedom: Celebrating and Living the Eucharist*. T&T Clark, 1997.

Geus, Arie de. *The Living Company: Growth. Learning, and Longevity in Business*. London: Nicholas Brealey, 1999.

Giussani, Luigi. *The Journey to Truth Is an Experience*, transl. John E. Zucchi. McGill-Queen's University Press, 2006.

Goodchild, Philip. *The Theology of Money*. Durham, NC: Duke University Press, 2009.

Gray, John. *Beyond the New Right: Markets, Government and the Common Environment*. London and New York: Routledge, 1993.

Guardini, Romano. *Conscience*. London: Sheed & Ward, 1932.

_____. *Letters from Lake Como: Explorations in Technology and the Human Race*. Grand Rapids: Eerdmans, 1994.

Habig, Marion A. (ed.). *St Francis of Assisi: Omnibus of Sources*. Chicago: Franciscan Herald Press, 1973.

Hani, Jean. *Divine Craftsmanship: Preliminaries to a Spirituality of Work*.

San Rafael: Sophia Perennis, 2007.

Healy and Schindler (eds). *Being Holy in the World: Theology and Culture in the Thought of David L. Schindler*. Grand Rapids: Eerdmans, 2011.

Heidegger, Martin. *The Question Concerning Technology and Other Essays*. New York: Harper & Row, 1977.

Henry, Michel. *Barbarism*. London: Continuum, 2012.

————. *Words of Christ*. Grand Rapids: Eerdmans, 2012.

Hitchcock, James. *Recovery of the Sacred: Reforming the Reformed Liturgy*. Ignatius Press, 1995.

Hoelscher, Ludger. *The Reality of the Mind: St Augustine's Philosophical Arguments for the Human Soul as Spiritual Substance*. London and New York: Routledge & Kegan Paul, 1986.

Huff, Peter A. *Allen Tate and the Catholic Revival: Trace of the Fugitive Gods*. Mahwah, NJ: Paulist Press, 1996.

Hughes, John. *The End of Work: Theological Critiques of Capitalism*. Oxford: Blackwell, 2007.

Hyde, Lewis. *The Gift: How the Creative Spirit Transforms the World*. Edinburgh: Canongate, 2006.

Jeanrond, Werner G. *A Theology of Love*. London: T&T Clark, 2010.

Jenson, Robert W. *Essays in the Theology of Culture*. Grand Rapids: Eerdmans, 1995.

John Paul II, *Man and Woman He Created Them: A Theology of the Body*. Boston: Pauline, 2006.

Keeble, Brian (ed.). *A Holy Tradition of Working: Passages from the Writings of Eric Gill*. Ipswich: Golgonooza Press, 1983.

————. *Art: For Whom and For What?*. Ipswich: Golgonooza Press, 1998.

————. (ed.). *Every Man An Artist: Readings in the Traditional Philosophy of Art*. Bloomington: World Wisdom Books, 2005.

————. *God and Work: Aspects of Art and Tradition*. Bloomington: World Wisdom Books, 2009.

Lanz, Tobias J. *Beyond Capitalism and Socialism: A New Statement of an Old Ideal*. Norfolk, VA: IHS Press, 2008.

Leask, Ian, and Eoin Cassidy. *Givenness and God: Questions of Jean-Luc Marion*. Fordham, 2005.

Long, D. Stephen. *Divine Economy: Theology and the Market*. London and New York: Routledge, 2000.

Lubac, Henri de SJ., *Aspects of Buddhism*. London: Sheed & Ward, 1953.

————. *Catholicism: Christ and the Common Destiny of Man*. San Francisco: Ignatius Press, 1988.

————. *The Mystery of the Supernatural*. New York: Crossroad, 1998.

Lubicz, Isha Schwaller de. *Her-Bak*, Vol. 1: "Chick-Pea." Baltimore: Penguin Books, 1972.

Luttwak, Edward. *Turbo-Capitalism: Winners and Losers in the Global Economy.* London: Weidenfeld & Nicolson, 1998.

McGregor, Bede, and Thomas Norris (eds). *The Beauty of Christ.* Edinburgh: T&T Clark, 2001.

McPartlan, Paul. *The Eucharist Makes the Church: Henri de Lubac and John Zizioulas in Dialogue.* Edinburgh: T&T Clark, 1993.

Marcel, Gabriel. *Men Against Humanity.* London: Harvill Press, 1952.

Maritain, Jacques. *Art and Scholasticism with Other Essays.* London: Sheed & Ward, 1947.

————. *True Humanism.* New York: Scribner's, 1938.

Mark of Whitstable, *Gospel Chivalry: Franciscan Romanticism.* Leominster: Gracewing, 2006.

Mathews, Race. *Jobs of Our Own: Building a Stakeholder Society, Alternatives to the Market and the State.* Irving, TX: Distributist Review Press, 2009.

Médaille, John. *Equity and Equilibrium: The Political Economy of Distributism.* Irving, TX: Distributist Review Press, 2013.

Michel, Virgil OSB. *The Liturgy of the Church According to the Roman Rite.* New York: Macmillan, 1937.

Milbank, John. *The Future of Love: Essays in Political Theology.* London: SCM Press, 2009.

————. *Theology and Social Theory: Beyond Secular Reason.* Oxford: Blackwell, 1990.

Moll, Helmut (ed.). *The Church and Women.* San Francisco: Ignatius Press, 1988.

Murata, Sachiko, and William Chittick. *The Vision of Islam: The Foundations of Muslim Faith and Practice.* London and New York: I.B. Tauris, 1996.

Nasr, Seyyed Hossein. *Traditional Islam in the Modern World.* London: KPI, 1987.

Nichols, Aidan OP. *Christendom Awake: On Re-energizing the Church in Culture.* Edinburgh: T&T Clark, 1999.

————. *Looking at the Liturgy: A Critical View of Its Contemporary Form.* Ignatius Press, 1996.

————. *Redeeming Beauty: Soundings in Sacral Aesthetics.* Aldershot: Ashgate, 2007.

Novak, Michael. *The Catholic Ethic and the Spirit of Capitalism.* New York: The Free Press, 1993.

_____. *The Spirit of Democratic Capitalism*. New York: Simon & Schuster, 1982.

Olsen, Glenn W. *The Turn to Transcendence: The Role of Religion in the Twenty-First Century*. Washington, DC: CUA Press, 2010.

Ostermann, Charlotte. *Souls at Rest: An Exploration of the Idea of Sabbath*. (Angelico Press, forthcoming.)

Ouspensky, Leonid, and Vladimir Lossky. *The Meaning of Icons*. Crestwood, NY: St Vladimir's Seminary Press, 1983.

Pabst, Adrian. *The Crisis of Global Capitalism: Pope Benedict XVI's Social Encyclical and the Future of Political Economy*. Eugene, OR: Cascade Books, 2011.

_____. *Metaphysics: The Creation of Hierarchy*. Grand Rapids: Eerdmans, 2012.

Patmore, Coventry. *The Rod, The Root, and the Flower*. London: Bell & Sons, 1923.

Pearce, Joseph. *Small is Still Beautiful: Economics as if Families Mattered*. Wilmington: ISI Books, 2006.

Pieper, Josef. *Divine Madness: Plato's Case Against Secular Humanism*, San Francisco: Ignatius Press, 1995.

_____. *Josef Pieper: An Anthology*. San Francisco: Ignatius Press, 1989.

Pinckaers, Servais OP. *Morality: The Catholic View*. South Bend: St Augustine's Press, 2001.

_____. *The Sources of Christian Ethics*. Washington, DC: CUA Press, 1995.

Plato, *Complete Works*, ed. John M. Cooper. Indianapolis: Hackett, 1997.

Pontifical Council for Justice and Peace, *Handbook for Business Leaders: Practical Principles in Serving the Common Good*. London: CTS, 2012.

Ratzinger, Joseph. *A Turning Point for Europe? The Church in the Modern World—Assessment and Forecast*. San Francisco: Ignatius Press, 1994.

_____. *God is Near Us: The Eucharist, the Heart of Life*. San Francisco: Ignatius Press, 2003.

_____. *Introduction to Christianity*. San Francisco: Ignatius Press, 2004.

_____. *Jesus of Nazareth* 2: Holy Week: From the Entrance Into Jerusalem to the Resurrection. San Francisco: Ignatius Press, 2011.

_____. *The Spirit of the Liturgy*. San Francisco: Ignatius Press, 2000.

Read, Alcuin (ed.). *Looking Again at the Question of the Liturgy with Cardinal Ratzinger: Proceedings of the July 2001 Fontgombault Conference*. Farnborough: St Michael's Abbey Press, 2003.

Root, Andrew. *The Children of Divorce: The Loss of Family as the Loss of Being*. Ada, MI: Baker Academic, 2010.

Rowland, Tracey. *Culture and the Thomist Tradition After Vatican II.* London: Routledge, 2003.

Saward, John, John Morrill, and Michael Tomko (eds). *Firmly I Believe and Truly: The Spiritual Tradition of Catholic England—An Anthology of Writings from 1483 to 1999.* Oxford University Press, 2011.

Scheeben, Matthias J. *The Mysteries of Christianity.* London: Herder, 1946.

Schindler, David L. *Ordering Love: Liberal Societies and the Memory of God.* Grand Rapids: Eerdmans, 2011.

Schmemann, Alexander. *For the Life of the World: Sacraments and Orthodoxy.* Crestwood, NY: St Vladimir's Seminary Press, 2000.

———. *The Eucharist: Sacrament of the Kingdom.* Crestwood, NY: St Vladimir's Seminary Press, 1987.

Schmitz, Kenneth L. *The Gift: Creation.* Marquette University Press, 1982.

Schönborn, Christoph *From Death to Life: The Christian Journey.* San Francisco: Ignatius Press, 1995.

Schumacher, E. F. *Good Work.* London: HarperCollins, 1980.

Schurmann, Heinz, Joseph Ratzinger, and Hans Urs von Balthasar. *Principles of Christian Morality.* San Francisco: Ignatius Press, 1986.

Short, Edward. *Culture and Abortion.* Leominster: Gracewing, 2013.

Sokolowski, Robert. *Eucharistic Presence.* Washington: CUA Press, 1994.

Speyr, Adrienne von. *The Victory of Love: A Meditation on Romans 8.* San Francisco: Ignatius Press, 1990.

Staniloae, Dumitru. *Orthodox Spirituality: A Practical Guide for the Faithful and a Definitive Guide for the Scholar.* South Canaan, PA: St Tikhon's Seminary Press, 2002.

Taylor, Charles. *A Secular Age.* Harvard University Press, 2007.

Torevell, David. *Losing the Sacred: Modernity and Liturgical Reform.* Edinburgh: T&T Clark, 2000.

Tornielli, Andrea. *Francis: Pope of a New World.* San Francisco and London: CTS and Ignatius Press, 2013.

Vauchez, André. *Francis of Assisi: The Life and Afterlife of a Medieval Saint.* Yale University Press, 2012.

Ward, Maisie. *Gilbert Keith Chesterton.* London: Sheed & Ward, 1949.

Wojtyla, Karol (John Paul II), *Love and Responsibility.* Boston: Pauline, 2013.

NAME INDEX

Adam 21, 37, 102–104, 108, 112, 114, 129, 194
Albert, Prince 138
Alighieri, see Dante
Anderson, Gary A. 51
Aristotle 94, 176, 230, 247
Arizmendiaretta, Jose-Maria 237
Augustine, Saint 10, 11, 13–15, 17–18, 45, 110–111, 119–120

Bacon, Francis 84
Bacon, Friar Roger 202
Baker, Augustine 126
Balthasar, Hans Urs von 26, 37, 43, 78, 80, 84, 90, 126, 145, 151, 172, 182, 186–188, 214, 249–251
Barber, Benjamin 86
Barker, Margaret 30–32
Bauman, Zygmunt 148, 215
Belloc, Hillary 77, 170, 226–227, 230–231, 232–233, 236
Benedict XVI (pope) 2, 5, 10, 44, 49, 51, 60, 62–66, 70–74, 82, 86, 89, 91–93, 98, 116–117, 121–122, 125, 134, 150, 153, 170–171, 181, 184, 211, 213, 245, 248, 254
Bergoglio, Jorge (see Francis, Pope)
Bernadone, Peter 196
Bernanos, Georges 75, 214
Berry, Wendell 67, 169, 238–239
Black, Michael 86, 88
Blake, William 140, 142, 226, 230

Boethius 118–119
Bolton, Robert 186–187

Caritas in Veritate 2, 5, 49, 60–72, 91–93, 169, 213, 216, 244, 248
Carlson, Allan 64
Carson, Rachel 81
Casarella, Peter 135
Caussade, J.-p. de 134
Cavanaugh, William T. 41–42, 215
Centesimus Annus 57, 59, 64, 81, 125, 134, 210, 212–213
Charles II (king) 230
Charles, Roger 5, 52–53
Chesterton, G. K. 141, 145, 170, 197, 226–236, 239, 241–242
Childe, V. Gordon 29
Chittick, William 163
Clare of Assisi, Saint 200
Clément, Olivier 128
Clement, Pope 52
Clement, Saint 78
Cobb, John B. 239
Coomaraswamy, Ananda K. 165
Corbin, Henry 175

Daly, Herman E. 239
Dante 22, 38, 202
D'Arcy, Eric 122
Darwin, Charles 138
Dawson, Christopher 76, 136, 144
Day, Dorothy 236
De Lubac, Henri 36–37, 39, 50, 65,

TOPIC INDEX

Made in the USA
Coppell, TX
05 December 2020